A HEART FOR MISSIONS
THE CLASSIC MEMOIR OF SAMUEL PEARCE

D1279253

A
HEART FOR MISSIONS

THE CLASSIC MEMOIR OF SAMUEL PEARCE

WHO WAS UNITED WITH WILLIAM CAREY AND OTHERS
IN ESTABLISHING MISSIONS IN INDIA, 1793

ANDREW FULLER

WITH ADDITIONS FROM HIS CORRESPONDENCE
WITH WILLIAM CAREY AND OTHERS

BY HIS SON, REV. W.H. PEARCE
MISSIONARY TO CALCUTTA, INDIA

"To me to live is Christ, and to die is gain." –Phil. 1:21
"That life is long which answers life's great end." –Edward Young

SOLID GROUND CHRISTIAN BOOKS
BIRMINGHAM, ALABAMA USA

Solid Ground Christian Books
715 Oak Grove Road
Birmingham, AL 35209
205-443-0311
sgcb@charter.net
http://solid-ground-books.com

A Heart for Missions
THE CLASSIC MEMOIR OF SAMUEL PEARCE

Andrew Fuller (1754-1815)

Solid Ground Classic Reprints

From expanded edition by the American Tract Society, New York

First printing of new edition May 2006

Cover work by Borgo Design, Tuscaloosa, AL
Contact them at nelbrown@comcast.net

Special thanks to –
Dr. Michael Haykin for his enthusiastic support of this project,
his helpful and informative Introduction, and his patience displayed
in waiting over a year for this project to be completed.
Pete and Barbara Nuckols who graciously took over re-typing
this material and proof-reading it with painstaking care.

ISBN: 1-932474-74-9

TABLE OF CONTENTS

INTRODUCING SAMUEL PEARCE [1]

For English-speaking people, the eighteenth century was an era of highly significant achievements. Through military conquest and exploration, for instance, they established themselves as the masters of a far-flung empire that encircled the globe. It was in the middle of this century that British troops under the command of Robert Clive (1725-1774) defeated an Indian army at the Battle of Plassey (1757), which paved the way for the British conquest of Bengal. Two years later, on September 13, 1759, General James Wolfe (1727-1759) defeated the French General Louis Joseph Montcalm (1712-1759) at the Battle of the Plains of Abraham, then outside the walls of city of Quebec. Though Wolfe was killed in this engagement, the British victory meant the end of French rule in Canada. Ten or so years later, Captain James Cook (1728-1779), a British naval officer, entered upon his world-changing discoveries in the South Pacific, discovering and mapping the coastlines of New Zealand and Australia.

Running parallel to this empire-building by the British, though initially quite distinct from it, was the building of God's kingdom by various English-speaking missionaries. Up until the latter part of the eighteenth century, Evangelical Christianity was primarily confined to northern Europe and the Atlantic seaboard of North America. But suddenly in the last decade of the century Evangelicals launched out from these two geographical regions and began to establish the presence of their faith throughout Asia, Africa, and Australasia.

At the heart of this missionary outreach was William Carey (1761-1834), whose centrality in this endeavour is well captured in a remark by John Newton (1725-1807). "Such a man as Carey," he once said, "is more to me than bishop or archbishop: he is an apostle."[2] In the course of the nineteenth century thousands upon thousands came to share Newton's opinion. The life of Carey and his archetypal ministry in the Indian sub-continent—told over and over again in a never-ending stream of biographies—captured the imagination of untold numbers of evangelicals in the nineteenth century and was thus central to the start of the modern missionary movement. It is not surprising that later authors, so taken with the historic nature of Carey's mission, have unwittingly minimized or overlooked the vital role played by Carey's co-workers, both at home in England and on the field in India.

When his contemporaries, though, spoke William Carey's name, it was yoked together first with the names of Joshua Marshman (1768-1837) and William Ward (1769-1823)—vital colleagues to Carey's work in India. Then, among Evangelicals of that day, Carey's name was linked with four devoted friends in England: Andrew Fuller (1754-1815), John Sutcliff (1752-1814), John Ryland, Jr. (1753-1825), and Samuel Pearce (1766-1799). The commitment of these men to one another is well captured in some Greek words from Acts 4:32 that Samuel Pearce wrote in the front of a New Testament that he sent to Carey in the autumn of 1797: "one heart and one soul."[3]

This book focuses on the life of one of these friends, Samuel Pearce. Written by another of Carey's friends, Andrew Fuller, it was said by one American reviewer in the mid-nineteenth century that if Fuller had written "nothing besides this biography, he would have been a benefactor of the Christian public."[4] Though scarcely known today, Samuel Pearce was in his own day well known for the anointing that attended his preaching and for the depth of his spirituality. In fact, for some decades after his death it was not uncommon to hear him referred to as the "seraphic Pearce."[5]

Pearce's early years

The youngest of two sons, Pearce was born in Plymouth on the English Channel on July 20, 1766, to devout Baptist parents.[6] His mother died when he was but an infant, and so he was raised by his godly father, William Pearce (d.1805) and an equally pious grandfather. As Pearce came into his teen years, however, he consciously spurned the rich heritage of his godly home and the Plymouth Baptist community in which he had been raised. According to his own testimony, "several vicious school-fellows" became his closest friends and he set his heart on what he would later describe as "evil" and "wicked inclinations."[7]

But God had better plans for his life. In the summer of 1782, a young preacher by the name of Isaiah Birt (1758-1837) came to preach for a few Sundays in the Plymouth meeting-house.[8] The Spirit of God drove home Birt's words to Pearce's heart. The change in Pearce from what he later called "a state of death in trespasses and sins" to a "life in a dear dying Redeemer" was sudden but genuine and lasting. A year or so later, on the day when he celebrated his seventeenth birthday, he was baptized and joined the Plymouth congregation in which he had been raised.

It was not long after his baptism that the church perceived that Pearce had been endowed with definite gifts that marked him out as one called to pastoral ministry. So, in November of 1785, when he was only nineteen years of age and serving as an apprentice to his father who was a silversmith, Pearce received a call from the church to engage in the ministry of the Word. The church recommended that Pearce first pursue a course of study at the Bristol Baptist Academy. From August, 1786 to May, 1789 Pearce thus studied at what was then the sole Baptist institution in Great Britain for the training of ministers for the Calvinistic Baptist denomination.

In February 1789 Pearce received and accepted a call to serve on probation—a common procedure of that day in the British Baptist community—as the pastor of Cannon Street Baptist Church in Birmingham. By June of that year, his studies finished, he was with them.[9] The following year he was formally called to be the pastor of the church. It would turn out to be his only pastoral charge. His ministry at Cannon Street occupied ten all-too-brief years. Yet they were ones of great fruitfulness. No less than 335 individuals were baptized during his ministry and received into the membership of Cannon Street. This figure does not include those converted under his preaching who, for one reason or another, did not join themselves to the Birmingham cause.[10]

Guilsborough, Northamptonshire

A prominent characteristic of Pearce's life was a passion for the salvation of his fellow human beings. This passion is strikingly revealed in two stories. The first took place when he was asked to preach at the opening of a Baptist meeting-house in Guilsborough, Northamptonshire, in May 1794. The previous meeting-house had been burnt down at Christmas, 1792, by a mob that was hostile to Baptists. Pearce had spoken in the morning on Psalm 76:10 ("Surely the wrath of man shall praise thee: the remainder of wrath shalt thou restrain"). Later that day, during the midday meal, it was quite evident from the conversation that was going at the dinner tables that Pearce's sermon had been warmly appreciated. It was thus no surprise when Pearce was asked if he would be willing to preach again the following morning. "If you will find a congregation," Pearce responded, "I will find a sermon." It was agreed to have the sermon at 5 a.m. so that a number of farm labourers could come who wanted to hear Pearce preach and who would have to be at their tasks early in the morning.

After Pearce had preached the second time, and that to a congregation of more than 200 people, and he was sitting at breakfast with a few others, including Andrew Fuller, the latter remarked to Pearce how pleased he had been with the content of his friend's sermon. But, he went on to say, it seemed to him that Pearce's sermon was poorly structured. "I thought," Fuller told his friend, "you did not seem to close when you had really finished. I wondered that, contrary to what is usual with you, you seemed, as it were, to begin again at the end—how was it?" Pearce's response was terse: "It was so; but I had my reason." "Well then, come, let us have it," Fuller jovially responded. Pearce was quite reluctant to divulge the reason, but after a further entreaty from Fuller, he consented and said:

"Well, my brother, you shall have the secret, if it must be so. Just at the moment I was about to resume my seat, thinking I had finished, the door opened, and I saw a poor man enter, of the working class; and from the sweat on his brow, and the symptoms of his fatigue, I conjectured that he had walked some miles to this early service, but that he had been unable to reach the place till the close. A momentary thought glanced through my mind—here may be a man who never heard the gospel, or it may be he is one that regards it as a feast of fat things; in either case, the effort on his part demands one on mine. So with the hope of doing him good, I resolved at once to forget all else, and, in despite of criticism, and the apprehension of being thought tedious, to give him a quarter of an hour."[11]

As Fuller and the others present at the breakfast table listened to this simple explanation, they were deeply impressed by Pearce's evident love for souls. Not afraid to appear as one lacking in homiletical skill, especially in the eyes of his fellow pastors, Pearce's zeal for the spiritual health of *all* his hearers had led him to minister as best he could to this "poor man" who had arrived late.

India

The second story has to do with India. Given Pearce's ardour for the advance of the gospel it is only to be expected that he would be vitally involved in the formation in October, 1792, of what would eventually be termed the Baptist Missionary Society, the womb of the modern missionary movement. In fact, by 1794 Pearce was so deeply gripped by the cause of missions that he had arrived at the conviction that he should offer his services to the Society and go out to India to join the first missionary team the Society had sent out, namely, William Carey, John Thomas (1757-1801), and their respective families. He began to study Bengali on his own.[12] And for the entire month of October, 1794, which preceded the early November meeting of the Society's administrative committee where Pearce's offer would be evaluated, Pearce set apart "one day in every week to secret prayer and fasting" for direction.[13]

The decision of the Society as to Pearce's status was ultimately a negative one. When the executive committee of the Society met at Roade, Northamptonshire, on November 12, it was of the opinion that Pearce could best serve the cause of missions at home in England. Pearce's response to this decision is best seen in an extract from a letter sent to William Carey over four months later.

"Instead of a letter, you perhaps expected to have seen the writer; and had the will of God been so, he would by this time have been on his way to Mudnabatty: but it is not in man that walketh to direct his steps. Full of hope and expectation as I was, when I wrote you last, that I should be honoured with a mission to the poor heathen, and be an instrument of establishing the empire of my dear Lord in India, I must submit now to stand still, and see the salvation of God."

Pearce then told Carey some of the details of the November meeting at which the Society executive had made their decision regarding his going overseas. In response to this decision, which dashed some of Pearce's deepest longings, he was, he said, "enabled cheerfully to reply, 'The will of the Lord be done;' and receiving this answer as the voice of God, I have, for the most part, been easy since, though not without occasional pantings of spirit after the publishing of the gospel to the Pagans."[14]

Final days

Between 1794 and his death in 1799, Pearce expended much of his energy in going about the country preaching the cause of foreign missions and raising support for the work in India. One of the meetings at which Pearce preached was at Kettering on 16 October 1798. Returning back to Birmingham from this meeting Pearce was caught in a heavy downpour of rain, drenched to the skin, and subsequently developed a severe chill. Neglecting to rest and foolishly thinking what he called "pulpit sweats" would effect a cure, he continued a rigorous schedule of preaching at Cannon Street as well as in outlying villages around Birmingham. His lungs became so inflamed that Pearce was necessitated to ask William Ward to supply the Cannon Street pulpit for a few months during the winter of 1798-1799.

By the spring of 1799 Pearce was desperately ill with pulmonary tuberculosis. Leaving his wife and family—he and Sarah had five children by this time—he went to the south of England from April to July in the hope that rest there in the warmer climate of southern England might effect a cure. Sarah and the children had gone to stay with her family in Alcester, twenty or miles or so from Birmingham. Eventually Sarah could no longer bear being absent from her husband. Leaving their children with Birmingham friends, she headed south in mid-May, where she stayed with her husband until the couple slowly made their way home to Birmingham in mid-July.[15]

By his time Samuel's voice was so far gone that he could not even whisper without pain in his lungs. His suffering, though, seemed to act like a refiner's fire to draw him closer to Christ. Not long before his death he could say to Sarah:

"Blessed be his dear name who shed his blood for me. ...Now I see the value of the religion of the cross. It is a religion for a dying sinner. ...Yes, I taste its sweetness, and enjoy its fulness, with all the gloom of a dying-bed before me; and far rather would I be the poor emaciated and emaciating creature that I am, than be an emperor with every earthly good about him, but without a God."[16]

He fell asleep in Christ on Thursday, 10 October 1799. William Ward, who had been profoundly influenced by Pearce's zeal and spirituality, well summed up his character when he wrote not long before the latter's death:

"Oh, how does personal religion shine in Pearce! What a soul! What ardour for the glory of God! ...you see in him a mind wholly given up to God; a sacred lustre shines in his conversation... I have seen more of God in him than in any other person I ever met."[17]

Dr. Michael A.G. Haykin
Toronto Baptist Seminary

---

[1] Much of this introduction was given as a talk at the Campus Crusade for Christ Winter Conference, Toronto, December 28, 2002

[2] *The Autobiography of William Jay*, eds. George Redford and John Angell James (1854 ed.; repr. Edinburgh: The Banner of Truth Trust, 1974), 275; S. Pearce Carey, *William Carey* (London: Hodder and Stoughton, [1923]), 134.

[3] John Taylor, comp., *Biographical and Literary Notices of William Carey, D.D.* (Northampton: Dryden Press, Taylor & Son/London: Alexander & Shepheard, 1886), 27. For the story of this circle of friends, see Michael A. G. Haykin, *One Heart and One Soul: John Sutcliff of Olney, his friends and his times* (Darlington, Co. Durham: Evangelical Press, 1995).

[4] "*The complete Works of the Rev. Andrew Fuller, with a Memoir of his life*", *The Biblical Repertory and Princeton Review*, 18 (1846), 551.

[5] See, for example, *The Life and Letters of John Angell James*, ed. R. W. Dale (3rd. ed.; London: James Nisbet and Co., 1861), 67; John Angell James, *An Earnest Ministry the Want of the Times* (4th. ed.; London: Hamilton, Adams, & Co., 1848), 272. The phrase appears to have originated with Pearce's friend, John Ryland, Jr.: see Ernest A. Payne, "Samuel Pearce" in his *The First Generation: Early Leaders of the Baptist Missionary Society in England and America* (London: Carey Press, [1936]), 46.

6 "Memoir of the Late Rev. Samuel Pearce, A.M.", *The Evangelical Magazine*, 8 (1800), 177.

[7] See p. 3 of this new reprint.

[8] For the life of Birt, see the memoir by his son: John Birt, "Memoir of the Late Rev. Isaiah Birt", *The Baptist Magazine*, 30 (1838), 54-59, 107-116, 197-203.

[9] S. Pearce Carey, *Samuel Pearce, M. A., The Baptist Brainerd* (3rd. ed.; London: The Carey Press, n.d.), 93-94.

[10] Carey, *Samuel Pearce, M. A., The Baptist Brainerd*, 113; Arthur S. Langley, *Birmingham Baptists: Past and Present* (London: The Kingsgate Press, 1939), 34. Even after Pearce's death, his wife Sarah could rejoice in people joining the church who had been saved under her husband's ministry. See Andrew Fuller, "Memoir of Mrs. Pearce" in his *Memoirs of the Late Rev. Samuel Pearce, A. M.* (Philadelphia: Amercian Sunday School Union, 1829), 160-161.

[11] F. A. Cox, *History of the Baptist Missionary Society*, I, 52-53. Pearce's friendship with Fuller drew him into the circle of friends mentioned above. For the story of this circle, see Michael A. G. Haykin, *One Heart and One Soul: John Sutcliff of Olney, his friends and his times* (Darlington, Co. Durham: Evangelical Press, 1995).

[12] Payne, "Samuel Pearce", 50.

[13] See p. 55 of this new reprint.

[14] Letter to William Carey, 27 March 1795 [*Missionary Correspondence: containing Extracts of Letters from the late Mr. Samuel Pearce, to the Missionaries in India, Between the Years 1794, and 1798; and from Mr. John Thomas, from 1798, to 1800* (London: T. Gardiner and Son, 1814), 26, 30-31].

[15] Ernest A. Payne, "Some Samuel Pearce Documents", *The Baptist Quarterly*, 18 (1959-1960), 31.

[16] See p. 135 of this new reprint.

[17] Cited Carey, *Samuel Pearce*, 188.

Original Preface

It was observed by this excellent man, during his affliction, that he never till then gained any personal instruction from our Lord's telling Peter by *what death* he should glorify God. To die by a consumption had used to be an object of dread to him; but, "O my dear Lord," said he, "if by *this death* I can most *glorify thee, I* prefer it to all others." The lingering death of the cross, by which our Savior himself expired, afforded him an opportunity of uttering some of the most affecting sentences which are left on sacred record; and to the lingering death of this his honored servant we are indebted for a considerable part of the materials which appear in these Memoirs. Had he been taken away suddenly, there had been no opportunity for him to have expressed his sentiments and feelings in the manner he has now done in letters to his friends. While in health, his hands were full of labor, and consequently his letters were written mostly upon the spur of occasion; and related principally to business, or to things which would be less interesting to Christians in general. It is true, even in them it was his manner to drop a few sentiments, towards the close, of an experimental kind; and many of these hints will be interspersed in this brief account of him; but it was during his affliction, when being laid aside nearly a year, and obliged to desist from all public concerns, that he gave scope to all the feelings of his heart. Here, standing as on an eminence, he reviewed his life, re-examined the ground of his hope, and anticipated the crown which awaited him, with a joy truly *unspeakable and full of glory.*

Like Elijah, he has left the "chariot of Israel," and ascended as in a "chariot of fire;" but not without having first communicated of his eminently Christian spirit. Oh that a double portion of it may rest upon us!

Andrew Fuller

Preface to the Revised Edition

The late venerable Dr. Ryland said of the subject of this memoir, "He possessed such an assemblage of lovely graces and acceptable qualifications as are seldom found united, even in truly Christian ministers. He had the firmest attachment to evangelical truth, and the most constant regard to practical godliness; he united remarkable soundness of judgment with uncommon warmth of affection. I never saw, at least in one of his years, such active, ardent zeal, conjoined with such gentleness, modesty, and deep humility; so much of the little child, and so much of the Evangelist—I can scarcely forbear saying of the Apostle of Jesus Christ." "One thing I will say, which I could say of very few others, though I have known many of the excellent of the earth,—that I never saw or heard of any thing respecting him which grieved me, unless it was his inattention to his health;—and that I believe was owing to a mistaken idea of his constitution."

In the funeral discourse preached by Rev. Mr. Fuller, he says, "There are but few characters in this imperfect state that will bear an impartial scrutiny; and which do not require, if exhibited to advantage, that a number of their words and deeds should be overlooked, or thrown, as by a painter, into the shade. But I solemnly declare that were I disposed to say all I know of our deceased friend, both bad and good, I should be utterly at a loss on one side, nor have I any fear of speaking too much on the other; but rather am persuaded that it is not in my power to do him justice. He was, doubtless, a sinful and imperfect creature before God; but he was also a singular instance of the holy and happy efficacy of divine grace, whose imperfections were as few, and whose excellences as many, as I have ever witnessed in a mortal man. Some, who knew but little of him, may think this too strong. I only say, they that knew him best will be the least disposed to think so."

Rev. W.H. Pearce

MEMOIRS

CHAPTER I

HIS PARENTAGE, CONVERSION CALL TO THE MINISTRY, AND SETTLEMENT AT BIRMINGHAM

Mr. Samuel Pearce was born at Plymouth, on July 20th, 1766. His father, who survives him, is a respectable silversmith, and many years a deacon of the Baptist church in that place.

When a child, he lived with his grandfather, who was very fond of him, and endeavored to impress his mind with the principles of religion. At about eight or nine years of age he came home to his father with a view of learning his business. As he advanced in life, his evil propensities, as he has said, began to ripen; and forming connections with several vicious school-fellows, he became more and more corrupted. So greatly was his heart at this time set in him to do evil, that had it not been for the restraining goodness of God, which somehow, he knew not how, preserved him in most instances from carrying his wicked inclinations into practice, he supposed he should have been utterly ruined.

At times he was under strong convictions, which rendered him miserable; but at other times they subsided, and then he would return with eagerness to his sinful pursuits. When about fifteen years old he was sent by his father to inquire after the welfare of a person in the neighborhood, in dying circumstances, who (though before his departure he was in a happy state of mind) at that time was sinking into deep despair. While in the room of the dying man, he heard him cry out with inexpressible agony of spirit, "I am damned for ever!" These awful words pierced his soul; and he felt a resolution at the time to serve the Lord; but the impression soon wore off, and he again returned to folly.

When about sixteen years of age, it pleased God effectually to turn him to himself. A sermon delivered by Mr. *Birt,* who was then co-pastor with Mr. *Gibbs* of the Baptist church at Plymouth, was the first means of impressing his heart with a sense of his lost condition, and of directing him to the gospel remedy. The change in him appears to have been sudden, but effectual; and though his vicious propensities were bitter to his recollection, yet, being now sensibly subdued, he was furnished with so much the clearer evidence that the work was of God. "I believe," he says, "few conversions were more joyful. The change produced in my views, feelings, and conduct was so evident to myself, that I could no more doubt of its being from God than of my existence. I had the witness in myself, and was filled with peace and joy unspeakable."

His feelings being naturally strong, and receiving a new direction, he entered into religion with all his heart; but not having known the devices of Satan, his soul was injured by its own ardor, and he was thrown into great perplexity. Having read Doddridge's *Rise and Progress of Religion in the Soul,* he determined formally to dedicate himself to the Lord, in the manner recommended in the seventeenth chapter of that work. The form of a covenant, as there drawn up, he also adopted as his own; and, that he might bind himself in the most solemn and affecting manner, *signed it with his blood.* But afterwards, failing in his engagements, he was plunged into great distress, and almost into despair. On a review of his covenant, he seems to have accused himself of a pharisaical reliance upon the strength of his own resolutions; and therefore, taking the paper to the top of his father's house, he tore it into small pieces, and threw it from him to be scattered by the wind. He did not however consider his obligation to be the Lord's as hereby nullified; but, feeling more suspicion of himself, he depended solely upon *the blood of the cross.*

Soon after his first awakening, he wrote the following letter to Rev. Mr. Birt,[1] his pastor:

"*Plymouth, October 27, 1782.*

My very dear Mr. Birt,

"Were I to make the least delay in answering your very affectionate letter, I should deem myself culpable of the greatest

---

[1] The excellent and venerable Isaiah Birt (1758-1837), about fourteen years after the death of Mr. Pearce, succeeded him in the pastoral office at Birmingham. His piety, public spirit, and success endeared him to a very large circle of friends, and make his name fragrant now that he has joined Pearce, and Fuller, Hall and Ryland, and the rest of his early companions on earth, in a better world.

ingratitude. You almost commence your kind letter with mentioning that my tears at parting with you demanded your fervent prayers. But do, my dear sir, consider that separating from an earthly parent, the author of animal life, must, where a filial affection subsists, be an affecting scene. How much more moving must it be to part with a father in Christ Jesus! To part with one whom the Almighty has made the happy means of raising from a state of death in trespasses and sins, to that of life in a dear dying Redeemer!

"O, sir, such was the case when I parted with my ever dear Mr. Birt. Did this require your fervent prayers? Has this caused you to remember me when prostrate at a footstool of mercy? Let me beseech you, my dear sir, still to continue it; and, whenever you bow the suppliant knee at a throne of grace, not to fail beseeching the Author of mercy to extend his mercy to an object so unworthy. O! beg of him, that, since he has begun a good work in me, he would carry it on. As he has enabled me to put my hand to the gospel plough, may I never look back: but may he grant me grace and strength to hold on, and hold out to the end; to conquer every foe; to be continually pressing forward toward the mark and prize of my high calling in Christ Jesus; and, in the end, to come off more than conqueror through him who, I trust, has loved me and given himself for me. O! beg of him that he will ever keep me from possessing a lukewarm, a Laodicean spirit! May my affections to the crucified Savior be continually on a flame!

"I am 'prone to wander;' yes, 'I feel it; prone to leave the God I love.' O that my affections may be more and more united to him! My dear sir, pray for me. Use your interest at a throne of grace on my behalf; and as God has promised to be a God hearing and answering prayer, I doubt not but it will meet with a gracious reception, and perhaps with a gracious answer too. O, sir! let me once more entreat you never to forget me whilst offering up prayers to your God. Religion, you may well say, is worthy the choice of all: it makes a beggar superior to a king; whilst, destitute of it, a king is inferior to a beggar. What—oh! what—can equal the felicity, the enjoyments of a Christian? Nothing, surely, on this transitory globe! Nothing this world calls good or great can be put in competition with it,—with the joyous feeling of him who has the unspeakable happiness of experiencing himself interested in a dear Redeemer.

"Surely, no tongue can express, no heart can conceive, what God has prepared for those who love him! O how thankful ought those to be whom he has called by divine grace to the knowledge of himself! What an unspeakable mercy is it that he has distinguished me in such a peculiar manner (give me leave to use your own words) as to be taken into his service, adopted into his family, made an heir of God, a joint heir with Jesus Christ! What now is required of me? What am I now required to do? When I reflect on this, how short do I find I come in my duty! How backward am I to it! How unwilling to perform it! Even when I would do good, evil is present with me.

> 'What shall I do with this my heart?
> Where shall I bring my sin?
> O Lamb of God, who bore my smart,
> `Tis thou must make me clean.'

"I have no righteousness of my own, no merits of mine to bring; the best of my performances come infinitely short of the holy law of God. On Jesus alone I must depend for salvation. Here I rest. Hence I draw all my hope. Jesus Christ has died, and Jesus shall not die in vain. The Redeemer's blood cleanses from all sin. Happy, thrice happy, they who have washed and made their robes white in the blood of the Lamb! May it be the blessed experience of my dear friend and myself.

"I thank you, sir, for your kind admonitions. I hope the God of all grace will enable me to abide by them. Tribulations, trials, and temptations, I am sensible, are the lot of all God's children here below; but I am equally certain that as long as we rely upon our God, and confide in him only, he that has given us a sure word of promise, whereby he has caused us to hope, will with them all work out a way for our escape, that we may be able to bear them.

"And now, that it may be our joint happiness, my dear sir, to be kept in a holy, happy fellowship with our God; that we may be often brought to Pisgah's summit, and behold the promised *Canaan;* that we may often, whilst there, anticipate the pleasures of the heavenly world; and, when we have passed the floods of Jordan, meet around the throne above, there to chant eternal lays to Him that sitteth upon the throne, and to the Lamb, for ever, is, dear sir, the constant prayer of him who is, and wishes ever to remain,

"Your affectionate friend,   Samuel Pearce"

On July 20, 1783, the day he was seventeen years old, he was he was baptized, and became a member of the Baptist church at Plymouth, the ministers and members of which, in a few years, perceived in him talents for public work. Being solicited by both his pastors, he exercised as a probationer; and receiving a unanimous call from the church, entered on the work of the ministry in November, 1786. Soon after this he went to the academy at Bristol, then under the superintendence of Dr. Caleb Evans.

Mr. Birt, now pastor of the Baptist church, in the Square, Plymouth Dock, in a letter to the compiler of these Memoirs, thus speaks of him:—"Though he was, so far as I know, the very first-fruits of my ministry on my coming hither, and though our friendship and affection for each other were great and constant, yet previously to his going to Bristol I had but few opportunities of conversing with him, or of making particular observations on him. All who best knew him, however, well remember and most tenderly speak of his loving deportment; and those who attended the conferences with him soon received the most impressive intimations of his future eminence as a minister of our Lord Jesus Christ."[2]

"Very few," adds Mr. Birt, "have entered upon and gone through their religious profession with more exalted piety or warmer zeal than Samuel Pearce; and as few have exceeded him in the possession and display of that *charity* which 'suffereth long, and is kind, that envieth not, that vaunteth not itself, and is not puffed up, that doth not behave itself unseemly, that seeketh not her own, is not easily provoked, thinketh no evil, that beareth all things, believeth all things, endureth all things.'[3] But why should I say this to you? You know him yourself."

While at the academy he was much distinguished by the amiableness of his spirit and behavior. It is sometimes observable, that where the talents of a young man are admired by his friends, and his early efforts flattered by crowded auditories, effects have been produced which have proved fatal to his future respectability and usefulness. But this was not the case with Mr. Pearce.

---

[2] The excellent and venerable Isaiah Birt, about fourteen years after the death of Mr. Pearce, succeeded him in the pastoral office at Birmingham. His piety, public spirit, and success endeared him to a very large circle of friends, and make his name fragrant now that he has joined Pearce, and Fuller, Hall and Ryland. and the rest of his early companions on earth, in a better world.

[3] 1 Corinthians 13:4-7.

Notwithstanding the popularity which even at that early period attended his ministerial exercises, his tutors have more than once remarked that he never appeared to them to be in the least elated, or to have neglected his proper studies; but was uniformly the serious, industrious, docile, modest, and unassuming young man.

In July, 1789, he came to the church in Cannon Street, Birmingham, to whom he was recommended by Mr. Hall, now of Cambridge, at that time one of his tutors. After preaching to them awhile on probation he was chosen to be their pastor, and was ordained August 18, 1790. Dr. Evans gave the charge, and the late venerable Mr. Hall, of Arnsby, delivered an address to the church on the occasion.

About two months after this he wrote to his friend, Mr. Summers, of London. Whether the sentiments contained in that letter arose from the recollection of his late solemn engagement is uncertain; but they were certainly very appropriate to the occasion. Requesting his friend to pray for him, he says,—"Paul speaks of blessings received through the prayers of his fellow Christians; no wonder, therefore, he so often solicits their continuance. But if it be well to be interested in the prayers of fellow Christians, how much more to believe the great High Priest of our profession, Jesus the Son of God, is gone into the holy of holies, with our names on his breastplate, ever to plead in the presence of God for us—for us; O transporting thought! Who can doubt of the success of such an Intercessor?

"I have of late had my mind very pleasantly, and I hope profitably, exercised on this subject, more than ever, and find increasing pleasure from a well-grounded faith in the *Divinity* of my incarnate Advocate. I see the glory of his office, arising from the infinite extent of his knowledge, power, and love, as well as from the efficacy of his atoning sacrifice.

"I do not wonder at those men who deny the priestly office of Christ, when they have refused him *the honors of Deity.* I rejoice in that he who *pleads for us knows our wants individually,* as well as the necessities of the whole church collectively. Through his intercession alone I expect my sins to be pardoned, my services accepted, and my soul preserved, guided, and comforted; and, with confidence in his intercession, I cannot doubt but I shall enjoy all. Oh how sweet is it, my dear friend, to exercise a lively faith in a living Savior! May you and I do this daily. Thus for us to live will be Christ, and to die gain; living or dying, we shall be the Lord's."

The following letters to his friend Mr. Staughton, exhibit the same spirit of piety and self-dedication:

"Birmingham, June 4, 1791.

"I received yours, my dear brother, just before I left Birmingham, on Wednesday last; it did me good, and gave me pleasure. I rejoice in your joy; I thank God for the assistance he grants you in public work. O, let all the strength and power you have, be devoted as the Divine will may see fit; let it all be employed to exalt the Savior: aim at that, and that only, my dear brother, in all your sermons. It will give us more pleasure, another day, that He was exalted by us, than that we exalted ourselves. Would to God we could live more on Him personally! We should then speak with more pleasure of him publicly. 'It is pleasant speaking of God when we walk with him.' May your experience and mine confirm it.

"Your very affectionate brother,   S.P."

"Plymouth Dock, July 29, 1791.

"My dear Friend,

One of the students, Mr. Rowland, is now dangerously ill at Plymouth Dock, of a fever, which is very prevalent here; and he lodges in a house where another student from the same country (Wales) died not long since. Lord, what is man! O, my brother, let us improve diligently the moments we possess; let us watch for souls; let us spend ourselves in its service for them. I preached thrice yesterday, not without pleasure; God grant it may be with profit. How is it with your soul? How do you find closet duties? I have had some precious seasons at a throne of grace since I reached Plymouth; I could say it was good, very good, to draw nigh to God. I am more and more convinced that our private devotion, or want of devotion, will materially affect the tenor of our deportment. God help us to give him our hearts; no fear, then, but he will have our services too. I wish you much of the divine presence; still pray for your unworthy brother, and still help him to praise.

"I am, yours affectionately,   S.P."

A similar spirit of ardent devotedness to the work of his divine Master, and of affectionate interest in the welfare of his friends, is displayed in the following letters to his friend Mr. Summers.

"Birmingham, Feb. 3, 1791.

"Friendship and ceremony seldom coalesce;—the ardor of affection and the chilling punctilios of formality cannot be united. Possessed of the former, averse to the latter, my kind friend receives a line from me, although my last is still unanswered. The occasion of my writing is a source of joy inexpressible to myself— a joy in which I know you will participate. Your amiable friend, Miss H. permitted me to call her my own yesterday. One dwelling now contains us both, and Paul's Square contains that dwelling.

"Thus far the good hand of my God has been with me; and I would hope, that not without his smiles, I have pursued the path which at length has led me to the felicity I now enjoy in the society of the most amiable of women; without them, I am still sensible, all created good is valueless, is vanity and vexation of spirit.

"How pleasing, my dear friend, to a pious mind, is the reflection that all our goings are in his hands whose love inclines him to every thing that is kind—whose purity connects with his conduct every thing that is good—whose wisdom infallibly adopts the best means, and whose power cannot fail to accomplish all his will. With his blessing, our felicity cannot fail of being accomplished—without it, it can never be attained. May it be our happiness to possess an interest in your prayers, that this all gracious, wise, and good Being, may continue still to bless, and cause that our union to each other may be a means of leading us more to communion with him.

"Besides this, I have, my dear friend, more mercies to be thankful for than I could enumerate on a quire of paper. Religion still flourishes among us, beneath the auspices of the Sun of Righteousness. Our congregations are quite as numerous as when you were at Birmingham; and we have had several pleasing additions since that period to our church. About eight weeks since, I baptized nine persons; last Sabbath I administered the same ordinance to eight more; and an equal or superior number appear in the way to join us soon. May this accession to our numbers be an increase to our joy.   S. P."

"Birmingham, September 30, 1791,

'My very dear friend,

". . . . The riots in Birmingham occasioned our stay in Bristol to be prolonged to a fortnight, so that we had not above three weeks to spend at Plymouth, from whence I purposed writing to you. This inch of time was wholly engrossed in making Mrs. P. witness the beauties of the West, and in introducing her to my numerous acquaintances in Devonshire.

"On our return we found our habitation had been quite emptied of furniture, and, though we found the goods replaced, yet my books and papers were so deranged that to this hour they are not all restored to order again.

"It is now Saturday evening; I have finished my usual preparations for the morrow. I have an hour to spare, and that hour I devote to intercourse with a friend I much esteem.

"I anticipate with some degree of holy pleasure the work of the approaching day. I have for my evening's discourse the best subject in all the Bible. Eph. 1:7.—Redemption! How welcome to the captive! Forgiveness! How delightful to the guilty! Grace! How pleasing to the heart of a saved sinner! O my dear friend, how much do we lose of Gospel blessings for want of realizing our personal connection with them! Hence it is that we are no more humble, thankful, watchful, prayerful, joyful. We view the glories of the Gospel at a distance, and for want of that faith which is the 'substance of things hoped for, and evidence of things not seen,'[4] think too lightly of them. O Lord, increase our faith!

"There are two things we should be always doing. First, we should identify the promises and things promised, satisfy ourselves respecting the certain existence of them—that they are not shadows, but substances—not fancies, but realities. This would have a commanding influence upon our meditations, desires, and prayers. Then, secondly, realize our interests in them, saying, 'These things are so, there is a far more exceeding and eternal weight of glory—there are enjoyments reserved in the heavenly world surpassing all human thought—and these joys, these glories, this inheritance is mine; then, how would our hearts be where our treasure is! How pure would be our affections! How burdensome would sin be! How precious would Christ be! How much prized would Sabbaths and ordinances be! How dear would the Scriptures be!—In short; death itself would be welcome, for the soul would long to depart and be with Christ, which is far better.

---

[4] Hebrews 11:1.

"I wish to be very thankful that I have had some rich experience of divine things since my return, both in the closet and in the pulpit; at some seasons I could have said, 'O that I had wings like a dove, that I might fly away and be at rest.' The twentieth hymn in Dr. Watts's second book has been the most experimental piece of poetry I ever read; when I say this, you need not be told that I am not upon the mount always; alas! no; but then why should I complain? My Lord knows best when to take me thither, and how long to keep me there; yet I know that if I had not an evil heart of unbelief I should not thus depart from the living and the true God. I hope you enjoy much of heaven on earth. O it is good to draw nigh to God.

> "'Tis heaven to rest in his embrace,
> And no where else but there."

"May we know more and more experimentally the blessing of the beloved disciple. John 21:20.

S.P."

"*Birmingham, October 8, 1792.*

"My very dear Friend,

"'Our law judgeth not a man before it heareth him'—let me beseech you to listen candidly to my defense, and then pronounce judgment on my silence as your wisdom directs. First, I have been out three considerable journeys since I returned from Wales, and all on my Master's business: into Oxfordshire, Shropshire, Leicestershire, and twice into Northamptonshire. This necessarily occasioned my being more busily employed on my return. But, secondly, my hands have been unusually full lately at home, partly from the prevalence of Antinomian poison among many professors in our town and congregation, and partly from greater success than ordinary attending my poor labors for my dear Master. Several have been under great awakenings; ten have lately joined us; yesterday I was rejoiced to hear that nineteen inquiring souls met at the house of one of our members; one besides has been with me this morning, and I expect two more tonight. My dear brother, it is pleasant to write to you under the endearing idea of Christian friendship; but you will, I know, forgive me when I say it is sweeter still to listen to the lispings of so many babes in grace, who are just beginning to say, 'Abba, Father,' and to regard them as 'children whom the Lord hath given me,'—poor unworthy me! O how I should rejoice to contemplate you in a similar, or more prosperous situation. You sometimes sit with your dear Mrs. S. by your side, and your little family around you; and, as you look, you love and are delighted. 'These children of mine (you say) will support my old age, and administer comfort when the springs of life begin to decline.' 'Blessed be God, I can sometimes contemplate my children in the faith, and say, 'ye are my hope and my joy, and shall be my crown of rejoicing in the day of the Lord Jesus.' Amen, so be it.

"Never was the sentiment of the text and sermon which you have transcribed from my manuscript more exemplified since God deigned to put gospel treasure into the brittle contemptible vessels of human nature, than it is in *Cannon-street;* surely the excellency of the power is not of man, but of God.

"O when will the time, the longed-for time arrive, when the Messiah's ensign shall be lifted high, and Jews and Gentiles, Pagans and Mohammedans, Africans and Indians, be gathered unto it?

> 'Fly abroad, thou mighty gospel,
> Win and conquer, never cease;
> Spread from eastern coast to western,
> Multiply and still increase:
> Hasten, Lord, this glorious day.'

"One journey I made to Northamptonshire was with a view to assist in *setting on foot a mission to the unconverted heathen.* It has long engaged the unusual concern of many ministers in our connection about the centre of the kingdom. Brother Carey, of Leicester, published on the subject; and last Wednesday evening we drew out a sketch of an institution for so great a design. May He, whose glory I trust we have in view, direct all future deliberations, and make the embryo effort ripen and succeed, till future ages prove that the plan begun at Kettering, October 3, 1790, comprehended in its consequences the salvation of the world. 'Soon,' my brother, 'soon (it is said) Ethiopia shall stretch forth her hands unto God.' May we, like our divine Master, not fail nor be discouraged, until the gospel be established in the earth, and the waiting isles have received the law of him who is the approaching 'desire of all nations!'

"O that our little selves were more lost and swallowed up in the general interests of mankind, and the honors of our illustrious Lord! Never did I feel myself a more contemptible reptile than when preaching last night from Prov. 19:21. The immutability of the divine counsels, and the omnipotence of the divine arm, exhibit a striking contrast with the limited power of mutable man. Well may we stand on the shore, and, gazing on the ocean of divine perfections, exclaim, 'O the depths, &c. Great God, 'I am a worm, and no man;' I am but an atom composed of the meanest matter, and in myself unqualified for the meanest service; but, in thy hand, 'a straw shall thresh a mountain,' and a 'barley cake put a host of thine enemies to flight.' Work, Lord, as thou wilt; send by whom thou wilt; for, when 'thou dost work, who shall let it?'

"We take a part in the pleasure which you must feel in reflecting on the gracious interposition of the Lord on behalf of Mrs. S. Who is a God like ours? O, what praising, living Christians should we be if we lived as our obligations to sovereign mercy teach us; dead to the world—alive to God—far from gloom —full of joy! Heaven would be begun below; and, like saints in apostolic ages, we should be 'praising God, and in favor with all his people.' Well! the tiresome days of sad complaint are rolling fast away; many are already gone; ere this reaches you, another will have been numbered with those beyond the flood; soon the night of death will come—a short night, but it will usher in a day, O how permanent! an eternal day! which shall be succeeded by night no more! Come Lord Jesus, come quickly.

"I have lately been much reconciled to death! First, from a persuasion that the Lord can accomplish all his purposes of grace as well without the use of so poor a worm as with him; and, secondly, from a comparison of this sinful state with that sinless world. O, my brother, it is sin, cursed sin, that turns man to a devil, and earth to hell. It is holiness, perfect holiness, which forms the heaven of God, of angels, and of the spirits of just men made perfect; and I can say this is the heaven I want. O, if the kingdom of glory contained a million of blessings, and God were to bid me choose, my heart would reply, 'Lord! give me the blessing of perfect conformity to thee, and then bestow the rest on angels: I'll envy not their portion, having enough in possessing thy image, and in thy image thee.   S. P."

In the year 1791 he married Miss Sarah Hopkins, daughter of Mr. Joshua Hopkins of Alcester—a connection which appears to have been all along a source of great enjoyment to him. The following lines addressed to Mrs. Pearce when he was on a journey, a little more than a year after their marriage, seem to be no more than a common letter; yet they show, not only the tenderness of his affection, but his heavenly-mindedness, his gentle manner of persuading, and how every argument was fetched from religion, and every incident improved for introducing it:

"Chipping Norton, August 15, 1792.

"I believe, on retrospection, that I have hitherto rather anticipated the proposed time of my return, than delayed the interview with my dear Sarah for an hour. But what shall I say, my love, now to reconcile you to my procrastinating my return for several days more? Why I will say—It appears I am called of God; and I trust the piety of both of us will submit and say, Thy will be done.

"You have no doubt perused Mr. Ryland's letter to me, wherein I find he solicits an exchange. The reason he assigns is so obviously important, that a much greater sacrifice than we are called to make should not be with-held to accomplish it. I therefore propose, God willing, to spend the next Lord's Day at Northampton. I thought of taking tea with you this evening: *that* would have been highly gratifying to us both; but it must be our meat and drink to do and submit to the will of our heavenly Father. All is good that comes from him, and all is done right which is done in obedience to him. Oh to be perfectly resigned to his disposal—how good is it! May you, my dearest Sarah, and myself, daily prove the sweetness of this pious frame of soul: then all our duties will be sweet, all our trials will be light, all our pleasures will be pure, and all our hopes sanctified.

"This evening I hope to be at Northampton. Let your prayers assist my efforts on the ensuing Sabbath. You will, I trust, find in Mr. Ryland a ship richly laden with spiritual treasures. Oh for more supplies from the exhaustless mines of grace!"

The exemplary diligence with which he pursued the duties of his pastoral office, about this time, will be evident from the following letter to Mr. Stoughton.

"Birmingham, March 30, 1792.

"My dear Brother,

"A violent head-ache prevents my attending our prayer-meeting this evening; but, as I am a letter in your debt, I will endeavor to repay you, notwithstanding my complaint; you must expect me to be brief. If I fill the sheet it must be deemed a work of supererogation.

"You have, probably, heard of the late transaction of our church; we were under the disagreeable necessity of separating two of our members. It was done publicly, with much solemnity, on Lord's Day; the members seemed much affected; we appointed the following day to be set apart for fasting and prayer; we met at nine, and continued confessing and supplicating till half past one. I believe the Lord was with us, both to notice and approve. We began the next day a prayer-meeting at five o'clock in the morning, to be continued every day without intermission, except Lord's Day; then, as usual, to be at seven. Beyond my expectations, we have had between thirty and fifty persons present most mornings since. I have found it to my advantage to attend regularly; the effects have been already seen; the young people have been amazingly revived; they meet four or five times for prayer every Lord's Day, besides the public opportunities. In preaching, I have enjoyed more of the substantial assistance of divine grace than usual; several persons, in darkness of soul, have been brought into the marvelous light of divine comfort; the hearers have been quickened; ten persons have applied for admission to the church in a less number of days, which, with one before, make eleven candidates; seven of them, I believe, were called in Cannon-street; among them the youth of sixteen, concerning whom I wrote you last. Next Lord's Day week, April 8th, I shall baptize some of them; we have not time to receive the experience of all; the rest must wait another month; who can tell but God may bring more to join them, who are yet in obscurity? I know of some who indeed appear 'inquiring the way to Zion, with their faces thither-ward.'

"We are next to divide the whole church into district meetings, similar to that of brother Eld's, with which you sometimes attended; I am in hopes it will wonderfully conduce to promote the union and affection of the body.

"In addition to all this, each member is numbered in the church book, &c.; cards with his or her name, and the corresponding number, thus are delivered to every individual, who is to put one on the poor's plate at each ordinance; the deacons and ministers afterwards compare the numbers and names, and whoever is found wanting is to be waited upon in the course of the ensuing week, to inquire the cause of absence. Thus shall we come at a pretty general knowledge of the state of the church at large; may we have wisdom to guide us as angels of God.

"I am, my dear friend,

"Yours, very affectionately,   S. P."

The soul of Mr. Pearce was formed for friendship; it was natural therefore to suppose that, while engaging in the pursuit of his studies at the academy, he would contract religious intimacies with some of his brethren; and it is worthy of notice, that the grand cement of his friendship was *kindred piety*. In the two following letters, addressed to his friend Mr. Steadman, the reader will perceive the justness of this remark, as well as the encouraging prospects which soon attended his labors at Birmingham:

"*May* 9, 1792.

"My Very Dear Brother,

"You live so remote that I can hear nothing of your prosperity at Broughton. I hope you are settled with a comfortable people, and that you enjoy much of your Master's presence, both in the study and in the pulpit. For my part, I have nothing to lament but an insensible, ungrateful heart, and that is sufficient cause for lamentation. This, only this, bows me down; and under this pressure I am ready to adopt the words I preached from last evening—'*Oh that I had wings like a dove: for then would I fly away and be at rest!*'

"As a people we are generally united; I believe more so than most churches of the same dimensions. Our number of members is about 295, between forty and fifty of whom have joined us since I saw you, and most of them I have the happiness of considering as my children in the faith.—There is still a crying out amongst us after salvation; and still, through much grace, it is my happiness to point them to 'the Lamb of God, who taketh away the sins of the world.'

"In preaching, I have often peculiar liberty; at other times barren. I suppose my experience is like that of most of my brethren; but I am not weary of my work. I hope still that I am willing to spend and be spent, so that I may win souls to Christ, and finish my course with joy: but I want more heart religion; I want a more habitual sense of the Divine presence; I want to walk with God as Enoch walked. There is nothing that grieves me so much, or brings so much darkness on my soul, as my little spirituality, and frequent wanderings in secret prayer. I cannot neglect the duty; but it is seldom that I enjoy it.

> 'Ye that love the Lord indeed,
> Tell me, is it so with you?'

"When I come to the house of God, I pray and preach with freedom. Then I think the presence of the people seems to weigh more with me than the presence of God, and deem myself a hypocrite, almost ready to leave my pulpit, for some pious preacher. But the Lord does own the word; and again I say, If I go to hell myself, I will do what I can to keep others from going thither; and so in the strength of the Lord I will.

"An observation once made to me helps to support me above water: 'If you did not plough in your closet, you would not reap in the pulpit.' And again I think, the Lord *dwelleth in Zion,* and loveth it *more* than the dwellings of Jacob.'   S.P."

"Feb. 1, 1793.

"The pleasure which your friendly epistle gave me rises beyond expression; and it is one of the first wishes of my heart ever to live in your valued friendship. Accept this, and my former letters, my dear brother, as sufficient evidences of my ardent wishes to preserve, by correspondence, that mutual remembrance of each other which on any part will ever be pleasurable, and on yours, I hope, never painful.

"But, ah, how soon may we be rendered incapable of such an intercourse! When I left Bristol, I left it with regret. I was sorry to leave my studies to embark, inexperienced as I am, on the tempestuous ocean of public life, where the high blowing winds, and rude noisy billows, must more or less inevitably annoy the trembling voyager. Nor did it make a small addition to my pain that I was to part with so many of my dear companions, with whom I had spent so many hours, either in furnishing or unburdening the mind. I need not say, amongst the first of these I considered Josiah Evans.[5] But ah, my

---

[5] The following extract from the account of this excellent young man, drawn up by Mr. Pearce, who had been his fellow student at Bristol, for Dr. Rippon's Register,

friend, we shall see his face no more! Through Divine grace I hope
we shall go to him; but he will not return to us. 'He wasted away, he
gave up the ghost, and where is he?' I was prepared for the news
because I expected it. The last time I heard directly from him was by
a very serious and affectionate letter, which I received, I think, last
September. To it I replied; but received no answer. I conjectured—I
feared; and now my conjectures and fears are all realized. Dear
departed youth! Thy memory will ever be grateful to this affectionate
breast. May thy amiable qualities live again in thy surviving friend,
that, to the latest period of his life, he may thank God for the
friendship of Josiah Evans!

"I assure you, my dear Steadman, I feel, keenly feel, the force of
the sentiment which Blair thus elegantly expresses:

> 'Of joys departed, ne'er to he recalled,
> How painful the remembrance!'

"But I sorrow not as one without hope. I have a two-fold hope; I
hope he is now among the spirits of the just made perfect and that
he will be of the blessed and holy number who has part in the first
resurrection; and I hope also, through the same rich, free, sovereign,
almighty, matchless grace, to join the number too. Pleasing thought!
United to divide no more!

---

will serve at once as a specimen of that endearing intimacy which Mr. P. and his
associate cultivated, and as a model of that friendship which Christians, and
especially students for the gospel ministry, should ever seek to enjoy.

"Mr. Evans had one essential qualification for friendship, which was
faithfulness. I believe he never discerned any thing in my temper or conduct which
he thought would be injurious to my proficiency as a student, or to my spirituality
as a Christian, (after our intimacy commenced,) but he watched the first
opportunity of laying it before me, with the reasons of his disapprobation. On some
of those occasions he would give his friendly admonitions and counsels with such
affectionate eloquence, that the result has been our retiring together with tears,
lamenting our mutual imperfections before God, and beseeching wisdom and grace
from above, to adorn our profession, and in every step to pursue something worthy
of our being and character. Some of the moments we thus spent, I believe, were
marked with as true humiliation of heart as ever we knew; for, as we did not
conceal the various states of our minds from each other, we had no occasion to
restrain our feelings, and guard our expressions, in these exercises; on the contrary,
we felt as much freedom as though we had been apart, and realized the presence of
none but our Maker.

"*A world, for such a friend, to lose is gain.*"

I preached last night from Rev. 21:6, 'I will give unto him that is athirst of the fountain of the water of life freely.' I took occasion to expound the former part of the chapter, and found therein a pleasure inexpressible; especially when speaking from the first verse—'*and there was no more sea.*' The first idea that presented itself to me was this—*There shall be no bar to intercourse.* Whether the thought be just, or not, I leave with you and my hearers to determine; but I found happy liberty in illustrating it. What is it that separates one nation, and one part of the globe, from another? Is it not the sea? Are not Christians, though all of one family, the common Father of which is God, separated by this sea, or that river, or the other stream below? Yes; but they are one family still. *There shall be none of these obstructions to communion, of these bars to intercourse; nothing to divide their affections or disunite their praise for ever.—Forgive my freedoms. I am writing to a friend, to a brother."

S.P."

There are few, if any, thinking men but who at some seasons have had their minds perplexed with regard to religious principles, even those which are of the greatest importance. In the end, however, where the heart is right, such exercises commonly issue in a more decided attachment to the truth. Thus it was with Mr. Pearce. In another part of the above letter, he thus writes to his friend Steadman:

"I have, since I saw you, been much perplexed about some doctrinal points, both Arminian and Socinian, I believe through reading very attentively, but without sufficient dependence on the Spirit of truth, several controversies on those subjects; particularly the writings of Whitby, Priestley, and others. Indeed, had the state of mind I was in about ten weeks since continued, I should have been incapable of preaching with comfort at all. But in the mount of the Lord will he be seen. Just as I thought of giving up, He who hath the hearts of all men in his hand, and turneth them as the rivers of water are turned, was pleased, by a merciful though afflicting providence, to set me at a happy liberty.

"I was violently seized with a disorder very rife here, and which carried off many, supposed to be an inflammation of the bowels. One Sabbath evening I felt such alarming symptoms that I did not expect to see the Monday morning. In these circumstances I realized the feelings of a dying man. My mind had been so accustomed to reflect on virtue and moral goodness, that the first thing I attempted was a survey of my own conduct; my diligence and faithfulness in the ministry, my unspotted life, &c. &c. But, ah, vain props these for dying men to rest on! Such heart sins, such corruptions, and evil propensities, recurred to my mind, that if ever I knew the moment when I felt my own righteousness to be as loathsome and filthy rags, it was then. And where should I, where could I, where did I flee, but to Him whose glory and grace I had been of late degrading, at least in my thoughts? Yes, there I saw peace for guilty consciences was to be *alone* obtained through an almighty Savior. And oh, wonderful to tell, I again came to him; nor was I sent away without the blessing. I found him full of all compassion, ready to receive the most ungrateful of men.

> 'Oh to grace how great a debtor
> Daily I'm constrained to be!'

Thus, my dear brother was the snare broken, and thus I escaped.

> 'A debtor to mercy alone,
> Of covenant mercy I sing.'

Join with me in praising Him who remembered me in my low estate, because his mercy endureth for ever. Yet this is among the *all things*. I have found it has made me more spiritual in preaching. I have prized the gospel more than ever, and hope it will be the means of guarding me against future temptations."

S.P.

From his first coming to Birmingham, his meekness and patience were put to the trial by an Antinomian spirit which infected many individuals, both in and out of his congregation. It is well known with what affection it was his practice to beseech sinners to be reconciled to God, and to exhort Christians to the exercise of practical godliness; but these were things which they could not endure. Soothing doctrine was all they desired. Therefore it was that his ministry was traduced by them as Arminian, and treated with neglect and contempt. But, like his Divine Master, he bore the contradiction of sinners against himself, and this while he had the strongest satisfaction that, in those very things to which they objected, he was pleasing God. And though he plainly perceived the pernicious influence of their principles upon their own minds, as well as the minds of others, yet he treated them with great gentleness and long forbearance; and when it became necessary to exclude such of this description as were in communion with him, it was with the greatest reluctance that he came into that measure, and not without having first tried all other means in vain. He was not apt to deal in harsh language; yet, in one of his letters about that time, he speaks of the principles and spirit of these people as a "cursed leaven."

Among his numerous religious friendships; he seems to have formed one for the special purpose of *spiritual improvement.* This was with Mr. Summers, of London, who often accompanied him in his journeys; to whom, therefore, it might be expected he would open his heart without reserve. Here, it is true, we sometimes see him, like his brethren, groaning under darkness, want of spirituality, and the remains of indwelling sin; but frequently rising above all, as into his native element, and pouring forth his ardent soul in the expression of joy and praise.

On Aug. 19, 1793, he writes thus:

"My Dear Brother,

"When I take my pen to pursue my correspondence with *you,* I have no concern but to communicate something which may answer the same end we propose in our annual journeys; namely, lending some assistance in the important object of *getting and keeping nearer to God.* This, I am persuaded, is the mark at which we should be continually aiming, nor rest satisfied until we attain that to which we aspire. I am really ashamed of myself, when, on the one hand, I review the time that has elapsed since I first assumed the Christian name, with the opportunities of improvement in godliness which have crowded on my moments since that period; and when, on the other, I *feel* the little advance I have made! More *light,* to be sure, I have; but light *without heat* leaves the Christian half dissatisfied. Yesterday, I preached on the duty of engagedness in God's service, from Jer. 30:21, 'Who is this that engaged his heart to approach unto me? saith the Lord' (a text for which I am indebted to our last journey). While urging the necessity of *heart* religion, including sincerity and ardor, I found myself much assisted by reflecting on the ardor which our dear Redeemer discovered in the cause of sinners. 'Ah,' I could not help saying, 'if our Savior had measured his intenseness in his engagements for us, by our fervency in fulfilling our engagements to him,—we should have been now further from hope than we are from perfection.'

> 'Dear Lord, the ardor of *thy* love
> Reproves my cold returns.'

"Two things are causes of daily astonishment to me:—The readiness of Christ to come from earth to heaven for me; and my backwardness to rise from earth to heaven with him. But, oh, how animating the prospect! A time approaches when we shall rise to sink no more; to 'be for ever with the Lord.' To be with *the Lord* for a week, for a day, for an hour; how sweetly must the moments pass! But to be *forever* with the Lord, *that* enstamps salvation with perfection; that gives an energy to our hopes, and a dignity to our joy, so as to render it *unspeakable and full of glory!* I have had a few realizing moments since we parted, and the effect has been, I trust, a broken heart. O my brother, it is desirable to have a broken heart, were it only for the sake of the pleasure it feels in being helped and healed by Jesus! Heart-affecting views of the cursed effects of sin are highly salutary to a Christian's growth in humility, confidence, and gratitude. At once how abasing and exalting is the comparison of our loathsome hearts with that of the lovely Savior! In Him we see all that can charm an angel's heart; in *ourselves* all that can gratify a devil's. And yet we may rest perfectly assured that these nests of iniquity shall, ere long, be transformed into the temples of God; and these sighs of sorrow be exchanged for songs of praise.

"Last Lord's Day I spent the most profitable Sabbath to myself that I ever remember since I have been in the ministry; and to this hour I feel the sweet solemnities of that day delightfully protracted. Ah, my brother, were it not for past experience I should say,

> 'My heart presumes I cannot lose
> The relish all my days.'

But now I rejoice with trembling, desiring to 'hold fast what I have, that no man take my crown. Yet fearing that I shall find how,

> —'Ere one fleeting hour is past,
> The flattering world employs

Some sensual bait to seize my taste,
And to pollute my joys.'"

"Yours, in our dear Savior,   S.P."

In April, 1794, dropping a few lines to the compiler of these Memoirs, on a Lord's Day evening, he thus concludes:—"We have had a good day. I find, as a dear friend once said, *it is pleasant speaking for God when we walk with him.* Oh for much of Enoch's spirit! The Head of the church grant it to my dear brother, and his affectionate friend—S. P."

A few months before this, writing to Mr. Staughton, he says: "I rejoice, my dear brother, in the delightful prospect of usefulness which appears to be opening upon you. May the Dayspring from on high still continue to enlighten you, and by you the benighted souls of your fellow-men around you. O that we may preach him plainly, faithfully, constantly, practically; and he hath said that his word shall not return void. We may, as ministers, adopt the evangelical lines of that popular hymn, and with reference to the subject of our preaching, say,

'None but Jesus, none but Jesus,
Can do helpless sinners good.'"

In another letter to Mr. Summers, dated June 24, 1794, he thus writes:—"We, my friend, have entered on a correspondence of heart with heart; and must not lose sight of that avowed object. I thank you sincerely for continuing the remembrance of so unworthy a creature in your intercourse with Heaven; and I thank that sacred Spirit whose quickening influences, you say, you enjoy in the exercise. Yes, my brother, I have reaped the fruits of your supplications. I have been indulged with some seasons of unusual joy, tranquil as solitude, and solid as the Rock on which our hopes are built. In public exercises, peculiar assistance has been afforded; especially in these three things:—The exaltation of the Redeemer's glory—the detection of the crooked ways, false refuges, and self-delusions of the human heart—and the stirring up of the saints to press onward, making God's cause their own, and considering themselves as living not for themselves, but for *Him* alone.

"Nor hath the word been without its effect: above fifty have been added to our church this year, most of whom I rejoice in as the seals of my ministry in the Lord. Indeed, I am surrounded with goodness; and scarcely a day passes over my head but I say, 'Were it not for an *ungrateful heart,* I should be the happiest man alive; and *that* excepted, I neither expect nor wish to be happier in this world.' My wife, my children, and myself, are uninterruptedly healthy; my friends kind; my soul at rest; my labors successful, &c. Who should be content and thankful if I should not? O my brother, help me to praise!"

In a letter to Mrs. Pearce, from Plymouth, dated Sept. 2, 1794, the dark side of the cloud seems towards him:—"I have felt much barrenness," says he, "as to spiritual things, since I have been here, compared with my usual frame at home; and it is a poor exchange to enjoy the creature at the expense of the Creator's presence! A few seasons of spirituality I have enjoyed; but my heart, my inconstant heart, is too prone to rove from its proper center. Pray for me, my dear, my dearest friend: I do for you daily. O wrestle for me, that I may have more of Enoch's spirit! I am fully persuaded that a Christian is no longer really happy, and inwardly satisfied, than whilst he walks with God; and I would this moment rejoice to abandon every pleasure here for a closer walk with him. I cannot, amidst all the round of social pleasure, amidst the most inviting scenes of nature, *feel* that peace with God which passeth understanding. My thirst for preaching Christ, I fear, abates, and a detestable vanity for the reputation of *a 'good preacher'* (as the world terms it) has already cost me many conflicts. Daily I feel convinced of the propriety of a remark which my friend Summers made on his journey to Wales, that 'it is easier for a Christian to walk habitually near to God than to be irregular in our walk with him.' But I want resolution; I want a contempt for the world; I want more heavenly-mindedness; I want more humility; I want much, very much, of that which God alone can bestow. Lord, help the weakest Lamb in all thy flock!

"I preached this evening from Cant. 2:3,—*'I sat down under his shadow with great delight, and his fruit was sweet to my taste.'* But how little love for my Savior did I feel! With what little affection and zeal did I speak! I am by some praised. I am followed by many. I am respected by most of my acquaintance. But all this is nothing, yea, less than nothing, compared with possessing this testimony, *that I please God.* O thou Friend of sinners, humble me by repentance, and melt me down with love!

"Tomorrow morning I set off for Launceston. I write tonight, lest my stay in Cornwall might make my delay appear tedious to the dear and deserving object of my most undissembled love. O my Sarah, had I as much proof that I love *Jesus Christ* as I have of my love to *you*, I should prize it more than rubies! As often as you can find an hour for correspondence, think of your more than ever affectionate—S. P."

On the same subject, and the same occasion, about three weeks afterwards, (Sept. 23, 1794,) he wrote to Mr. Summers. His dissatisfaction with himself while spending his time in visits, and his satisfaction when engaged in his proper work, are well worthy of attention. "I was pretty much engaged in preaching," says he, "and often felt enlarged in public work; but, in private, my almost daily cry was, 'My leanness, my leanness!' Indeed it was a barren visit, as to the inward exercises of grace. Now and then I felt a brokenness of spirit, and a panting after God; but in general my mind was in a dissipated state. After so long an absence from so large an acquaintance, I was always crowded with company, some of whom, though amiable, were very gay. Their politeness and cheerfulness, joined with a high degree of indulgence, were too fascinating for my volatile mind. I admired, and was too much conformed to their spirit. I did indeed often struggle with myself, and watched for occasions of dropping some improving hint; but, either through want of opportunity or of fortitude, the hint seldom produced a long conversation, or a permanent effect. New visits, or excursions, were every day proposed, and my heart was continually divided between painful recollection and flattering hopes. One lesson, indeed, I have thoroughly learned—that real, solid satisfaction is to be found in nothing but God. May I have grace to improve it throughout my future life.

"The last week I have known more of the power of inward religion than all the four which I have spent from home. I devoted the week to my Lord's service entirely, and I found in keeping his commandments great reward."

In another letter to Mr. Summers, dated Nov. 10, 1794, he says—"I suppose I shall visit London in the spring: prepare my way by communion both with God and man. I hope your soul prospers. I have enjoyed more of God within this month than ever since the day of my espousals with him. O my brother, help me to praise! I cannot say that I am quite so exalted in my frame today; yet still I acknowledge what I have lived upon for weeks—that were there no being or thing in the universe beside God and me, I should be at no loss for happiness. Oh,

> ''Tis heaven to rest in his embrace,
> And no where else but there.'''

CHAPTER II

HIS DEEP INTERST IN MISSIONS TO THE HEATHEN—HIS LABORIOUS EXERTIONS IN PROMOTING THEM—AND HIS OFFERING HIMSELF TO BECOME A MISSIONARY.

Mr. Pearce was uniformly the spiritual and the active servant of Christ; but neither his spirituality nor his activity would have appeared in the manner they have, but for his engagements in the *introduction of the gospel among the heathen.*

It was not long after his settlement at Birmingham that he became acquainted with Mr. William Carey, in whom he found a soul nearly akin to his own. When the brethren in the counties of Northampton and Leicester formed themselves into a missionary society at Kettering, in October, 1792, he was there, and entered into the business with all his heart. On his return to Birmingham, he communicated the subject to his congregation with so much effect, that, in addition to the small sum of 13 pounds, 2s. 6d., with which the subscription was begun, 70 pounds were collected, and transmitted to the treasurer; and the leading members of the church formed themselves into an assistant society. Early in the following spring, when it was resolved that our brethren, Thomas and Carey, should go on a mission to the Hindus, and a considerable sum of money was wanted for the purpose, he labored with increasing ardor in various parts of the kingdom; and when the object was accomplished, he rejoiced in all his labor, smiling in every company, and blessing God.

During his labors and journeys on this important object he wrote several letters to his friends, an extract or two from which will disclose the state of his mind at this period, as well as the encouragements that he met with in his work at home:

To Mr. Steadman.[6]

Birmingham, Feb. 8, 1793

"My Very Dear Brother,

"Union of sentiment often creates friendship among carnal men, and similarity of feeling never fails to produce affection among pious men, as far as that similarity is known. I have loved you ever since I knew you. We saw, we felt alike, in the interesting concerns of personal religion. We formed a reciprocal attachment. We expressed it by words. We agreed to do so by correspondence; and we have not altogether been wanting to our engagements. But our correspondence has been interrupted, not, I believe, through any diminution of regard on either side; I am persuaded not on mine. I rather condemn myself as the first aggressor; but I excuse while I condemn, and so would you, did you know half the concerns which devolve upon me in my present situation. Birmingham is a central place; the inhabitants are numerous; our members are between three and four hundred. The word preached has lately been remarkably blessed. In less than five months I baptized nearly forty persons, almost all newly awakened. Next Lord's Day week I expect to add to their number. These persons came to my house to propose the most important of all inquiries—'What must we do to be saved?' I have been thus engaged some weeks, during the greatest part of most days. This, with four sermons a week, will account for my neglect. But your letter, received this evening, calls forth every latent affection of my heart for you. We are, my dear brother, not only united in the common object of pursuit—salvation; not only rest our hopes on the same foundation—Jesus Christ; but we feel alike respecting the poor heathens. Oh how Christianity expands the mind! What tenderness for our poor fellow sinners! What sympathy for their moral misery! What desires to do them everlasting good doth it provoke! How satisfying to our judgments is this evidence of grace! How gratifying to our present taste are these benevolent breathings! Oh how I love that man whose soul is deeply affected

---

[6] This excellent man lived to a good old age; for many years before his death he was the beloved and eminently successful pastor of the first Baptist church at Bradford, Yorkshire, and the not less excellent president of the Baptist College near that town. Not a few of his students in England, in these states, and in the missionary field, bless his memory, and refer with delight to the man whom good Dr. Ryland, in his own peculiar manner and voice, used to call "that great lump of goodness, Dr. Steadman."

with the importance of the precious gospel to idolatrous heathens! Excellently, my dear brother, you observe, that, great as its blessings are in the estimation of a sinner called in a Christian country,—inexpressibly greater must they shine on the newly illuminated mind of a converted pagan.

"We shall be glad of all your assistance in a pecuniary way, as the expense will be heavy. Dear brother Carey has paid us a visit of love this week. He preached excellently tonight. I expect Brother Thomas next week, or the week after. I wish you would meet him here. I have a house at your command, and a heart greatly attached to you."   S.P.

To Mr. Fuller.
"Feb. 23, 1793.

"I am willing to go any where, and do any thing in my power, but I hope no plan will be suffered to interfere with the affecting— hoped for—dreaded day, March 13 (the day of our brethren Carey and Thomas's solemn designation at Leicester). Oh how the anticipation of it at once rejoices and afflicts me! Our hearts need steeling to part with our much-loved brethren, who are about to venture their all for the name of the Lord Jesus. I feel my soul melting within me when I read the 20th chapter of the Acts, and especially verses 36-38. But why grieve? We shall see them again. Oh yes; them and the children whom the Lord will give them;—we and the children whom the Lord hath given us. We shall meet again, not to weep and pray, but to smile and praise."   S.P.

From the day of the departure of the missionaries, no one was more importunate in prayer than Mr. Pearce; and on the news of their safe arrival, no one was more filled with joy and thankfulness. The following extracts of letters to them will exhibit the interest he felt in their welfare as well as in the prosperity of the church of Christ at large.

(To Mr. Thomas and Mr. Carey)
"Kettering, May 26, 1794

"My Dear Brethren,
"Where you now are, where this may find you, or whether it will ever reach you, I know not; but be your present sojourning where it may, whether at Tranquebar, Calcutta, Malda, or elsewhere, I feel the

most affectionate attachment to your persons, and the highest degree of concern for your prosperity. Nor am I singular; the message you took to the Christian brethren in Hindostan I may now convey to yourselves, and say, 'Thousands of prayers have been, and still are, offered unto God on your behalf.' A more convincing proof of our regard we cannot give you; nor, I am persuaded, do you desire. O my dear, dear brethren, our separate prayers will be exchanged ere long for united praises, whilst our hearts glow with an ardor of gratitude and joy now unknown. What a motive is this to 'our always abounding in the work of the Lord!' Our reward will be great; our time both for working and suffering is but short; but the importance of the object we all pursue is infinite.

"You, brethren, are called to the most arduous part of this important service; but I doubt not you find in Asia, what we do in Europe, that 'God is faithful who hath called you to *partnership* (koinonia) with his Son Jesus Christ,' and gives you strength equal to your day. I long to hear of and from you, and with anxious expectation wait for some accounts from India.

"Many things have transpired since you left us, which I should have t a k e n pleasure in communicating; had you no other medium of intelligence; but brother Fuller has rendered this needless, by the detail of occurrences which he is prepared to give you; and nothing is so tedious as a twice-told tale. A few asides, however, he may have omitted; or, if twice told, may be of importance enough to forbid disgust.

"Our Mission Society has been the means of provoking other Christians to love and good works. An association is formed by the Independent Brethren in Warwickshire, for the propagation of the Gospel in that county, and if possible among the heathen too. It goes on with spirit, and promises success. I preached a sermon for them about a fort-night ago from Gal. 5:13, *'By love serve one another;'* and put my people's generosity again to the test. It gave me pleasure to find that at the doors 11 pounds, 1s. 3d. were contributed by them. I hope it will be a means of uniting us more firmly in the common cause. Another association was formed December 11, 1793, at Kidderminster, of seven churches in Worcestershire, for the purpose of promoting evangelical truth and union.

"The resolutions both of the Warwickshire and Worcestershire Associations are in print. To the former added a large extract from brother Carey's account of the state of the world, &c. Were I at home, I would send you a copy of both these publications, not doubting but you would derive considerable pleasure from a perusal; but I am now at Kettering, and preached yesterday for brother Fuller who is in London,——a successful pleader for the heathen, and the Society formed for their spiritual advantage. I will desire him to procure them for you in London, if possible, and hope he will succeed.

"We have had a considerable work of God to rejoice in at Cannon-Street the last winter: many have been converted unto him, and professed his name. Nor are other churches without occasion for praise; eight have been added at Arnsby; twelve I baptized at Leicester; and seven more I hear are about to join the dear people in Harvey Lane (Leicester) soon. A young man from our church at Birmingham has been preaching to them for above six months. He is generally approved. The congregation is upon the increase; and the prospect is at present very encouraging. The sermon I preached on the morning of baptism, at the request of the church, is now in the press; but I fear will not be out in time to admit the sending a few copies with this letter.

"At Walgrave there are nearly twenty young people under hopeful concern. Some have been added at: Northampton since brother Ryland has removed to Bristol, where he was formally settled the week before last: he is to spend some time with his friends at College Lane after the association; and I hear that seven candidates are waiting to receive baptism by his hands. At Chenies too, and at Earl's Barton, (where Mr. Shrewsbury was ordained over a congregation last Thursday,) and other places, the dear Redeemer's cause appears to be considerably advancing. What reason we have to praise the Lord, and give thanks to his holy name!

"I forget whether Guilsborough meeting-house was destroyed by some incendiaries before you sailed or not; be that as it may, a very good house, capable of containing 600 people, was opened last Wednesday fortnight; brother Sutcliff and I preached; I, from *'The wrath, of man shall praise thee;'* he from *'Save now, I beseech thee, 0 Lord; 0 Lord, I beseech thee, send now prosperity.'* It was a solemn and delightful day. Brother Blundell preached at night from Judges 5:31; and I again, to above two hundred people, the next morning at five o'clock. I recollect nothing more but what brother Fuller has written for your information already, and have therefore only to add the strongest assurances of my fraternal regard, and desire of hearing from you soon. Do give my love to brethren Ram Ram and Parbotee. It would give me great pleasure if you would prevail on the former (by profession a scribe) to write me; but I must get you to English it before it is sent off. I confess there is something of fancy in the request; but I think more of brotherly love. The idea of an epistle from a pious Hindu will be peculiarly gratifying; and perhaps a means of serving the good cause, by opening the heart, at well as convincing the judgments of some whose assistance in this good work may be solicited. Adieu, my dear brethren, pray for me, and do not forget me when an opportunity offers for sending to England.

"I am, most affectionately, yours in the dear Redeemer, S.P."

(To Mr. Thomas and Mr. Carey.)

"Birmingham, July 24, 1794.

"My very dear Brethren,

"It has rejoiced all our hearts to hear that you arrived safe in India, although the information would have afforded double joy had it been conveyed by letters from yourselves. All we knew for certainty, till yesterday, was that the Princess Maria had passed the Downs on her return to Denmark. Long we waited, and many letters of inquiry passed between brethren Ryland, Fuller, &c. the substance of which was, 'Have you beard from India?' All answered, 'No!' At last I got Mr. Potts, who does business with the captain, to write to him about you. Yesterday I received the joyful news that he 'landed you all in perfect good health.' I sat up all night to copy his letter for the satisfaction of various interested brethren; and now I have but five minutes left to write to you. What shall I say, dear brethren? We love you in the bowels of Christ, and we ardently pray for you every day. Our closets, our families, our stated and occasional meetings always witness our supplications for your peace, health, prudence, fortitude, perseverance and success. Not knowing where you were, Brother Fuller, who was in London collecting this year, sent £50 worth of goods for your use at a venture. We only want to know your necessities in order to supply them: but why have you not written at least to one of us? Perhaps you have before now: but the first three homeward bound East Indiamen this season have been captured by the French. Do write by more ships than one, and tell us all about your work and reward. The cause of Christ in England has not experienced much alteration since you left it. In some churches the sun of righteousness shines; in others, a wintry gloom prevails. Leicester church is, without exception, the most prosperous in the whole association. Seventeen have been lately added. At Birmingham I have baptized about sixty in the last twelve months.

"I can only say, my wife joins in the most affectionate regards to both of you and yours. Do my dear, dear brethren, write very soon to

"Your affectionate, though unworthy brother, S.P."

(To Mr. Carey)

"Birmingham, August 9, 1794.

"My very dear Brother,

"It was but a day or two after I had written my last letters that I had the inexpressible joy of receiving yours, dated Bay of Bengal, and Calcutta. That moment more than compensated for all the anxieties which my affection for you, and concern for the prosperity of the good cause in which you have embarked, had created. Yes, the harvest already begins to be gathered in; and though, in some respects, I, with my brethren here, went forth weeping; now I bear my sheaves, rejoicing in the prospect of a still larger crop.

"I need not acquaint you that, last Monday the Committee, with other warm friends to the mission, met at Guilsborough. Brother Fuller's letter will render all that information mere tautology. The account you gave us inspired us with new vigor, and greatly strengthened our hands in the Lord. We read, and wept, and praised, and prayed. O, who but the Christian feels such pleasures as are connected with friendship for our dear Lord Jesus Christ? Were there no hereafter, my dying breath should praise him for giving me a heart decidedly for him and his glorious cause on earth. May my whole life be spent for Him! O, I feel, indeed I feel, that nothing is worth living for but his glory, and the good of his church. I hope I feel a daily conviction that I am a mere atom in creation—less than nothing, and vanity: yet, with all my conscious meanness and unworthiness, I cannot help feeling myself dignified in my relation to the Son of God; and the highest ambition of my heart is to do something for him while I live. There is no part of my life which I reflect on with so much pleasure as that which has been spent in behalf of the Society under whose patronage you are; and *thrice happy should I be, were the path of duty plain, if I could personally share the toils and pleasures of the mission with you.* At times I indulge a hope that my Lord will put me in a similar station; but then again, I think, he well knows I am inadequate to a task so arduous. Well, 'tis his to appoint—mine to acquiesce, submit, and obey. I trust, whenever, or wherever he calls, I shall have grace immediately to say, 'Speak, Lord, for thy servant heareth.' It is our mercy, my brother, that he chooses our inheritance for us: he knows best our fitness for the various posts in his spiritual kingdom; and so that we are but where he would have us, and doing what he bids us, we may rejoice in the common hope that be will at last say to us all, 'Well done.'

"Last Lord's day I read a part of your letter from the pulpit. It would have done you good had you seen the effects. It made the lame to leap as a hart, and caused the tongue of the dumb to sing! The following evening, being the monthly prayer-meeting, a crowd of Christians came to testify their joy and gratitude; and you may assure yourselves that you have the prayers of the Israel of God. Next Monday morning I purpose leaving Birmingham, for five or six weeks on a journey to my friends in Devonshire. It is now long past the hour of mid-night and tomorrow, or rather this day, is our ordinance day. I mention this to account for my not writing you two or three sheets of paper, as I should rejoice to do had I the time.

"Few occurrences have taken place in the circle of our acquaintance since my last letter. At Sutton, in the Elms, a young man from Bristol was ordained a few days ago. Brother Ryland gave the charge—Brother Fuller addressed the people—I spoke at night: It was a good day. The young man from our church is to be ordained over your dear friends, at Leicester, on the 21st of September. He has been, and is likely to be useful there: twenty-five persons, I think, have been baptized within the last five months, and more are on the way. At Birmingham the Lord has not forsaken us. I enclose two copies of the sermon I preached at Leicester—one for yourself, the other for Mr. Thomas. Had I more time, (for it was not till this evening that I had notice of your goods going so soon,) I would have made up a larger packet. The Society have voted you a Polyglot Bible and, Malay Testament, both of which brother Fuller has procured. Do write often; and be as particular as to your progress as your convenience will admit; especially give us such things respecting the natives, their customs, Shasters;[7] and attention to the Gospel, as are likely to interest Europeans. A few extracts of this kind from your letters will go a wonderful way in procuring support to the Society, and greatly facilitate our applications for the public benevolence. One well attested fact goes farther than a hundred speculations, however pious and promising. My, and my dear Mrs. P's. affectionate wishes attend all

---

[7] What the Koran is to the Muslim, the Shasters is to the Hindu. It is their accepted holy book.

your family. I hope you will tell the Society all your wants. No exertions on our part shall be wanting to make your situation comfortable. I rejoice that you and Mr. T. love one another. The God of love and peace be with you always,

"I am, my dear brother, with the most unfeigned respect and affection, your unworthy brother, in our dear Lord Jesus,   S.P."

Hitherto we had witnessed his zeal in promoting this important undertaking *at home*; but this did not satisfy him. In October, 1794, we were given to understand that he had for some time had it in serious contemplation to go himself, and to cast in his lot with his brethren in India. When his designs were first discovered, his friends and connections were much concerned, and endeavoured to persuade him that he was already in a sphere of usefulness too important to be relinquished. But his answer was, that they were too interested in the affair to be competent judges. And nothing would satisfy him short of his making a formal offer of his services to the committee: nor could he be happy for them to decide upon it without their appointing a day of solemn prayer for the purpose, and, when assembled, hearing an account of the principal exercises of his mind upon the subject, with the reasons which induced him to make the proposal, as well as the reasons alleged by his connections against it.

On October 4, 1794, he wrote to an intimate friend, of whom he entertained a hope that he might accompany him, as follows:

"Last Wednesday I rode to Northampton, where a ministers' meeting was held on the following day. We talked much about the mission. We read some fresh and very encouraging accounts. We lamented that we could obtain no suitable persons to send out to the assistance of our brethren. Now what do you think was said at this meeting? My dear brother, do not be surprised that *all* present united in opinion that in all our connection there was no man known to us so suitable as *you,* provided you were disposed for it, and things could be brought to bear. I thought it right to mention this circumstance; and one thing more I cannot refrain from saying, that, were it manifestly the will of God, I should call that the happiest hour of my life which witnessed our *both* embarking with our families on board one ship, as helpers of the servants of Jesus Christ already in Hindustan. Yes, I could unreluctantly leave Europe and all its contents for the pleasures and perils of this glorious service.

Often my heart in the sincerest ardors thus breathes forth its desires unto God,—'Here am I, send me.' But I am ignorant whether you from experience can realize my feelings. Perhaps you have friendship enough for me to lay open your meditations on this subject in your next. If you have had half the exercises that I have, it will be a relief to your laboring mind; or if you think I have made too free with you, reprove me, and I will love you still. Oh if I could find a heart that had been tortured and ravished like my own in this respect, I should form a new kind of alliance, and feel a friendship of a novel species. With eagerness should I communicate all the vicissitudes of my sensations, and with eagerness listen to a recital of kindred feelings. With impatience I should seek, and with gratitude receive, direction and support, and I hope feel a new occasion of thankfulness when I bow my knee to the Father of mercies and the God of all comfort. Whence is it that I thus write to you, as I have never written to any one before? Is there a fellowship of the spirit; or is it the confidence that I have in your friendship that thus directs my pen? Tell me, dear—! Tell me how you felt, and how you still feel, on this interesting subject, and do not long delay the gratification to your very affectionate friend and brother—S. P."

About this time he wrote to Mr. Carey the following letter, which is full of his usual zeal and self-dedication.

"Birmingham, October 24, 1794.

"My dear, dear Brother,

"Never did I take pen in hand with such a combination of interesting feelings before. Love for your person, respect for your character, joy at your prospects, gratitude for your communications, desire for your success, and, withal, a hope that we shall yet meet in the flesh, so variously affect me, that I can scarcely compose myself to write at all.

"Blessed by the God and Father of our Lord Jesus Christ, who inclines your heart to undertake his cause among the heathen—a cause which European Christians may blush that they have neglected so long. But I hope the day is dawning when we shall all feel and sing as angels—'Peace on earth, and good will to men.' We have indeed been seeking every man his own things, not the things of others. Ah, cursed self! how have Christians been bowing down to thy altar, forgetful that true philanthropy is a leading feature of that religion which they profess, and of the character of him whose name they bear. We talk of morals, whilst our neglect of the duties of the second table too plainly demonstrate that we have imbibed but a small portion of the spirit of the first. We abide the greatest part of our lives beneath the power of the common lethargy; and if perchance a desire ever rises in our bosom for the good of others, we congratulate ourselves on our superior love for mankind, and dose, and dose, whilst millions of immortal souls, as precious as our own, drop into hell without an effort for their salvation. Ah, wither is the apostolic spirit fled from the churches? Unlike the translated prophet who bequeathed a double portion of his spirit to his successor, the apostle of the Gentiles and his contemporaries seem to have taken all their heroism, affection, zeal, greatness of design, and comprehension of effort, with them to the skies, whilst we exist to gaze at what we scarce hope ever to obtain. But why? Where is the Lord God of Elijah? Where is the Lord God of Paul? Still he is near unto us, ready to animate with equal ardor the bosom of every faithful soldier who is willing to obey the injunctions of the Lord. You, my brother, have caught the falling mantle; but we in Europe are ready to ask 'hast thou not a blessing for us also?' Shall we not share the pains and pleasures, the conflicts and the conquests of our distant brethren? Who denies us the privilege? What forbids our standing in the same rank with them, and enjoying the honor of the foremost in the charge of Immanuel's troops upon the infernal powers among the heathen? Brother, I long to stand by your side, and participate in all the vicissitudes of the attack—an attack which nothing but cowardice can make unsuccessful. Yes, the Captain of our salvation marches at our head. Sometimes he may withdraw his presence (but not his power) to try our prowess with our spiritual arms and celestial armor. O, what cannot a lively faith do for the Christian soldier! It will bring the Deliverer from the skies; it will array him as with a vesture dipped in blood; it will place him in the front of the battle, and put a new song into our mouths—'These made war with the Lamb; but the Lamb shall overcome them.' Yes, he shall—the victory is sure before we enter the field; the crown is already prepared to adorn our brows, even that crown of glory which fadeth not away, and already we have resolved what to do with it.—we will lay it at the conqueror's feet, and say, 'Not unto us, O Lord, not unto us, but to thy name give glory,' while all heaven unites in the chorus, 'Worthy the Lamb.'

"Whither hath the subject of the conversion of the heathen world led me? Forgive the style, so much more like that of a declaimer than a correspondent; but I feel the immense magnitude of my subject, and (as a brother minister in an enclosed pamphlet says) 'I must write what I feel.' I will try to be more composed whilst I unbosom myself (at 15,000 miles distant) to one whom I so dearly love in the bowels of Christ Jesus.

"Neither of us has forgot a conversation a little before you left us, on the exercises of my mind respecting an effort for the spread of the gospel in foreign lands, which for ten years now have more or less attended me. I cannot forget your prediction, with which the conversation ended,—'well, you will come after us.' From that time to the present, the desire has been increasing with scarcely any intermission, except when spiritual things have been at a low ebb with me; but for several weeks past I have been too full to contain, and I resolved to come to a point either about going or staying. For this purpose, I first attentively considered my situation in every relation at home, and the duty of ministers arising from the general commission of our Lord, together with the disproportion of means to the multitude of mankind; and I concluded that it was my duty to join hands with you in your great and laudable undertaking. I expected opposition from many quarters; I thought I would take every prudent step the know the mind of God; and therefore, secondly, determined, after setting apart a certain day in every week, for some weeks, on purpose to pray, with fasting, to God, for his direction, and examining the matter on every side, I would (if the same views remained or were confirmed) lay the case before the Society and leave it with them to decide, resolving in the strength of God to abide by their judgment. The time I proposed to wait is now nearly expired. I have met with heart-breaking trials of a domestic nature since I made known my inclination; but I thank God I faint not, and every day more fully convinces me that I ought to go. Now, as I mean to adhere to my plan, I have not yet acquainted the Society with my views. There is a meeting at Road, on the 12th of November, 1794. That opportunity I intend to embrace, God willing, and then, whether my Master will count me worthy of so high a calling, or whether his providence will check my temerity, will be determined. I wish I had time to delay sending this letter till that period is past; but the ships sail in a few days, and I was unwilling that you should be unacquainted with the state of my mind. I have reason to be thankful that, notwithstanding I have been severely tried from quarters most afflictive, yet I never enjoyed so much of God since I have been in the ministry; where no friend would or could sympathise with me, I have found him ever nigh; and yesterday my wife told me that, on mature deliberation, she approved of the plan I have adopted, and was much more comfortable in her mind than ever before since she had known my wishes, and was willing to leave it to the judgment of the ministers as I proposed, hoping that she should see in it the hand of God. O help me to praise! It is a relief inexpressible. If I come, I am not without hopes of a companion in the good work. Brother—,(a man of the first-rate piety, deep humility, great zeal, and good sense) and I correspond on it; and he says nothing but a fear that he is not qualified keeps him from deciding. I think his judgment will be governed here by the opinion of the Society; and I have the pleasure of conveying to him, in their name, their opinions, that in all our connection, there was not a man so suitable as himself. Besides him, a brother who is not in the ministry, and his wife, have offered to accompany me if I go; a pair the most suitable that I can conceive of—poor people. Affection for my wife inclines the good woman to the voyage, and zeal and affection operate on her husband. I could not but think it a kind providence that the same afternoon on which my wife had been objecting, on account of her being incapable to do the work of a nurse and servant too, that same afternoon these good people offered their services; they are both my own children in the faith, of five years standing; active, simple, faithful, hospitable people, and are willing to be in the steerage rather than not go. If we all come, it will be no small addition to your church, or rather the church of the dear Lord Jesus in Asia.

"I have had Halhed's grammar about a fortnight; and have made myself master of most of the characters, the rules for the formation of nouns, and part of the chapter on pronouns; but I fear I shall be able to do but little to purpose, for want of a tutor to teach me the pronunciation. Of one character in the Sanskrit pronouns I can find no account anywhere: you will tell me readily when we meet; but I must leave it for the present. O how happy shall I be to sound the name of my dear Lord Jesus in the Bengalee tongue, on the plains of Hindostan! Give my love to dear Ram Boshoo; tell him I long to take him by the hand, and call him brother. I suppose ere now he has felt the constraints of divine love overcoming the fears of man, and that he has become an avowed disciple of the lowly and lovely Jesus. The Lord be with you when you partake together of the memorials of the Redeemer's sorrows. I want much to hear from you about Parbotee; so do all our friends. Perhaps some interesting account is now on the way for Europe. The Lord send us good news from a far country. In my next, I hope I shall be able with propriety to ask you withal to 'prepare me a lodging.' If I come next year, and any ship goes before me, by that you shall know all particulars.

"It is late on Saturday evening. I propose preaching tomorrow from 1 Cor. 13:13. The comprehension of Christian love as to its object—the sweetness, universality, and energy of its operations—with the permanency of its nature—have occurred as illustrative of its superiority to every other grace. The afternoon subject I think will be on 2 Cor. 3:8, including, among other things, the extent of the gospel dispensation. It comprehends gentiles as well as Jews, and Hindoos as well as Englishmen. I have not fixed on a subject for the evening yet. Adieu, my dear, dear, brother; the God of love, peace, and glory, be with you, and with

"Your unworthy, but affectionate brother in Christ Jesus, S.P."

About the same period he wrote the following letter, which, besides exhibiting evidences of the piety and zeal which animated his own breast, illustrates the happy talent he possessed of exhorting and persuading others to their duty in regard to the heathen. For many years after this letter was written, American Christians did little for this object——they are now happily awakening to their duty, and appear taking the foremost place in the army of the Lamb.

(To Mr. Rogers, of Philadelphia)
"Birmingham, Oct. 27, 1794

"My very dear Friend,

"It is certainly as impossible for Christians to maintain a pious intercourse without love, as for the magnetic needle to point any where but to the pole. Suffer me, then, if I address you in a less distant form than heretofore. I think of you with no less respect, nor of myself, I hope, with less humility, though I approach you with this unwonted familiarity. The difference arising from conscious inferiority, is not inconsistent, I presume, with the unrestrained effusions of Christian love.

"In situation, in publicity of character, in mental vigor, in age, in literary acquirements, in a thousand things, we may differ; but still we are *one in Christ Jesus*, that dear centre of union to holy angels and holy men, to perfect saints above and imperfect saints below. Allow me, then, in the exercise of that godlike grace, which has the precedence even to that *faith* which is unto salvation, and that *hope* which fastens upon immortality, to throw the arms of my affection across the Atlantic, and embrace you as a beloved brother in the Lord. Yes, you will allow it; you will not disdain my youth, nor want of name; you will regard me as participating of his paternal regards of whom the whole family in heaven and earth is named; you will give me the right hand of fellowship, and say, 'Affection without rudeness deserves no censure.'

"There is something in a similarity of circumstances which gives both tenderness and energy to our affectionate sensations. When I read the very affecting account of the late trial of your faith and patience, I felt as if affliction can strengthen the bonds of affection. I felt a fellowship with you unknown before. Mine was indeed but a taste compared with yours: your heavenly Father saw fit that you should drink the cup even to the dregs; but his wisdom and his love have an equal share in his conduct towards his people. During the few days my dearest friend lay senseless, on what we all expected would be the bed of death, I found his *sovereignty* silenced all my complaints, and his *love* sweetened all my sorrows. No doubt, you also have found strength equal to your day; and you daily see enough in God to compensate for the loss of every less good. It is thither I am obliged to fly for all substantial comfort; and, blessed be Jehovah, there I daily find it! Were there no being in the universe besides Jehovah and myself, I see enough in him to ravish and satisfy my soul. Well did the pious Psalmist say, 'Whom have I in heaven but thee; and there is none upon earth that I desire besides thee!' Lord, help us ever to say so too!

"Most sincerely do I thank you for your friendly epistle of June 18. Your account for Mr. M.'s conversion warmed my heart, and the hearts of many others to whom I read it. What a trophy of Immanuel's grace! But are we less so? The gradual rising of the sun is no less an effort of the divine energy; than the eccentric movements of the blazing comet; the latter may produce more surprise in the minds of a gazing crowd, but not more admiration in the heart of the devout philosopher. By whatever methods we became Christians, *all, all* must acknowledge, that 'by the grace of God we are what we are.' O that like him who first made that acknowledgement, your friend may be assisted to spend himself in successfully preaching that faith which once he destroyed!

"I know not how to make adequate acknowledgements for your introducing me to Mr. Jones, whose valuable correspondence I shall hope to retain. I love the man who tenderly feels for the souls of the poor heathen. What a reflection is it on the philanthropy of every Christian country that no more pains have been taken to carry the light of eternal life to those nations that sit in darkness and in the shadow of death! What a lapse of time since the Reformation! but how have its wasting years been improved to this important end? We and our fathers have thought, and spoken, and written, and heard, and read about Christian benevolence; we have investigated its nature, admired its beauty, contended for its importance to the Christian character, whilst, like the unapproved servant, though we knew our Master's will, we did it not. Almost the whole Christian world have partaken of the common lethargy; and if here and there a few have thought about the state of pagan nations, and felt a faint desire for their salvation, or at most mentioned the ingathering of the Jews and the fullness of the Gentiles as a thing of course in their prayers, they have felt a self-complacency on account of their superior zeal; comparing their feelings, not with the greatness of the subject, but with those of their yet more lethargic neighbors. They have satisfied themselves without any positive exertions, and lain down dozing, dozing at their ease, whilst thousands of immortal souls, as precious as their own, have been daily dropping into hell, without an effort made for their salvation! But I hope the time is come when we shall, every man, look no longer at his own things only, but the things of others. Zion already travails in birth, and soon she shall bring forth her children. Already heaven is besieged with earnest supplications: 'they who make mention of the Lord keep no longer silence, and will give him no rest until he make Jerusalem a praise in the earth.'   S.P."

About a month preceding the decision of this affair, he drew up *a narrative* of his experience respecting it; resolving at the same time to set apart one day in every week for secret fasting and prayer to God for direction; and to keep a *diary* of the exercises of his mind during the month.

When the committee were met at Northampton, according to his desire, he presented to them the narrative, which was as follows:

"October 8, 1794.

"Having had some peculiar exercises of mind relative to my personally attempting to labor for the dear Redeemer amongst the heathen, and being at a loss to know what is the will of the Lord in this matter respecting me, I have thought that I might gain some satisfaction by adopting these two resolutions: First, that I will, in the presence of God, faithfully endeavour to recollect the various workings of my mind on this subject, from the first period of my feeling any desire of this nature until now, and commit them to writing; together with what considerations do now, on the one hand, impel me to the work, and, on the other, what prevent me from immediately resolving to enter upon it. Secondly, that I will from this day keep a regular journal, with special relation to this matter.

"This account and journal will, I hope, furnish me with much assistance in forming a future opinion of the path of duty; as well as help any friends whom I may hereafter think proper to consult to give me suitable advice in the business. Lord, help me!

"It is very common for young converts to feel strong desires for the conversion of others. These desires immediately followed the evidences of my own religion; and I remember well they were particularly fixed upon the poor heathen. I believe the first week that I knew the grace of God in truth I put up many fervent cries to heaven in their behalf, and at the same time felt a strong desire to be employed in promoting their salvation. It was not long after that the first settlers sailed for Botany Bay. I longed to go with them, although in company with the convicts, in hopes of making known the blessings of the great salvation in New Zealand. I actually had thought of making an effort to go out unknown to my friends; but, ignorant how to proceed, I abandoned my purpose. Nevertheless I could not help talking about it; and at one time a report was circulated that I was really going, and a neighboring minister very seriously conversed with me upon the subject.

"While I was at the Bristol Academy, the desire remained; but not with that energy as at first, except on one or two occasions. Being sent by my tutor to preach two Sabbaths at Coleford, I felt *particular sweetness in devoting the evenings of the week to going from house to house among the colliers*, who dwelt in the Forest of Deane, adjoining the town, conversing and praying with them, and preaching to them. In these exercises I found the most solid satisfaction that I have ever known in discharging the duties of my calling. In a poor hut, with a stone to stand upon, and a three-legged stool for my desk, surrounded with thirty or forty of the smutty neighbors, I have felt such an unction from above that my whole auditory have been melted into tears, whilst directed to "the Lamb of God which taketh away the sin of the world;" and I, weeping among them, could scarcely speak, or they hear, for interrupting sighs and sobs. Many a time did I then think, thus it was with the apostles of our Lord, when they went from house to house among the poor heathen. In work like this I could live and die. Indeed, had I at that time been at liberty to settle, I should have preferred that situation to any in the kingdom with which I was then acquainted.

"But the Lord placed me in a situation very different. He brought me to Birmingham; and here, amongst the novelties, cares, and duties of my station, I do not remember any wish for foreign service, till, after a residence of some months, I heard Dr. Coke preach at one of Mr. Wesley's chapels, from Psalm 68:31, 'Ethiopia shall soon stretch out her hands unto God.' Then it was that, in Mr. Horne's phrase, 'I felt a passion for missions.' Then I felt an interest in the state of the heathen world far more deep and permanent than before, and seriously thought how I could best promote their obtaining the knowledge of the crucified Jesus.

"As no way at that time was open, I cannot say that I thought of taking a part of the good work among the heathen abroad; but resolved that I would render them all the assistance I could at home. My mind was employed during the residue of that week in meditating on Psalm 67:3, 'Glorious things are spoken of thee, O city of God;' and the next Sabbath morning I spoke from those words, on the promised increase of the church of God. I had observed that our monthly meetings for prayer had been better attended than the other prayer-meetings, from the time that I first knew the people in Cannon street; but I thought a more general attention to them was desirable. I therefore preached on the Sabbath day evening preceding the next monthly prayer-meeting from Matt. 6:10: 'Thy kingdom come;' and urged with ardor and affection a universal union of the serious part of the congregation in this exercise. It rejoiced me to see three times as many the next night as usual; and, for some time after that, I had nearly equal cause for joy.

"As to my own part, I continued to preach much upon the

promises of God respecting the conversion of the heathen nations; and by so doing, and always communicating to my people every piece of information I could obtain respecting the present state of missions, they soon imbibed the same spirit; and from that time to this they have discovered so much concern for the more extensive spread of the gospel, that at our monthly prayer-meetings, both stated and occasional, I should be as much surprised at the case of the heathen being omitted in any prayer as at an omission of the name and merits of Jesus.

"Indeed it has been a frequent means of enkindling my languid devotion, in my private, domestic, and public engagements in prayer. When I have been barren in petitioning for myself, and other things, often have I been sweetly enlarged when I came to notice the situation of those who were perishing for lack of knowledge.

"Thus I went on praying and preaching, and conversing on the subject, till the time of brother Carey's ordination at Leicester, May 24, 1791. On the evening of that day he read to the ministers a great part of his manuscript, since published, entitled, '*An Inquiry into the Obligations of Christians to use Means for the Conversion of the Heathen.*' This added fresh fuel to my zeal. But to pray and preach on the subject was all I could then think of doing. But when I heard of a proposed meeting at Kettering, October 2, 1792, for the express purpose of considering our duty in regard to the heathen, I could not resist my inclination for going, although at that time I was not much acquainted with the ministers of the Northamptonshire association. There I got my judgment informed, and my heart increasingly interested. I returned home resolved to lay myself out in the cause. The public steps I have taken are too well known to need repeating; but my mind became now inclined to go among the heathen myself. Yet a consideration of my connections with the dear people of God in Birmingham restrained my desires, and kept ore from naming my wishes to any body, (as I remember,) except to brother Carey. With him I was pretty free. We had an interesting conversation about it just before he left Europe. I shall never forget the *manner of* his saying, 'Well, you will come after us.' My heart said amen! and my eagerness for the work increased; though I never talked freely about it, except to my wife, and we then both thought that my relation to the church in Cannon Street, and usefulness there, forbad any such an attempt. However, I have made it a constant matter of prayer, often begging of God, as I did when first I was disposed for the work of the ministry, either that he would take away the desire, or open a door for its fulfillment. And the result has uniformly been, that the more spiritual I have been in the frame of my mind, the more love I have felt for God; and the more communion I have enjoyed with him, so much the more disposed have I been to engage as a missionary among the heathen.

"Until the accounts came of our brethren's entrance on the work in India, my connections in Europe pretty nearly balanced my desire for going abroad; and though I felt quite devoted to the Lord's will and work, yet I thought the scale rather preponderated on the side of my abiding in my present situation.

"But since our brethren's letters have informed us that there are such prospects of usefulness in Hindostan, and that preachers are a thousand times more wanted than people to preach to, my heart has been more deeply affected than ever with their condition; and my desires for a participation of the toils and pleasures, crosses and comforts, of which they are the subjects, are advanced to an anxiety which nothing can remove, and time seems to increase.

"It has pleased God also lately to teach me, more than ever, that HIMSELF is the *fountain* of happiness; that likeness to him, friendship for him, and communion with him, form the basis of all true enjoyment; and that this can be attained as well in an Eastern jungle, amongst Hindoos and Moors, as in the most polished parts of Europe. The very *disposition* which, blessed be my dear Redeemer! he has given me, to be any thing, do any thing, or endure any thing, so that his name might be glorified,—I say, the *disposition* itself is heaven begun below! I do feel a daily panting after more devotedness to his service, and I can never think of my suffering Lord without dissolving into love—love which constrains me to glorify him with my body and spirit, which are his.

"I do often represent to myself all the possible hardships of a mission, arising from my own heart, the nature of the country, domestic connections, disappointment in my hopes, &c. And then I set over against them all these two thoughts,—I am God's servant; and God is my friend.' In this I anticipate happiness in the midst of suffering, light in darkness, and life in death. Yea, I do not count my life dear unto myself, so that I may win some poor heathen unto Christ; and I am willing to be offered as a sacrifice on the service of the faith of the gospel.

"Mr. Horne justly observes, 'that, in order to justify a man's undertaking the work of a missionary, he should be qualified for it, disposed heartily to enter upon it, and free from such ties as exclude an engagement.' As to the first, others must judge for me; but they must not be men who have an interest in keeping me at home. I shall rejoice in opportunities of attaining to an acquaintance with the ideas of judicious and *impartial* men in this matter, and with them I must leave it. A willingness to embark in this cause I do possess; and I can hardly persuade myself that God has for ten years inclined my heart to this work without having any thing for me to do in it. But the third thing requires more consideration; and here alone I hesitate."

He then goes on to state all the objections from this quarter, with his answers to them, leaving it with his brethren to decide, when they had heard the whole.

The committee, after the most serious and mature deliberation, though they were fully satisfied as to brother Pearce's qualifications, and greatly approved of his spirit, yet were unanimously of opinion that he ought not to go; and that not merely on account of his connections at home, which might have been pleaded in the case of brother Carey, but on account of the mission itself, which required his assistance in the station which he already occupied.

In this opinion brother Carey himself, with singular disinterestedness of mind, afterwards concurred; and wrote to brother Pearce to the same effect.[8]

On receiving the opinion of the committee, he immediately wrote to Mrs. P. as follows:

Northampton, Nov. 13, 1794.

"My Dear Sarah,

"I am disappointed, but not dismayed. I ever wish to make my Savior's will my own. I am more satisfied than ever I expected I should be with a negative upon my earnest desires, because the business has been so conducted that I think (if by any means such an issue could be insured) the mind of Christ has been obtained. My dear brethren here have treated the affair with as much seriousness and affection as I could possibly desire, and I think more than so insignificant a worm could expect. After we had spent the former part of this day in fasting and prayer, with conversation on the

---

[8] See Periodical Accounts, Vol. I. p. 374.

subject, till nearly two o'clock, brother Potts, King, and I retired. We prayed, while the committee consulted. The case seemed difficult, and I suppose they were nearly two hours in deciding it. At last, *time* forced them to a point, and their answer I enclose for your satisfaction. Pray take care of it; it will serve for me to refer to when my mind may labor beneath a burden of guilt another day. I am my dear Sarah's own—S. P."

With reference to the same subject, he soon after wrote to his dear friend, Mr. Carey, as follows:

"Birmingham, March 27, 1795.

"My very dear Brother,

"Instead of a letter, you perhaps expected to have sent the writer; and, had the will of God been so, he would by this time have been on his way to Mudnabatty; but 'it is not in man that walketh to direct his steps.' Full of hope and expectation as I was, when I wrote you last, that I should be honored with a mission to the poor heathen, and be an instrument of establishing the empire of my dear Lord in India, I must submit now to 'stand still, and see the salvation of God.' Judging from the energy of my feelings, together with their long continuance and growing strength, I scarcely entertained a doubt but I should this year go to assist you in your evangelical undertaking, and under those circumstances I wrote to you. It was not long after, that some of our church, guessing from the strain of my preaching the state of my mind, questioned me upon the subject, and I frankly told them all my heart. On this, various meetings of consultation were held, and I suffered much, but fainted not; and, during that struggle, I felt, for the first time, the plenary import of that phrase, 'The world is crucified unto me, and I unto the world.' No domestic attachment, nor flattering prospects of reputation nor wealth, which, in unworthier moments, have had too much ascendancy over me, and had now any influence. Love to Christ, and love to sinners—heathen sinners—reign triumphant in my soul; and I trust I did then feel what it was to be wholly devoted to God.

"At length, a full church-meeting was called, and I was requested to be present. I went accordingly; and, having stated my views and feelings, I told them that though I should be glad of their opinion, yet I should not think myself bound to abide their decision;

because their affection for me would incline them to partiality in their judgment. I then withdrew.

"The issue of the meeting was unfavorable to my going; and, as I had expressed my design of finally submitting to the opinion of a meeting of disinterested ministers the church appointed two of the deacons to represent them at this meeting, whenever it should be. In the mean time, I lay the case before three or four of our brethren, whose piety and experience I thought best enabled them to judge. I was both disappointed and grieved to find them all decidedly against me. The following is an extract from one beloved brother and father in the ministry.

"'I really think you must not leave England. The heathen will get more by you here than they will abroad; and surely your post must not be given up. Who is there in your neighborhood to make a stand against false religion, my dear brother? I bless God for your zeal, but surely I think it will hurt the cause in various ways if you go. Churches will be afraid of the consequences of encouraging missions, if the most important stands at home are deserted by those that God has greatly prospered in them. You know brother Fuller's infirmity.[9] If you run away we shall want a man too of activity, to keep alive the attention of the public to the cause, and give a great argument to them that are averse to it. I am pleased with the measures you propose to follow for determining the point, and trust God will direct you.'

"I copy out this, just as I received it, that you may better enter into my situation. The week after this we had a very solemn day of fasting and prayer, on the business of Northampton. Some brethren of the Society, and some who were not, attended. Brethren Ryland and Sutcliff were not able to be present; but their opinions, and those of some of the London ministers were known. On this occasion I read a narrative of my feelings for some time past, together with the views and motives which induced me to desire employment among the heathen, and such answers to objections arising from my connection in the family, the church, and the mission Society, as appeared to me satisfactory and full. I shall ever

---

[9] Referring to a paralytic affection in his face, which came upon him in 1793, the effects of which were not removed in less than four or five years.

love my dear brethren the more, for the tenderness with they treated me, and the solemn prayer they repeatedly put up to God for me. At last, I withdrew for them to decide; and whilst I was apart from them, and engaged in prayer for divine direction, I felt all anxiety forsake me, and an entire resignation of will to the will of God, be it what it would, together with a satisfaction that so much praying breath would not be lost; but that He who hath promised to be found of all that seek him, would assuredly direct the hearts of my brethren to that which was most pleasing to himself, and most suitable to the interest of his kingdom in the world. Between two and three hours were they deliberating, after which time a paper was put into my hands of which the following is a copy:

"'The brethren at this meeting are fully satisfied of the fitness of brother P's qualifications, and greatly approve of the disinterestedness of his motives, and the ardor of his mind. But another missionary not having been requested, and not being in our view immediately necessary, and brother P. occupying already a post very important to the prosperity of the mission itself, we are unanimously of the opinion that, for the present, he should continue in the situation which he now occupies.'

"To this I was enabled cheerfully to reply, 'the will of the Lord be done;' and, receiving this answer as the voice of God, I have for the most part been easy since, though not without occasional pantings of spirit after the publishing of the Gospel to pagans.

"What particularly weighed with me was an apprehension of the necessity of the language being known to more evangelical men than two, lest, in case they should die, or be by any means laid aside, the work should materially suffer through the long chasm occasioned by their seeking out proper successors, the time occupied by the voyage, and, after all, their inability to speak to the natives in the Bengalee tongue. It appeared to me highly important that provision should be made for such an event, which at sometime must take place; and I conceived that numerous advantages would arise from the mission being kept up by men who had been on the spot, were known to the natives, and already in the habit of instructing them in the way of righteousness. The preference of such persons to strangers was obvious; and, as no one offered himself for the work, I thought it my duty to propose myself for the undertaking; whether the Lord will ever honor me so far, I know not; but the state of my mind still inclines me to say daily, 'here am I, Lord, send me.'

"At present, however, I am better satisfied in staying, because the Lord has raised up some others for the work. We have all been diligently employed in inquiring after proper persons to assist you, but in vain, till a few days since, when two of the students at Bristol, both warm-hearted for Christ, offered themselves to brother Ryland as willing to embark in the glorious undertaking. He has communicated their wishes to brother Fuller and me, &c. I suppose they will formally propose themselves to the Society at the next committee meeting. I wish we could have your mind on the business, for our direction; but we must guess at it and act accordingly.

"I think I said in my last, that I had taken some pains, or rather pleasure, with the Bengalee language; but having no vocabulary, or dictionary, or book to read in the language, I was obliged to lay it aside. Could you furnish me with any helps, I should be very thankful; for I have not yet relinquished my hopes of telling the Hindoos how Jesus Christ came into the world to save sinners; or, if not, our brethren wish me to learn the language, as they say it is possible that, when you have translated the Bible, it may be found most convenient to print it in England; to do which, it is necessary to have the press under the inspection of some pious person who knows the language. This has its weight, though it just strikes me that probably it would be better (if types were procured) to look out for some good man who understands printing, and send him over to you, that the work may go on beneath your own care. This was done at Malabar, by the Danish mission; but no doubt you will give the Society your free opinion on this matter when the translation is in a good degree of forwardness.

"And now, my dear brother, how shall I express the joy I feel at the great goodness of our God unto you in a strange land. Your letters were read at a committee meeting, the 18th instant, at Guilsborough. We glorified God on your behalf, and earnestly prayed that the same mercy and goodness might still attend you; at the same time affectionately commending you to the grace of his Holy Spirit, that he might prevent your secular concerns from diminishing that pious ardor with which your spirit glows for the advancement of the kingdom of Christ among men. How securely may we leave you in his hands! Yes, my dear brother, we do rejoice that, though oceans divide us from each other, we are equally beneath his protection who filleth all in all. Daily in our closets and in our families do we remember you before God; and, in the sanctuary, the tribes of God's spiritual Israel wrestle hard for you Sabbath after Sabbath. Nor shall we pray in vain—God, even our own God, will bless you; his promise is on your side, and through him you shall do valiantly; never will he forsake his servants, nor leave them unassisted in their work; but your 'confidence is strong;' I rejoice that it is so, for 'this is the victory that overcometh the world, even our faith;' and he who hath been the author of that faith will, I doubt not, be the finisher of it too.

"The Periodical Accounts, no. I, have been of great help to the funds of the Society. We sent a copy to every church of our denomination: brother Fuller and I have had handsome collections after preaching upon the subject; and, from other places, unvisited, we have received many tokens of benevolence. I know it will give you pleasure to know that on Christmas-day, after preaching at Leicester on the subject, we received about thirty guineas towards the mission.

"We are thinking now about Africa. It will be the subject of our consideration next meeting; and I will take care that you shall have the earliest account of the result by the later ships.

"Anxiously do we wait for your journal. Extracts from it will be put in No. II. You can hardly imagine how the public are interested in these accounts; and I hope that, now you see the nature of the plan, you will furnish the Society with such information, from time to time, as may preserve the respectability and celebrity of the work. But I must close; my time is quite exhausted, and I really have not enough left to read over what I have written in such haste, unless I omit a letter to brother T. Excuse blunders. Accept my warmest love, in which Mrs. P., brother King, and others (whose name is legion) join with your very, very affectionate, though unworthy brother. S.P."

"P.S. Pray favor me with a long letter by the first conveyance, and any helps toward the Bangalee language which you can send me. Adieu.

"With this I shall send an octavo volume on the Moravian Missions. I am compiling a piece which I desire may deserve to be called, The History and Present State of Protestant Christian Missions."

The decision of the committee, though it rendered him much more reconciled to abide in his native country than he could have been without it, yet did not in the least abate his zeal for the object. As he could not promote it abroad, he seemed resolved to lay himself out more for it at home. In March, 1795, after a dangerous illness, he says, in a letter to Mr. Fuller—"Through mercy I am almost in a state of convalescence. May my spared life be wholly devoted to the service of my dear Redeemer I do not care where I am, whether in England or in India, so I am employed as he would have me; but surely we need pray hard that God would send some more help to Hindostan."

In January, 1796, when he was first informed by the secretary of a young man (Mr. Fountain) being desirous of going, of the character that was given of him by our friend Mr. Savage of London, and of a committee-meeting being in contemplation, he wrote thus in answer: "Your letter, just arrived, put, I was going to say, another soul into my little body; at least it has added new life to the soul I have. I cannot be contented with the thought of being absent from your proposed meeting. No, no; I must be there, (for my own sake I mean,) and try to sing with you, 'O'er the gloomy hills of darkness.' S.P."

In August, the same year, having received a letter from India, he wrote to Mr. Fuller as follows: "Brother Carey speaks in such a manner of the effects of the gospel in his neighbourhood as in my view promises a fair illustration of our Lord's parable, when he compared the kingdom of heaven to a little leaven, hid in three measures of meal, which insinuated itself so effectually as to leaven the lump at last. Blessed be God, the leaven is already in the meal; the fermentation is begun; and my hopes were never half so strong as they are now that the whole shall be effectually leavened. OH THAT I WERE THERE TO WITNESS THE DELIGHTFUL PROCESS! But whither am I running?....I LONG TO WRITE YOU FROM HINDOSTAN!"
"S.P."

On receiving other letters from India, in January, 1797, he thus writes: "Perhaps you are now rejoicing in spirit with me over fresh intelligence from Bengal. This moment have I concluded reading two letters from brother Thomas: one to the Society, and the other to myself. He speaks of others from brother Carey. I hope they are already in your possession. If his correspondence has produced the same effects on your heart as brother Thomas's has on mine, you are filled with gladness and hope. I am grieved that I cannot convey them to you immediately. I long to witness the pleasure their contents will impart to all whose hearts are with us. Oh that I were accounted worthy of the Lord to preach the gospel to the Booteas!"

Being detained from one of our missionary meetings by preparing the periodical accounts for the press, he soon after wrote as follows: "We shall now get out No. IV very soon. I hope it will go to the press in a very few days. Did you notice that the very day on which we invited all our friends to a day of prayer on behalf of the mission (December 28, 1796) was the same in which brother Carey sent his best and most interesting accounts to the Society? I hope you had solemn and sweet seasons at Northampton. On many accounts I should have rejoiced to have been with you; yet I am satisfied that on the whole I was doing best at home.'

It has been already observed, that, for a month preceding the decision of the committee, he resolved to devote one day in every week to secret prayer and fasting, and to keep a *diary* of the exercises of his mind during the whole of that period. This diary was not shown to the committee at the time, but merely the preceding *narrative*. Since his death a few of them have perused it; and have been almost ready to think, that if they had seen it before, they would not have dared to oppose his going. But the Lord hath taken him to himself. It no longer remains a question now whether he shall labor in England, or in India. A few passages, however, from this transcript of his heart, while contemplating a great and disinterested undertaking, will furnish a better idea of his character than could be given by any other hand; and with these we shall close the present chapter.

"Oct. 8, 1794.—Had some remarkable freedom and affection this morning, both in family and secret prayer. With many tears I dedicated myself, body and soul, to the service of Jesus; and earnestly implored full satisfaction respecting the path of duty. I feel an increasing deadness for all earthly comforts; and derive my happiness immediately from God himself. May I still endure, as Moses did, by seeing him who is invisible.

"Oct. 10.—Enjoyed much freedom today in the family. Whilst noticing in prayer the state of the millions of heathen who know not God, I felt the aggregate value of their immortal souls with peculiar energy.

"Afterwards was much struck, whilst, on my knees before God in secret, I read the fourth chapter of Micah. The ninth verse I fancied very applicable to the church in Cannon Street; but what reason is there for such a cry about so insignificant a worm as I am? The third chapter of Habakkuk too well expresses that mixture of *solemnity* and *confidence* with which I contemplate the work of the mission.

"Whilst at the prayer-meeting to-night, I learned more of the meaning of some passages of Scripture than ever before. Suitable frames of soul are like good lights, in which a painting appears to its full advantage. I had often meditated on Phil. 3: 7, 8, and Gal. 6:14, but never *felt* crucifixion to the world, and disesteem for all that it contains, as at that time. All prospects of pecuniary independence, and growing reputation, with which in unworthier moments I had amused myself, were now chased from my mind; and the desire of living *wholly* to Christ swallowed up every other thought. Frowns and smiles, fullness and want, honor and reproach, were now equally indifferent; and when I concluded the meeting, my whole soul felt, as it were, going after the lost sheep of Christ among the heathen.

"I do feel a growing satisfaction in the proposal of spending my whole life in something nobler than the locality of this island will admit. I long to raise my Master's banner in climes where the sound of his fame hath but scarcely reached. He has said, for my encouragement, that '*all* nations shall flow unto it.'

"The conduct and success of Stach, Boonish, and other Moravian missionaries in Greenland, both confound and stimulate me. O Lord, forgive my past indolence in thy service, and help me to redeem the residue of my days for exertions more worthy a friend of mankind and a servant of God.

"Oct. 13.—Being taken up with visitors the former part of the day, I spent the after part in application to the Bengal language, and found the difficulties I apprehended vanish as fast as I encountered them. I read and prayed, prayed and read, and made no small advances. Blessed be God!

"Oct. 15.—There are in Birmingham 50,000 inhabitants; and, exclusive of the vicinity, ten ministers who preach the fundamental truths of the gospel. In Hindostan there are twice as many millions of inhabitants; and not so many gospel preachers. Now Jesus Christ has commanded his ministers to go into all the world, and preach the gospel to every creature: why should we be so disproportionate in our labors? Peculiar circumstances must not be urged against positive commands: I am therefore bound, if others do not go, to make the means more proportionate to the multitude.

"Tonight, reading some letters from brother Carey, in which he speaks of his wife's illness when she first came into the country, I endeavoured to realize myself not only with a sick, but a dead wife. The thought was like a cold dagger to my heart at first; but on recollection I considered the same God ruled in India as in Europe; and that he could either preserve her, or support me, as well there as here. My business is only to be where he would have me. Other things I leave to him. O Lord, though with timidity, yet I hope not without satisfaction, I look every possible evil in the face, and say, *'Thy will be done!'*

"Oct. 17.—This is the first day I have set apart for extraordinary devotion in relation to my present exercise of mind. Rose earlier than usual, and began the day in prayer that God would be with me in every part of it, and grant the end I have in view may be clearly ascertained—the knowledge of his will.

"Considering the importance of the work before me, I began at the foundation of all religion, and reviewed the grounds on which I stood,—the being of a God, the relation of mankind to him, with the Divine inspiration of the Scriptures—and the review afforded me great satisfaction.[10] I also compared the different religions which claimed divine origin, and found little difficulty in determining which had most internal evidence of its divinity. I attentively read and seriously considered Doddridge's three excellent Sermons on the Evidences of the Christian Religion; which was followed by such conviction that I had hardly patience to conclude the book before I fell on my knees before God, to bless him for such a religion, established on such a basis: and I have received more solid satisfaction this day upon the subject than ever I did before.

"I also considered, since the gospel is true, since Christ is the Head of the church, and his will is the law of all his followers, what

---

[10] There is a wide difference between admitting these principles in theory, and *making use of them*. David might have worn Saul's accoutrements at a parade; but, in meeting Goliath, he must go forth in an armor that had been *tried*. A mariner may sit in his cabin at his ease, while the ship is in harbor; but, ere he undertakes a voyage, he must examine its soundness, and inquire whether it will endure the storms which may overtake him.

are the obligations of his servants in respect of the enlargement of his kingdom. I here referred to our Lord's commission, which I could not but consider as universal in its object and permanent in its obligations. I read brother Carey's remarks upon it; and as the command has never been repealed—as there are millions of beings in the world on whom the command may be exercised—as I can produce no counter-revelation—and as I lie under no natural impossibilities of performing it—I concluded that I, as a servant of Christ, was bound by this law.

"I took the narrative of my experience, and statement of my views on this subject, in my hand, and, bowing down before God, I earnestly besought an impartial and enlightened spirit. I then perused that paper; and can now say that I have (allowing for my own fallibility) not one doubt upon the subject. I therefore resolved to close this solemn season with reading a portion of both Testaments, and earnest prayer to God for my family, my people, the heathen world, the Society, and particularly for the success of our dear brethren Thomas and Carey, and his blessing, presence, and grace to be ever my guide and glory. Accordingly I read the forty-ninth chapter of Isaiah; and with what sweetness! I never read a chapter in private with such feeling since I have been in the ministry. The eighth, ninth, tenth, twentieth, and twenty-first verses, I thought remarkably suitable.

"Read also part of the Epistle to the Ephesians, and the first chapter to the Philippians. Oh that for *me* to live may be *Christ* alone! Blessed be my dear Savior! in prayer I have had such fellowship with him as would warm me in Greenland, comfort me in New Zealand, and rejoice me in the valley of the shadow of death!

"Oct. 18.—I dreamed that I saw one of the Christian Hindoos. Oh how I loved him! I long to realize my dream. How pleasant will it be to sit down at the Lord's table with our swarthy brethren, and hear Jesus preached in their language! Surely then will come to pass the saying that is written, In Christ there is neither Jew nor Greek, Barbarian, Scythian, bond nor free, all are ONE in him.

"Have been happy today in completing the manuscript of Periodical Accounts, No. I. Any thing relative to the salvation of the heathen brings a certain pleasure with it. I find I cannot pray, nor converse, nor read, nor study, nor preach with satisfaction, without reference to this subject."

"Oct. 20.—Was a little discouraged on reading Mr. Zeigenbald's conferences with the Malabarians, till I recollected, what ought to be ever present to my mind, in brother Carey's words,— '*The work is God's.*'

"In the evening I found some little difficulty with the language; but, considering how merchants and captains overcome this difficulty for the sake of wealth, I sat confounded before the Lord that I should ever have indulged such a thought; and, looking up to him, I set about it with cheerfulness, and found that I was making a sensible advance, although I can never apply till eleven o'clock at night on account of my other duties.[11]

"Preached from 2 Kings 4:26, 'It is well;' was much enlarged both in thought and expression. Whilst speaking of the satisfaction enjoyed by a truly pious mind when it feels itself in all circumstances and times in the hand of *a good God,* I felt that were the universe destroyed, and I the only being in it besides God, HE is fully adequate to my complete happiness; and had I been in an African wood, surrounded with venomous serpents, devouring beasts, and savage men, in such a frame I should be the subject of perfect peace and exalted joy. Yes, O my God, thou hast taught me that THOU ALONE art worthy of my confidence; and, with this sentiment fixed in my heart, I am free from all solicitude about any temporal prospects or concerns. If *thy* presence be enjoyed, poverty shall be riches, darkness, light; affliction, prosperity; reproach, my honor; and fatigue, my rest: and thou hast said, 'My presence shall go with thee.' Enough, Lord! I ask for nothing, nothing more.

"But how sad the proofs of our depravity; and how insecure the best frames we enjoy! Returning home, a wicked expression from a person who passed me caught my ear, and recurred so often to my thoughts for some minutes as to bring guilt upon my mind, and overwhelm me with shame before God. But I appealed to God for

---

[11] Night studies, often continued till two or three o'clock in the morning, it is to be feared, were the first occasion of impairing Mr. Pearce's health, and brought on that train of nervous sensations with which he was afterwards afflicted. Though not much accustomed to converse on the subject, he once acknowledged to a brother in the ministry, that, owing to his enervated state, he sometimes dreaded the approach of public services to such a degree that he would rather have submitted to stripes than engage in them; and that while in the pulpit he was frequently distressed with the apprehension of falling over it.

my hatred of all such things, secretly confessed the sin of my heart, and again ventured to the mercy-seat. On such occasions how precious a Mediator is to the soul!

"Oct. 22.—I did not on the former part of the day feel my wonted ardor for the work of a missionary, but rather an inclination to consult flesh and blood, and look at the worst side of things. I did so; but when on my knees before God in prayer about it, I first considered that my judgment was still equally satisfied, and my conscience so convinced that I durst not relinquish the work for a thousand worlds! And then I thought that this dull frame had not been without its use, as I was now fully convinced that my desire to go did not arise from any fluctuation of inconstant passions, but the settled convictions of my judgment. I therefore renewed my vows unto the Lord, that, let what difficulties soever be in the way, I would, provided the Society approved, surmount them all. I felt a kind of unutterable satisfaction of mind in my resolution of leaving the decision in the hands of my brethren. May God rightly dispose their hearts. I have no doubt but he will.

"Oct. 23.—Have found a little time to apply to the Bengalee language. How pleasant it is to work for God! Love transforms thorns to roses, and makes pain itself a pleasure. I never sat down to any study with such peculiar and continued satisfaction. The thought of exalting the Redeemer in this language is a spur to my application paramount to every discouragement for want of a living tutor. I have passed this day with an abiding satisfaction respecting my present views.

"Oct. 24.—Oh for the enlightening, enlivening, and sanctifying presence of God today! It is the *second* of those days of extraordinary devotion which I have set apart for seeking God in relation to the mission. How shall I spend it? I will devote the morning to prayer, reading, and meditation; and the afternoon to visiting the wretched, and relieving the needy. May God accept my services, guide me by his counsel, and employ me for his praise!

"Having besought the Lord that he would not suffer me to deceive myself in so important a matter as that which I had now retired to consider, and exercised some confidence that he would be the rewarder of those who diligently seek him, I read the 119th Psalm at the conclusion of my prayer, and felt and wondered at the congruity of so many of the verses to the breathings of my own heart. Often with holy admiration I paused, and read, and thought, and prayed over the verse again, especially verses 20, 31, 59, 60, 112, 145, 146. 'My soul breaketh for the longing that it hath unto thy judgments at all times.'—'I have stuck unto thy testimonies: O Lord, put me not to shame.'

"Most of the morning I spent in seriously reading Mr. Horne's 'Letters on Missions,' having first begged of the Lord to make the perusal profitable to my instruction in the path of duty. To the interrogation, 'Which of you will forsake all, deny himself, take up his cross, and, if God pleases, die for his religion?' I replied spontaneously, 'Blessed be God, I am willing! Lord, help me to accomplish it!'

"Closed this season with reading the 61st and 62nd chapters of Isaiah, and prayer for the church of God at large, my own congregation, the heathen, the Society, brethren Thomas and Carey, all missionaries whom God hath sent of every denomination, my own case, my wife and family, and for assistance in my work.

"The after part of this day has been gloomy indeed. All the painful circumstances which can attend my going have met upon my heart, and formed a load almost insupportable. A number of things which have been some time accumulating have united their pressure, and made me groan being burdened. Whilst at a prayer-meeting I looked round on my Christian friends, and said to myself, 'A few months more, and probably I shall leave you all!' But in the deepest of my gloom I resolved, though faint, yet to pursue; not doubting but my Lord would give me strength equal to the day.

"I had scarcely formed this resolution before it occurred, my Lord and Master was a man of sorrows. Oppressed and covered with blood, he cried, 'If it be possible, let this cup pass from me.' Yet in the depth of his agonies he added, 'Thy will be done.' This thought was to me what the sight of the cross was to Bunyan's pilgrim; I lost my burden—spent the remainder of the meeting in sweet communion with God.

"But, on coming home, the sight of Mrs. P. replaced my load. She had for some time been much discouraged at the thoughts of going. I therefore felt reluctant to say any thing on this subject, thinking it would be unpleasant to her; but though I strove to conceal it, an involuntary sigh betrayed my uneasiness. She kindly inquired the cause. I avoided at first an explanation, till she, guessing the reason, said to this effect: 'I hope you will be no more uneasy on *my* account. For the last two or three days I have been more comfortable than ever in the thought of going. I have considered the steps you are pursuing to know the mind of God, and I think you cannot take more proper ones. When you consult the ministers, you should represent your obstacles as strongly as your inducements; and then, if they advise your going, though the parting from my friends will be almost insupportable, yet I will make myself as happy as I can, and God can make me happy any where.'

"Should this little diary fall into the hands of a man having the soul of a missionary, circumstanced as I am, he will be the only man capable of sharing my peace, my joy, my gratitude, my rapture of soul. Thus at evening tide it is light; thus God brings his people through fire and through water into a wealthy place; thus those who ask do receive, and their joy is full. 'O love the Lord, ye his saints: there is no want to them that fear him!'

"Oct. 26.—Had much enlargement this morning whilst speaking on the nature, extent, and influence of Divine love; what designs it formed—with what energy it acted—with what perseverance it pursued its object—what obstacles it surmounted—what difficulties it conquered—and what sweetness it imparted under the heaviest loads and severest trials. Almost through the day I enjoyed a very desirable frame; and, on coming home, my wife and I had some conversation on the subject of my going. She said, though in general the thought was painful, yet there were some seasons when she had no preference, but felt herself disposed to go or stay, as the Lord should direct.

"This day wrote to brother Fuller, briefly stating my desires, requesting his advice, and proposing a meeting of the committee on the business. I feel great satisfaction arising from my leaving the matter to the determination of my honored brethren, and to God through them.

"Oct. 27.—Today I sent a packet to our brethren in India. I could not forbear telling brother Carey all my feelings, views, and expectations; but without saying I should be entirely governed by the opinion of the Society.

"Oct. 28.—Still panting to preach Jesus among my fellow sinners to whom he is yet unknown. Wrote to Dr. Rogers of Philadelphia, to-day, upon the subject with freedom and warmth, and inquired whether, whilst the people of the United States were forming societies to encourage arts, liberty, and emigration, there could not a few be found among them who would form a society for the transmission of the word of life to the benighted heathen; or, in case that could not be, whether they might not strengthen our hands in Europe, by some benevolent proof of concurring with us in a design which they speak of with such approbation. With this I sent Horne's Letters. I will follow both with my prayers; and who can tell?

"Oct. 29.—Looked over the Code of Hindoo laws today. How much is there to admire in it, founded on the principles of justice! The most salutary regulations are adopted in many circumstances. But what a pity that so much excellence should be debased by laws to establish or countenance idolatry, magic, prostitution, prayers for the dead, false-witnessing, theft, and suicide. How perfect is the morality of the gospel of Jesus; and how desirable that they should embrace it! Ought not means to be used? Can we assist them too soon? There is reason to think that their Shasters were penned about the beginning of the Kollee Jogue, which must be soon after the deluge: and are not 4000 years long enough for 100,000,000 of men to be under the empire of the devil?

"Oct. 31.—I am encouraged to enter upon this day (which I set apart for supplicating God) by a recollection of his promises to those who seek him. If the sacred word be true, the servants of God can never seek his face in vain; and as I am conscious of my sincerity and earnest desire only to know his pleasure that I may perform it, I find a degree of confidence that I shall realize the fulfillment of the word on which he causeth me to hope.

"Began the day with solemn prayer for the assistance of the Holy Spirit in my present exercise, that so I might enjoy the spirit and power of prayer, and have my personal religion improved, as well as my public steps directed. In this duty I found a little quickening.

"I then read over the narrative of my experience, and my journal. I find my views are still the same; but my heart is much more established than when I began to write.

"Was much struck in reading Paul's words in 2 Cor. 1:17, when, after speaking of his purpose to travel for the preaching of the gospel, he saith, 'Did I then use lightness when I was thus minded? Or the things that I purpose, do I purpose according to the flesh, that with me there should be yea, yea, and nay, nay?' The *piety* of the apostle in not purposing after the flesh, the *seriousness* of spirit with which he formed his designs, and his *steadfast* adherence to them, were in my view worthy of the highest admiration and strictest imitation.

"Thinking that I might get some assistance from David Brainerd's experience, I read his life to the time of his being appointed a missionary among the Indians. The exalted devotion of that dear man almost made me question mine. Yet, at some-seasons, he speaks of sinking as well as rising. His singular piety excepted, his feelings, prayers, desires, comforts, hopes, and sorrows are my own; and if I could follow him in nothing else, I knew I had been enabled to say this with him, 'I feel exceedingly calm, and quite resigned to God respecting my future improvement (or station) *when* and *where* he pleased. My faith lifted me above the world, and removed all those mountains which I could not look over of late. I thought I wanted not the favour of man to lean upon; for I knew God's favour was infinitely better, and that it was no matter *where,* or *when,* or *how* Christ should send me, nor with what trials he should still exercise me, if I might be prepared for his work and will.'

"Read the second, third, fourth, fifth, and sixth chapters of the Second Epistle to the Corinthians. Felt a kind of placidity, but not much joy. On beginning the concluding prayer I had no strength to wrestle, nor power with God at all. I seemed as one desolate and forsaken. I prayed for myself, the Society, the missionaries, the converted Hindoos, the church in Cannon Street, my family, and ministry; but yet all was dullness, and I feared I had offended the Lord. I felt but little zeal for the mission, and was about to conclude with a lamentation over the hardness of my heart, when on a sudden it pleased God to smite the rock with the rod of his Spirit, and immediately the waters began to flow. Oh what a heavenly, glorious, melting power was it! My eyes, almost closed with weeping, hardly suffer me to write. I feel it over again. Oh what a view of the love of a crucified Redeemer did I enjoy! The attractions of his cross, how powerful! I was as a giant refreshed with new wine, as to my animation: like Mary at the Master's feet, weeping for tenderness of soul; like a little child, for submission to my heavenly Father's will; and like Paul, for a victory over all self-love, and creature love, and fear of man, when these things stand in the way of my duty. The interest that Christ took in the redemption of the heathen, the situation of our brethren in Bengal, the worth of the soul, and the plain command of Jesus Christ, together with an irresistible drawing of soul, which by far exceeded any thing I ever felt before, and is impossible to be described or conceived of by those who have never experienced it—all compelled me to *vow* that

I would, by his leave, serve him among the heathen. The Bible lying open before me, (upon my knees,) many passages caught my eye, and confirmed the purposes of my heart if ever in my life I knew any thing of the influence of the Holy Spirit, I did at this time. I was swallowed up in God. Hunger, fullness, cold, heat, friends, and enemies, all seemed nothing before God. I was in a new world. All was delightful; for Christ was all, and in all. Many times I concluded prayer, but, when rising from my knees, communion with God was so desirable that I was sweetly drawn to it again, till my animal strength was almost exhausted. Then I thought it would be pleasure to *burn* for God!

"And now while I write such a heavenly sweetness fills my soul that no exterior circumstances can remove it; and I do uniformly feel that the more I am thus, the more I pant for the service of my blessed Jesus among the heathen. Yes, my dear, my dying Lord, I am thine, thy servant; and if I neglect the service of so good a Master, I may well expect a guilty conscience in life, and a death awful as that of Judas or Spira!

"This evening I had a meeting with my friends. Returned much dejected. Received a letter from brother Fuller, which, though he says he has many objections to my going, yet is so affectionately expressed as to yield me a gratification.

"Nov. 3.—This evening received a letter from brother Ryland, containing many objections; but contradiction itself is pleasant when it is the voice of judgment mingled with affection. I wish to remember that *I may be mistaken,* though I cannot say I am at present convinced that it is so. I am happy to find that brother Ryland approves of my referring it to the committee. I have much confidence in the judgment of my brethren, and hope I shall be perfectly satisfied with their advice. I do think, however, if they knew how earnestly I pant for the work, it would be impossible for them to withhold their ready acquiescence. O Lord, thou knowest my sincerity; and that if I go not to the work, it will not be owing to any reluctance on my part! If I stay in England, I fear I shall be a poor useless drone; or if a sense of duty prompt me to activity, I doubt whether I shall ever know inward peace and joy again. O Lord, I am, thou knowest I am, *oppressed,* undertake for me!

Nov. 5—At times today I have been reconciled to the thought of staying, if my brethren should advise; but at other times I seem to think I could not. I look at brother Carey's portrait as it hangs in my study: I love him in the bowels of Jesus Christ, and long to join his labors: every look calls up a hundred thoughts, all of which inflame my desire to be a fellow laborer with him in the work of the Lord. One thing, however, I have resolved upon, that, the Lord helping me, if I cannot go abroad, I will do all I can to serve the mission at home.

"Nov. 7.—This is the last day of peculiar devotion before the deciding meeting. May I have strength to wrestle with God today for his wisdom to preside in the committee, and by faith to leave the issue to their determination!

"I did not enjoy much enlargement in prayer today. My mind seems at present incapable of those sensations of joy with which I have lately been much indulged, through its strugglings in relation to my going or staying; yet I have been enabled to commit the issue into the hands of God, as he may direct my brethren, hoping that their advice will be agreeable to his will."

The result of the committee-meeting has already been related; together with the state of his mind, as far as could be collected from his letters, for some time after it. The termination of these tender and interesting exercises, and of all his other labors, in so speedy a removal from the present scene of action, may teach us not to draw any certain conclusion, as to the designs of God concerning our future labors, from the ardor or sincerity of our feelings. He may take it well that "it was in our hearts to build him a house," though he should for wise reasons have determined not to gratify us. Suffice it that in matters of EVERLASTING MOMENT he has engaged to "perfect that which concerns us." In this he hath condescended to bind himself, as by an oath, for our consolation; here, therefore, we may safely consider our spiritual desires as indicative of his designs: but it is otherwise in various instances with regard to present duty.[12]

---

[12] I am aware that it becomes us to be extremely cautious in interpreting the conduct of Divine Providence; it is, however, worthy of remark, that the church at Birmingham were unwilling to part with their pastor to labor in the missionary field, and they were called to witness his affliction and to surrender him to death: while the church at Leicester cheerfully gave up their beloved Carey to the work, and in a few years after were blest with the labors of Robert Hall.

CHAPTER III

HIS EXERCISES AND LABORS, FROM THE TIME OF HIS GIVING UP THE IDEA OF GOING ABROAD TO THE COMMENCEMENT OF HIS LAST ILLNESS.

Had the multiplied labors of this excellent man permitted his keeping a regular diary, we may see, by the foregoing specimen of a single month, what a rich store of truly Christian experience would have pervaded these Memoirs. We should then have been better able to trace the gradual openings of his holy mind, and the springs of that extraordinary unction of spirit, and energy of action, by which his life was distinguished. As it is, we can only collect the gleanings of the harvest, partly from memory, and partly from letters communicated by his friends.

This chapter will include a period of about four years, during which he went twice to London, to collect for the *Baptist Mission,* and once he visited Dublin, at the invitation of the *Evangelical Society* in that city.

There appears throughout the general tenor of his life a singular submissiveness to the will of God; and, what is worthy of notice, this disposition was generally most conspicuous when his own will was most counteracted. The justness of this remark is sufficiently apparent from his letter to Mrs. Pearce, of November 13, 1794, after the decision of the committee; and the same spirit was carried into the common concerns of life. Thus, about a month afterwards, when his dear Louisa was ill of a fever, he thus writes from Northampton to Mrs. Pearce:

Northampton, Dec. 13, 1794.

"My Dear Sarah,

"I am just brought on the wings of celestial mercy safe to my Sabbath's station. I am well; and my dear friends here seem healthy and happy: but I feel for *you*. I long to know how our dear Louisa's pulse beats: I fear still feverish. We must not, however, suffer ourselves to be infected with a mental fever on this account. Is she ill? It is right. Is she very ill….dying? It is still right. Is she gone to join the heavenly choristers? It is all right, notwithstanding our repinings….Repinings! No; we will not repine. It is best she should go. It is best for *her:* this we must allow. It is best for us. Do we expect it? Oh what poor, ungrateful, short-sighted worms are we! Let us submit, my Sarah, till we come to heaven: if we do not *then* see that it is best, let us then complain. But why do I attempt to console? Perhaps an indulgent providence has ere now dissipated your fears: or if that same *kind providence* has removed our babe, you have consolation enough in Him who suffered more than we; and more than enough to quiet all our passions in that astonishing consideration,—'*God so* loved the world, that he *spared not his* own Son.' Did God cheerfully give the holy child Jesus for us; and shall we refuse our child to him? He gave his Son to *suffer:* he takes our children to *enjoy*. Yes; to enjoy himself.

"Yours with the tenderest regard,—S. P."

In June, 1795, he attended the association at Kettering, partly on account of some missionary business there to be transacted. That was a season of great joy to many, especially the last forenoon previous to parting. Thence he wrote to Mrs. Pearce as follows:

"From a pew in the house of God at Kettering, with my cup of joy running over, I address you by the hands of brother Simmons. Had it pleased Divine Providence to have permitted your accompanying me, my pleasures would have received no small addition, because I should have hoped that you would have been filled with similar consolation, and have received equal edification by the precious means of grace on which I have attended. Indeed, I never remember to have enjoyed a public meeting to such a high degree since I have been in the habit of attending upon them. Oh that I may return to you, and the dear church of God, in the *fullness* of the blessing of the gospel of Christ! I hope, my beloved, that you are not without the enjoyment of the sweetness and the supports of the blessed gospel. Oh that you may get and keep near to God, and in *Him* find infinitely more than you can possibly lose by your husband's absence!

"Mr. Hall preached, last evening, from 1 Pet. 1:8. A most evangelical and experimental season! I was charmed and warmed.

Oh that Jesus may go on to reveal himself to him as altogether lovely! I am unable to write more now. Today I set off for Northampton, and preach there to-night. The Lord bless you!" S.P.

The following letters, written to Mr. Carey, will exhibit the deep interest he continued to feel in the happiness, of his brethren in India, and in the success of their blessed undertaking. The first was written from London, where he was engaged in soliciting contributions for the Mission.

"London, August 27, 1795.

"My very dear Brother,

"Banished as you are from my eyes, I love you too well to be unmindful of your concerns, or uninterested in your best welfare. Our affectionate and I trust pious intercourse, before you left England, together with the letters I have received and seen from you since your arrival in India, have uniformly heightened that esteem which begun with our first acquaintance on the day of your ordination at Leicester. Hence I can suffer no opportunity of corresponding with you to pass unnoticed; and as my dear friend Mr. Savage tells me that he expects a vessel will sail for Bengal in a few days, I attempt to give you some pleasure by writing a friendly epistle.

"I am here raising subscriptions for our Society the third year. The times, indeed, are unfavorable to application, and I do not fail to meet with beggars' fare; yet on the whole I must not complain. I have been three days at work, and have received thirty-four guineas: whether I shall continue to succeed as well, I know not; my spirits often flag, but I would hope and do the best.

"Perhaps you have heard that the late Mr. Trinder, of Northampton, left about £400 to the Society, besides which I suppose we have £300 or £400 more in hand; so that we only want suitable persons to send, in order to extend our endeavors for the conversion of the heathen.

"In former letters we told you that we had resolved on an African mission, and that two pious, and apparently suitable young men, had offered their services for the work of the Lord in that benighted and miserable part of the world. I am happy now in being able to add, that although there was some difficulty at first in securing them a passage, it is at length obtained. Brother Fuller came to London, and met with some of the directors of the Sierra

Leone Company, who have agreed to allow them a passage in their ships, and to leave them at full liberty as to the conducting of the mission when they arrive in Africa.

"On Wednesday, the 16h of September next, we propose to have a parting meeting at Birmingham. Brother Ryland is to address the missionaries; the other parts of the service are not yet arranged. Early in October the vessels will sail, and with them six pious families of Wesleyan Methodists, who are to settle for one year at Free Town. They mean to proceed up the Foulah country; and having prepared suitable receptacles for their families, on the commencement of the second year they are to be removed also; when, by the practice of agriculture and the useful arts, together with frequent conversation on religious subjects, and a cheerful yet guarded behavior, they hope to civilize and Christianize the negro inhabitants. The better to promote their pious designs, it is proposed to send with them one or more missionaries, whose only work it will be to preach to the colony and evangelize the heathen.

"The plan strikes me as well calculated to answer its end. I remember reading of a similar plan formed by one John Oxenbridge, an ejected minister in the reign of Charles II, who went to South America on purpose to explore the country, and on his return published a book, recommending the going out of a colony for the purpose of spreading the Gospel there; but the time was not then come: both wise and foolish virgins then slumbered and slept. I trust that the friends of Christ are now recovering from their stupor. A general concern discovers itself in almost all denominations. The Independent brethren, in connection with Calvinistic Methodists and Churchmen, are about attempting a mission to the South Sea Islands, where they propose to send a large body of missionaries, if they can procure them. The Lord prosper the work of their hands!

"Your affectionate brother,   S.P."

"P.S. I have another minute to spare, and affection bids me to spend it in your company. I have heard, since I wrote the above, that the plan of the Wesleyan Colony in the Foulah country has been somewhat altered, and that Dr. C. will accompany them.

"Mr. La Trobe has furnished me with the last two numbers of the Brethren's Periodical Accounts: I enclose them for your gratification. You will rejoice to find that the Hottentots are seeking after Jesus, and be encouraged to continue your labors of love among the poor Hindoos. Be not discouraged, my dear brother, if you do not succeed immediately. You know the brethren labored nearly six years without effect in Greenland; but they persevered, and now a tenth part of the inhabitants of that country are professors of the faith of Christ. But when I consider by what means they achieved so great a work—by the simple preaching of the cross of Christ, and an exhibition of the love of his heart, I am constrained to say, 'Not be might, nor by power, but by thy Spirit, O Lord of Hosts.' I have lately been struck with a remark which applies to their labors and success. Facts interest more than speculations or abstract positions, however just. Talk to a child about any abstract subject, and it requires pains to secure his attention; but tell him a story, and he is all ear. So I should suppose an affectionate relation of the story of Jesus Christ, and his death and sufferings, would be the most likely way of engaging the heart of a heathen: but I, who am 15,000 miles from the seat of your labors, am almost ashamed to give my thoughts on a subject with which you must be so much better acquainted. Forgive my freedom, and again believe me,

"Most affectionately yours, in our dear Lord Jesus,
"S.P."

"Birmingham, Jan. 6, 1796

"My dearly beloved Brother,

"To neglect any opportunity of renewing the expressions of my warm attachment, would give me pain, especially after knowing how long you were in India before you received any communications from your friends in Europe. Long before now I hope you are convinced that your disappointment was not owing to any want of regard or attention in your brethren here. I have often pleased myself with an idea of the scene when the delayed correspondence poured in upon you too fast almost even for your keenest appetite to devour, and the abundance of packets at once annihilated all your suspicions of our want of friendship.

"I would now have written a long letter, but have been so much employed this last month in preparing our Periodical Accounts, No. 2, for the press; correcting the proofs, and sending them off to the different churches in the kingdom, that I almost fear being too late for this conveyance, as I must first send to Olney, that it may be enclosed in brother Sutcliff's parcel to you. He, brother

Fuller, and I suppose brother Ryland, will write, and probably give you all the intelligence that the state of the churches afford. My next, I hope, will be longer.

"What pleasure must it give you to hear of the great things God has done for Leicester! I was there last Christmas day, and preached for the Mission at Mr. Worthington's meeting. The congregation was very large, and many went away, not being able to get in. £36 were collected, and apparently given with the heart. I think I told you that above £30 were raised in Leicester the last year. Thus the seed you sowed, during your residence there, now springs up to the glory of God.

"Thank you, my dear brother, for your kind letter of January 18, 1795. It was as cold water to a thirsty soul. Do not fail to refresh me as often as you have leisure, and pray be particular in your communications respecting the work of God. A large portion of zeal now discovers itself among Christians of every name. I shall desire brother Sutcliff to enclose a copy of the Missionary Society's Sermons. I was in London when they were preached, attending our brethren, who soon after sailed for Africa. It was a Pentecost. The brethren who compose that society, stated publicly that our zeal kindled theirs: 'we lighted our torch at yours, and it was God who first touched your heart with fire from his holy altar.' To him be all the praise!

"I am, my dear, dear brother, affectionately yours.
                                          "S.P."

In July, 1795, he received a pressing invitation from the *General Evangelical Society* in Dublin to pay them a visit, and to assist in diffusing the gospel of the grace of God in that kingdom. To this invitation he replied in the following letter, addressed to Dr. M'Dowal:

Birmingham,.Aug. 3, 1795.
"Rev. and Dear Sir,

"I received your favour of the 22nd ult., and, for the interesting reason you assign, transmit a 'speedy answer.' The Society, on whose behalf you wrote, I have ever considered with the respect due to the real friends of the best of causes—the cause of God and of his Christ—a cause which embraces the most important and durable interests of our fellow men; and your name, dear sir, I have been taught to hold in more than common esteem by my dear brother and

father, Messrs. Birt and Francis. The benevolent institution which you
are engaged in supporting, I am persuaded, deserves more than the
good wishes or prayers of your brethren in the kingdom and patience
of Jesus, on this side the Channel; and it will yield me substantial
pleasure to afford personal assistance in your pious labours. But for
the present, I am sorry to say, I must decline your proposal, being
engaged to spend a month in London this autumn on the business of
our *mission society,* of which you have probably heard.

"When I formed my present connections with the church in
Birmingham, I proposed an annual freedom for six weeks from my
pastoral duties; and should the 'Evangelical Society' express a wish
for my services the ensuing year, I am perfectly inclined, God willing,
to spend that time beneath their direction, and at what part of the year
they conceive a visit would be most serviceable to the good design. I
only request that, should this be their desire, I may receive the
information as soon as they can conveniently decide, that I may
withhold myself from other engagements, which may interfere with
the time they may appoint. I entreat you to make my Christian
respects acceptable to the gentlemen who compose the Society; and
assure yourself that I am, dear sir, respectfully and affectionately,
your brother, in our Lord Jesus,—S. P."

The invitation was repeated, and he complied with their request,
engaging to go over in the month of June, 1796.

A little before this journey, it occurred to Dr. Ryland that an
itinerating mission into Cornwall might be of use to the cause of true
religion, and that two acceptable ministers might be induced to
undertake it; and that, if executed during the vacation at the Bristol
academy, two of the students might supply their place. He
communicated his thoughts to Mr. Pearce who wrote thus in answer:

May 30, 1796.

"My Very Dear Brother,

"I thank you a thousand times for your last letter. Blessed be
God, who hath put it into your heart to propose such a plan for
increasing the boundaries of Zion! I have read your letter to our
wisest friends here, and they heard it with great joy. The plan, the
place, the mode, the persons,—all, *all* meet our most affectionate
wishes. How did such a scheme never enter our minds before? Alas!

we have nothing in our hearts that is worth having, save what God puts there. Do write to me when at Dublin, and tell me whether it be resolved on, when they set out, &c. I hope, ere long, to hear that as many disciples are employed in Great Britain, as the Saviour employed in Judea. When he gives the word, great will be the company of the preachers.[13]

"O my dear brother, let us go on still praying, contriving, labouring, defending, until 'the little leaven leaven the whole lump, and the small stone from the mountain fill the whole earth.'

"What pleasure do those lose who have no interest in God's gracious and holy cause! How thankful should we be that we are not strangers to the joy which the friends of Zion feel, when the Lord turneth again Zion's captivity! I am, beyond expression, your affectionate brother in Christ,   S. P."

On May 31 he set off for Dublin, and "the Lord prospered his way," so that he arrived at the time appointed; and from every account it appears that he was not only sent *in the fullness of the blessing of the gospel of peace,* but that the Lord himself went with him. His preaching was not only highly acceptable to every class of hearers, but the word came from him with power; and there is abundant reason to believe that many will, through eternity, praise God for sending his message to them by this dear ambassador of Christ. His memory lives in their hearts, and they join with the other churches of Christ in deploring the loss they have sustained by his death.

He was earnestly solicited by the *Evangelical Society* to renew his visit to that kingdom in 1798. Ready to embrace every call of duty, he had signified his compliance; and the time was fixed: but the breaking out of the late rebellion prevented him from realizing his intention. This was a painful disappointment to many, who wished once more to see his face, and to hear the glad tidings from his lips.

Such is the brief account of his visit to Dublin given by Dr. M'Dowal. The following letter was written to Mrs. Pearce, when he had been there little more than a week.

---

[13] This plan was carried out by the committee of the foreign mission, and was successful As it was felt, however, to be a departure from the constitution of the society, they originated, in 1797, a new institution,—The *Baptist Home Missionary Society.*

Dublin, June 30, 1796.

"My Dear Sarah,

"I long to know how you do, and you will be as much concerned to know how I go on at this distance from you. I haste to satisfy your inquiries.

"I am in perfect health; am delightfully disappointed with the place and its inhabitants. I am very thankful that I came over. I have found much more religion here already than I expected to meet with during the whole of my stay. The prospect of usefulness is flattering. I have already many more friends (I hope *Christian* friends) than I can gratify by visits. Many doors are open for preaching the gospel in the city; and my country excursions will probably be few. Thus much for outline.

"But you will like to know how I spend my time, &c. Well, then, I am at the house of a Mr. Hutton, late high sheriff for the city, a gentleman of opulence, respectability, and evangelical piety. He is by profession a Calvinistic Presbyterian, an elder of Dr. M'Dowal's church; has a most amiable wife, and four children. I am very thankful for being placed here during my stay. I am quite at home— I mean as to ease and familiarity; for as to *style* of living, I neither do, nor desire to equal it. Yet, in my present situation, it is convenient. It would, however, be sickening and dull, had I not a GOD to go to, to converse with, to enjoy, and to call *my own.* Oh it is this, *it is this,* my dearest Sarah, which gives a point to every enjoyment, and sweetens all the cup of life.

"The Lord's Day after I wrote to you last, I preached for Dr. M'Dowal in the morning, at half past eleven; heard a Mr. Kilburne at five; and preached again at Plunket Street at seven. On Tuesday evening I preached at a hospital; and on Thursday evening at Plunket Street again. Yesterday, for the Baptists, in the morning; Dr. M'Dowal at five; and at Plunket Street at seven.

"The hours of worship will appear singular to you: they depend on the usual *meal times.* We breakfast at ten; dine between four and five, sometimes between five and six; take tea from seven to nine; and sup from ten to twelve.

"I thank God that I possess an abiding determination to aim at the *consciences* of the people in every discourse. I have borne the most positive testimony against the prevailing evils of professors here; as sensuality, gaiety, vain amusements, neglect of the Sabbath, &c.; and last night told an immense crowd of professors of the first rank, 'that if they made custom and fashion their plea, they were awfully deluding their souls; for it had always been the fashion to insult God, to dissipate time, and to pursue the broad road to hell: but it would not lessen their torments there that the way to damnation was the fashion.'

"I feared my faithfulness would have given them offence: but, I am persuaded, it was the way to please the Lord; and those who I expected would be enemies are not only at peace with me, but even renounce their sensual indulgences to attend on my ministry. I do assuredly believe that God hath sent me hither for good. The five o'clock meetings are miserably attended in general. In a house that will hold one thousand five hundred or two thousand people, you will hardly see above fifty! Yesterday morning I preached on the subject of *public worship,* from Psalm 5:7, and seriously warned them against preferring their bellies to God, and their own houses to his. I was delighted and surprised, at the five o'clock meeting, to see the place nearly full. Surely this is the Lord's doing, and it is marvelous in my eyes. Never, never did I more feel how weak I am in myself—a mere nothing; and how strong I am in the omnipotence of God. I feel a superiority to all fear, and possess a conscious dignity in being the ambassador of Christ. O help me to praise! for it is he alone who teacheth my hands to war, and my fingers to fight: and still pray for me; for if he withdraw for a moment, I become as weak and unprofitable as the briars of the wilderness.

"You cannot think how much I am supported by the assurance that I have left *a praying people* at Birmingham; and I believe that, in answer to their prayers, I have hitherto been wonderfully assisted in the public work, as well as enjoyed much in private devotion.

"I have formed a most pleasing acquaintance with several serious young men in the university here, and with two of the fellows of the college—most pious gentlemen indeed, who have undergone a world of reproach for Christ and his gospel, and have been forbidden to preach in the churches by the archbishop; but God has raised another house for them here, where they preach with much success, and have begun a meeting in the college, which promises fresh prosperity to the cause of Jesus." S.P.

The following particulars, in addition to the above, are taken partly from some notes in his own hand-writing, and partly from the account given by his friend Mr. Summers, who accompanied him during the latter part of his visits.

At his first arrival, the congregations were but thinly attended, and the Baptist congregation in particular, amongst whom he delivered several discourses. It much affected him to see the whole city given to sensuality and worldly conformity; and especially to find those of his own denomination amongst the lowest and least affected with their condition. But the longer he continued, the more the congregations increased, and every opportunity became increasingly interesting, both to him and them. His faithful remonstrances, and earnest recommendations of prayer-meetings to his Baptist friends, though at first apparently ill received, were well taken in the end; and he had the happiness to see in them some hopeful appearances of a return to God. On June the 20th he wrote to his friend Mr. Summers as follows:

"My Dear Friend,

"If you mean to abide by my opinion, I say, come to Dublin, and come directly! I have been most delightfully disappointed. I expected darkness, and behold light; sorrow, and I have had cause for abundant joy. I thank God that I came hither, and hope that many, as well as myself, will have cause to praise him. Never have I been more deeply taught my own nothingness—never hath the power of God more evidently rested upon me. The harvest here is great indeed; and the Lord of the harvest hath enabled me to labour in it with delight.

> 'I praise him for all that is past;
> I trust him for all that's to come.'

"The Lord hath of late been doing great things for Dublin. Several of the young men in the college have been awakened; and two of the *fellows* are sweet evangelical preachers. One of them is of a spirit serene as the summer's evening, and sweet as the breath of May. I am already intimate with them, and have spent several mornings in college with various students who bid fair to be faithful watchmen on Jerusalem's walls. But I hope you will come, and then you will see for yourself. If not, I will give you some pleasant details when we meet in England."

Mr. Summers complied with this invitation; and of the last seven or eight days of Mr. Pearce's continuance at Dublin, he himself thus writes:

"Monday, July 4.—At three in the afternoon I went with my friend, Mr. Summers, to Mr. K.'s. Spent a very agreeable day. Miss A. K. remarked two wonders in Dublin: A praying society composed of students at college, and another of lawyers. The family were called together. We sung: I read, and expounded the twelfth chapter of Isaiah; and prayed.—At seven we went to a prayer-meeting at Plunket Street—there was a very large attendance. Mr. R. and Mr. S. prayed; and I spoke from Rom. 10: 12, 13, "There is no difference between the Jew and the Greek; for the same Lord over all is rich unto all who call upon him. For whosoever shall call upon the name of the Lord shall be saved."— Many seemed affected.—After I had closed the opportunity, I told them some of my own experience, and requested that, if any present wished for conversation, they would come to me, either that evening or on Thursday evening, in the vestry. Five persons came in: one had been long impressed with religion, but could never summon courage enough to open her heart before. Another, a Miss W., attributed her first impressions, under God, to my ministry; and told me that her father had regularly attended of late, and that her mother was so much alarmed as to be almost in despair. Poor girl! she seemed truly in earnest about her own soul, and as much concerned for her parents.—The next had possessed a serious concern for some time, and of late had been much revived.—One young lady, a Miss H., stayed in the meeting-house, exceedingly affected indeed. Mr. K. spoke to her.—She said she would speak to me on Thursday.

"Tuesday, 5th.—Went to Lexlip. At seven preached to a large and affected auditory.

"Wednesday, 6th.—Mr. H. and myself went to Mrs. M'G., to inquire about the young lady who was so much affected at the meeting. Mrs. M'G. said her mother and sister were pious; that she had been very giddy; but that last Lord's Day she was seriously awakened to a sense of sin; had expressed her delight in religion, and fled for refuge to the blood of Jesus.—Her sister was introduced to me; a sweetly pious lady.—I agreed to wait for an interview with the young lady at Mr. H.'s., in Eccles Street, tomorrow.

"Thursday, 7th.—Miss H., her sister, and Mrs. M'G. came to Eccles Street.—A most delightful interview. Seldom have I seen such proficiency in so short a time.—That day a week, at Plunket Street, she received her first serious impressions. Her concern deepened at Mass Lane, on Lord's Day morning—more so in the evening at Plunket Street—but most of all on Monday night. I exhorted them to begin a prayer and experience meeting; and they agreed. Blessed be God! this strengthens my hands greatly.—At seven o'clock preached at Plunket Street, from Jer. 1: 4, 5, 'Going and weeping—they shall ask the way to Zion with their faces thitherward.' A full house; and an impressive season. Tarried after the public services were ended, to converse on religion. The most pleasing case was that of a young man of Mr. D.'s.

"Saturday, 9th.—Went with my friend, Mr. S., to call on Miss H.—Found her at her mother's.—We first passed the door.—She ran out after us.—Seemed happy; but agitated. Ran, and called her mother.—Soon we saw the door of the parlour open, and a majestic lady appeared; who, as she entered the room, thus accosted me:— 'Who art thou, O blessed of the Lord? Welcome to the widow's house! Accept the widow's thanks for coming after the child whom thou hast begotten in the gospel!'—I was too much overcome to do more than take by the hand the aged saint. A solemn silence ensued for a minute or two; when the old lady, recovering, expressed the fullness of her satisfaction respecting the reality of the change effected in her daughter, and her gratitude for great refreshment of her own soul, by means of my poor labours. She said she had known the Lord during forty years, being called under the ministry of John Fisher, in the open air, when on a visit to an officer, who was her brother-in-law. She told us much of her experience, and promised to encourage the prayer-meeting which I proposed to be held in her house every Lord's Day evening. They are to begin tomorrow, after preaching.—It was a pleasant meeting; and we returned with pleasure to Eccles Street. After we rose up to come away, the old lady affectionately said, 'May the good-will of Him who dwelt in the bush attend you wherever you go, for ever and ever.'"

The young lady, some months after, wrote to Mr. S., and says, amongst other things, "I have great reason to be thankful for the many blessings the Lord has been pleased to bestow upon me, and in particular for his sending Mr. Pearce to this city; and that through his means I have been convinced of sin. I am happy to inform you that, through grace, I am enabled to walk in the narrow path. The Lord has taken away all desire for worldly company; all my desires, now, are to attend on the means of grace. Blessed be his name! I often find him present in them. My mother and I often remember the happy time we spent in your company at our house. She often speaks of it with great pleasure, and blesses the Lord for the change which grace has wrought in me."

"Lord's Day, 10th (the last Sabbath)—Preached in the morning at Mary's Abbey, from Job 33: 27, 28, 'He looketh upon men, and if any say, I have sinned, and perverted that which was right, and it profited me not, he will deliver his soul from going into the pit, and his life shall see the light'—A happy season.—In the afternoon, having dined with Mr. W., he took me to Swift's Alley, the Baptist place of worship, where I gave an exhortation on brotherly love, and administered the Lord's supper. At Mr. W.'s motion, the church requested me to look out a suitable minister for them. In the evening I preached at Plunket Street, from 2 Tim. 1:18, 'The Lord grant unto him that he may find mercy of the Lord in that day!'—A very solemn season.

"Monday, 11th.—Met the dear Christian friends, for the last time, at a prayer-meeting in Plunket Street.—The Lord was there!— Several friends spent the evening with us afterwards at Mr. H.'s.

"Tuesday, 12th.—Went on board at four; arrived at Liverpool on Thursday, and safely at home on Friday, July 15th, 1796. Blessed be the Preserver of men, the Saviour of sinners, and the help of his servants, for evermore. Amen, amen!"

Some time after, writing to his friend who accompanied him, he says, "I have received several letters from Dublin: two from Master B., one from Miss H., one from M., three or four from our Baptist friends, and some from others whom I cannot recollect.—Mr. K. lately called on me, in his way from Bath to Holyhead. We talked of you, and of our Lord, and did not part till we had presented ourselves before the throne."

During his labours in Dublin, he was strongly solicited to settle in a very flattering situation in the neighbourhood;[14] and a very liberal salary was offered him.[15] On his positively declining it, mention was made of only six *months* of the year. When that was declined, *three months* were proposed; and when he was about to

---

[14] At the *Black Rock,* the residence of some of the most genteel families in the vicinity of Dublin.

[15] One lady of affluence engaged herself to contribute sufficient for the handsome support of Mr. Pearce and family, if he would reside in the neighborhood of Dublin; but he declined, telling her that he had found three things at Birmingham which determined him not to leave it—health, love, and usefulness.

answer this in the negative, the party refused to receive his answer, desiring him to take time to consider of it. He did so; and though he entertained a very grateful sense of the kindness and generosity expressed by the proposal, yet, after the maturest deliberation, he thought it his duty to decline it. Mr. Pearce's modesty prevented his talking on such a subject; but it was known at the time by his friend who accompanied him, and, since his death, has been frequently mentioned as an instance of his disinterested spirit.

His friends at Birmingham were ready to think it hard that he should be so willing to leave them to go on a mission among the heathen; but they could not well complain, and much less think ill of him, when they saw that such a willingness was more than could be effected by the most flattering prospects of a worldly nature, accompanied, too, with promising appearances of religious usefulness.

About a month after his return from Dublin, Mr. Pearce addressed a letter to Mr. Carey, in which he gives some further account of Ireland, as well as of some other interesting matters:

"Birmingham, Aug. 12, 1796.

"O my dear brother, did you but know with what feelings I resume my pen, freely to correspond with you after receiving your very affectionate letter to myself, and perusing that which you sent by the same conveyance to the Society, I am sure you would persuade yourself that I have no common friendship for you, and that your regards are at least returned with equal ardour.

"I fear (I had almost said) that I shall never see your face in the flesh; but if any thing can add to the joy which the presence of Christ, and conformity, perfect conformity to him, will afford in heaven, surely the certain prospect of meeting with my dear brother Carey there is one of *the greatest.* Thrice happy should I be if the providence of God would open a way for my partaking of your labours, your sufferings, and your pleasures, on this side the eternal world; but all my brethren here are of opinion that I shall be more useful at home than abroad; and I, though reluctantly, submit. Yet I am truly with you in spirit. My heart is at Mudnabatty, and at times I even hope to find my body there: but with the Lord I leave it; *He* knows my wishes, my motives, my regret; *He* knows all my soul; and, depraved as it is, I feel an inexpressible satisfaction that he does know it. However, it is a humbling thought to me that he sees I am unfit for such a station, and unworthy of such an honor as to bear his name among the heathen. But I must be thankful still, that though he appoints me not to a post in foreign service, he will allow me to stand sentinel at home. In this situation may I have grace to be faithful unto death!

"I hardly wonder at your being pained on account of the effects produced in the minds of your European friends, by the news of your engagement in the indigo business, because I imagine you are ignorant of the process of that matter among us. When I received the news, I glorified God in sincerity on account of it, and gave most hearty thanks to him for his most gracious appearance on your behalf: but at the same time I feared lest, through that undertaking, the work of the mission might in some way or other be impeded. The same impression was made on the minds of many others; yet no blame was attached, in our view, to you. Our minds were only alarmed for the future—not disposed to censure for the past. Had you seen a faithful copy of the prayers, the praises, and the conversation of the day in which your letters were read, I know you would not have entertained one unkind thought of the Society towards you. Oh, no, my dear brother, far be it from us to lay an atom upon your spirits of a painful nature. Need I say, we do love you, we do respect you, we do confide too much in you, to *design* the smallest occasion of distress to your heart. But I close this subject. In future we will atone for an expression that might bear a harsh construction. We will strengthen, we will support, we will comfort, we will encourage you in your arduous work; all, *all* shall be love and kindness; glory to God, and good will to men. If I have done aught that is wrong, as an individual, pardon me; if we have said aught amiss, as a society, pardon us. Let us forbear one another in love, 'forgiving one another, even as God for Christ's sake hath forgiven us.'

"By the time this reaches you, I hope you will have received Nos. I. and II. of Periodical Accounts. Should you find any thing in them which you think had better be omitted, pray be free in mentioning it, and in future your instructions shall be fully attended to. We have taken all the pains, and used all the caution, in our power to render them unexceptionable; but you can better judge in some respects than we. If you should not approve of all, (though we are not conscious of any thing that you will disapprove,) you will not be offended, but believe we have done our best, and, with your remarks, hope to do better still.

"With pleasure, approaching to rapture, I read the last accounts you sent us. I never expected immediate success; the prospect is truly greater than my most sanguine hopes. 'The kingdom of heaven is like to a *little* leaven hid in three measures of meal, till the *whole is* leavened. Blessed be God! the leaven is in the meal, and its influence is already discoverable. A great God is doing great things by you.[16] Go on, my dearest brother, go on; God will do greater things than these. Jesus is worthy of a *world* of praise: and shall *Hindostan* not praise him? Surely he shall see of the travail of his soul *there,* and the sower and the reaper shall rejoice together. Already the empire of darkness totters, and soon it shall doubtless fall. Blessed be the labourers in this important work; and blessed be He who giveth them hearts and strength to labour, and promises that they shall not labour in vain!

"Do not fear the want of money. *God* is for us, and the silver and the gold are his; and so are the hearts of those who possess the most of it; I will travel from the Land's End to the Orkneys but we will get money enough for all the demands of the mission. I have never had a fear on that head; a little exertion will do wonders; and past experience justifies every confidence. Men we only want; and God shall find them for us in due time.

"Is brother Fountain arrived? We hope he will be an acceptable remittance, and *viva voce,* compensate for the lack of epistolary communications from us.

"I rejoice in contemplating a church of our Lord Jesus Christ in Bengal, formed upon his own plan. Why do not the Hindoo converts join it? Lord, help their unbelief! But perhaps the drop is now withheld that you may by and by have the shower, and lift up your eyes and say, 'These, whence came they? They fly as clouds, or as doves to their windows.' For three years we read of few baptized by the first disciples of our Lord; but, on the fourth, three thousand, and five thousand, openly avowed him. The Lord send *you* such another Pentecost!

"I intend to write my dear brother a long letter. It will prove my *desire* to gratify him, if it do no more. I wish that I knew in what communications your other correspondents will be most deficient; then I would try to supply their omissions.

"I will begin with myself: but I have nothing good to say. I think I am the most vile, ungrateful servant that ever Jesus Christ

---

[16] Pearce is here reminding Carey of the latter's most famous sermon, *Expect Great Things from God; Attempt Great Things for God*

employed in his church. At some times, I question whether I ever knew the grace of God in truth; and at others I hesitate on the most important points of Christian faith. I have lately had peculiar struggles of this kind with my own heart, and have often half concluded to speak no more in the name of the Lord. When I am preparing for the pulpit, I fear I am going to avow fables for facts, and doctrines of men for the truths of God. In conversation I am obliged to be silent, lest my tongue should belie my heart. In prayer I know not what to say, and at times think prayer altogether useless. Yet I cannot wholly surrender my hope, or my profession.—Three things I find, above all others, tend to my preservation:—First, A recollection of a time when, at *once,* I was brought to abandon the practice of sins which the fear of damnation could never bring me to relinquish before: surely, I say, this must be the finger of God, according to the Scripture doctrine of regeneration

"Secondly, I feel such a consciousness of guilt, that nothing but the gospel scheme can satisfy my mind respecting the hope of salvation;—Thirdly, I see that what true devotion does appear in the world seems only to be found among those to whom Christ is precious.

"But I frequently find a backwardness to secret prayer, and much deadness in it; and it puzzles me to see how this can be consistent with a life of grace. However, I resolve, that, let what will become of me, I will do all I can for God while I live, and leave the rest to him; and this I usually experience to be the best way to be at peace.

"I believe, that if I were more fully given up to God, I should be free from these distressing workings of mind; and then I long to be a missionary, where I should have temptations to nothing but to abound in the work of the Lord, and lay myself entirely out for him. In such a situation, I think, pride would have but little food, and faith more occasion for exercise; so that the spiritual life and inward religion would thrive better than they do now.

"At times, indeed, I do feel, I trust, genuine contrition, and sincerely lament my short-comings before God. Oh the sweets that accompany true repentance! Yes, I love to be abased before God. 'There it is I find my blessing.' May the Lord daily and hourly bring me low, and keep me so.

"As to my public work, I find, whilst engaged in it, little cause to complain for want either of matter or words. My labours are acceptable and not altogether unprofitable to the hearers; but what is this to me, if my own soul starves whilst others are fed by me? O my brother, I need your prayers; and I feel a great satisfaction in the hope that you do not forget me. Oh that I may be kept faithful unto death! Indeed, in the midst of my strugglings, a gleam of hope that I shall at last awake in the likeness of God affords me greater joy than words can express. To be with Christ is far better than to continue sinning here; but if the Lord hath any thing to do by me, His will be done.

"I have never so fully opened my case to any one before. Your freedom on similar topics encourages me to make my complaint to you, and I think if you were near me I should feel great relief in revealing to you all my heart. But I shall fatigue you with my moanings, so I will have done on this subject.

"It is not long since I returned from a kind of mission to Ireland. A society is established in Dublin for the purpose of inviting from England ministers of various denominations to assist in promoting the interest of the kingdom of Christ there. Some of our Baptist brethren had been there before me, as Rippon, Langdon, Francis, and Birt; and I think the plan is calculated for usefulness. I have, at Dr. Rippon's request, sent him some remarks on any visit for the Register, but as it is probable you will receive this before that comes to hand, I will say something of my excursion here.

"Having engaged to spend six Lord's Days in that kingdom, I arrived there the day before the first sabbath in June. I first made myself acquainted with the general state of religion in Dublin. I found there were four Presbyterian congregations; two of these belong to the southern presbytery, and are Arians or Socinians; the other two are connected with the northern presbytery, and retain the Westminster confession of faith. One of these latter congregations is very small, and the minister, though orthodox, appears to have but little success. The other is large and flourishing; the place of worship is ninety feet by seventy, and in a morning well filled. Their times of public service are at half-past eleven and five. In the afternoon the stated congregations are small indeed; for five o'clock is the usual dining-hour in Dublin, and few of the hearers would leave their dinners for the gospel. Dr. M'Dowal is the senior pastor of this church—a very affectionate, spiritual man. The junior is Mr. Horner. The Doctor is a warm friend to the Society at whose request I went over to Ireland.

"There is one congregation of Burgher seceders, and another of Anti-burghers. The latter will not hear any man who is not of their own cast; the former are much more liberal. I preached for them once, and they affectionately solicited a repetition of my services.

"Lady Huntingdon's connection has one society here, the only one in the kingdom, perhaps, except at Sligo, where there is another. It is not large, and I fear rather declining There is not one Independent church in the whole kingdom. There were ten Baptist societies in Ireland; but they are now reduced to six: and are, I fear, still on the decline.

"The inhabitants of Dublin seem to be chiefly composed of two classes; the one assumes the appearance of opulence, the other exhibits marks of the most abject poverty; and as there are no parishes in Ireland which provide for the poor, many die every year for want of the common necessaries of life.

"Most of the rich are by profession protestants; the poor are nearly all papists, and strongly prejudiced against the Reformed religion. Their ignorance and superstition are scarcely inferior to your miserable Hindoos. On Midsummer day I had an affecting proof of the latter. On the public road, about a mile from Dublin, is a well, which was once included in the precincts of a priory dedicated to St. John of Jerusalem. This well is in high repute for curing a number of bodily complaints, and its virtues are said to be the most efficacious on the saint's own day. So from twelve o'clock at night, for twenty-four hours, it becomes the rendezvous for all the lame, blind, and otherwise diseased people, within a circuit of twenty miles. Here they brought old and young, and applied the 'holy water' both internally and externally; some by pouring, some by immersion, and all by drinking whilst, for the good of those who could not attend in person, their friends filled bottles with the efficacious water to use at home. Several I saw on their knees before the well at their devotions, which were not unfrequently interrupted with a glass of whiskey! With this they were supplied from a number of dealers in that article, who kept standings all round the well.

"Near to the spot was a church-yard, where great numbers kneeled upon the tombs of their deceased relatives, and appeared earnestly engaged in praying for the repose of their souls.

"It was truly a lamentable sight. My heart ached at their delusions, whilst I felt gratitude I hope unfeigned for an acquaintance with the 'water of life, of which if a man drink he shall live for ever!'

"There are few or none of the middle class to connect the rich and the poor, so that favourable access to them is far more difficult than to the lower orders of the people in England; and their priests hold them in such bondage, that if a catholic servant only attend on family worship in a protestant house, penance must be performed for the offence."—S.P."

Mention has already been made of his having "formed a pleasing acquaintance with several serious young gentlemen of the University of Dublin." The following letter was addressed to one of them, the Rev. Mr. Matthias, a few months after his return:

"Dear brother Matthias,

"I have been employed this whole day in writing letters to Dublin; and it is the first day I have been able to redeem for that purpose. I will not consume a page in apology. Let it suffice to say that necessity, not disinclination, has detained from my Irish friends those proofs of my gratitude and esteem which in other circumstances I ought to have presented three months ago. I thought this morning of answering all their demands before I slept; but I have written so many sheets, and all full, that I find my eyes and my fingers both fail; and l believe this must close my intercourse with Dublin this day. When I shall be able to complete my purpose I do not know. To form friendships with good men is pleasant; but to maintain *all that communion* which friendship expects is in some cases very difficult. Happy should I be could I meet my Irish friends *in propria persona,* instead of sitting in solitude, and maintaining, by the tedious medium of the pen, this distant intercourse. But "the Lord he shall choose our inheritance for us." Were all the planets of our system embodied and placed in close association, the light would be greater and the object grander; but then usefulness and systematic beauty consist in their dispersion; and what are we, my brother, but so many satellites to Jesus, the great Sun of the Christian system? Some, indeed, like burning Mercuries, keep nearer the luminary, and receive more of its light and heat, whilst others, like the ringed planet, or the Georgium Sidus, preserve a greater distance, and reflect a greater portion of his light; yet if, amidst all this diversity, *they belong to the system,* two things may be affirmed of all:—all keep true to one centre, and borrow whatever light they have from one source. True it is, that the further they are from the sun, the longer are they in performing their revolutions: and is not this exemplified in us'! The closer we keep to Jesus, the more brilliant are our graces; the more cheerful and active are our lives: but, alas! we are all comets; we all move in eccentric orbits: at one time glowing beneath the ray Divine, at another congealing and freezing into icicles. 'Oh what a miracle to man is man!'

"Little did I think when I began this letter that I should thus have indulged myself in allegory: but true friendship, I believe, always dictates extempore; and my friends must never expect from me a studied epistle. They can meet with better thoughts than I can furnish them with, in *any* bookseller's shop. It is not the dish, however well it may be cooked, that gives the relish, but the sweet sauce of friendship; and this I think sometimes makes even nonsense palatable.

"But I have some questions to put to you:—first, how are all my college friends, Messrs. Walker, Maturin, Hamilton, &c.? How is their health? But, chiefly, how are the interests of religion among you? Are there any praying students added to your number? Do all those you thought well of continue to justify their profession? You know what it is that interests me. Pray tell me all, whether it makes me weep or rejoice.

"I hope Mr. H—'s ministry was blessed in Dublin. Do you know any instances of it? We must sow in hope, and I trust that we shall all gather fruit to eternal life, even where the buddings have never appeared to us in this world. How is it with your own soul? I thank God, I never, I think, rejoiced habitually so much in him as I have done of late. '*God is love.*' That makes me happy. I rejoice that God reigns; that he reigns over all; that he reigns over *me;* over my crosses, my comforts, my family, my friends, my senses, my mental powers, my designs, my words, my preaching, my conduct; that he is *God over all,* blessed for ever. I am willing to live, yet I long to die, to be freed from all error and all sin. I have nothing else to trouble me; no other cross to carry. The sun shines without all day long; but I am sensible of internal darkness. Well, through grace it shall be all light by and by. Yes, you and I shall be *angels* of light; all Mercuries then; all near the Sun; always in motion; always glowing with zeal, and flaming with love. Oh for the new heavens and the new earth wherein dwelleth righteousness!

> 'Oh what love and concord there,
> And what sweet harmony
> In heaven above, where happy souls
> Adore thy majesty!
> Oh how the heavenly choirs all sing

> To him who sits enthroned above!
> What admiring!
> And aspiring!
> Still desiring:
> Oh how I long to taste this feast of love!'

"Will you tell brother M— that I wait an opportunity of sending a parcel to him? In that I will enclose a letter. My very affectionate respects to him and Mr. H—, and all my college friends as though named. If you be not weary of such an eccentric correspondent, pray do not be long ere you write to your unworthy but affectionate brother in Christ,—S. P."

Awhile after this, he thus writes to his friend Mr. Summers:

December, 1796.

"I rejoice that you have been supported under and brought through your late trials. I do not wonder at it; for it is no more than God has *promise;* and though we may well wonder that he promises any thing, yet his performance is no just ground of surprise: and when we find ourselves so employed, we had better turn our wonder to our own unbelief, that for one moment we suspected God would not be as good as his word.

"I have been lately more than ever delighted with the thought that God *has engaged* to do any thing for such worms as we. I never studied the deistical controversy so much, nor ever rejoiced in revelation more. Alas! what should we know if God had not condescended to teach us? Paul very justly remarks, that no one knoweth any thing of God, but the Spirit of God, and he to whom the Spirit revealeth him. Now the Spirit hath revealed God in the Bible; but to an unbeliever the Bible is a sealed book. He can know nothing from a book that he looks upon as an imposture, and yet there is no other book in which God is revealed: so that to reject the Bible is to immerse ourselves in darkness, and, whilst professing to be wise, actually to become fools: whereas no sooner do we believe what the Spirit saith, than unto us is God revealed, and in his light do we see light. S.P."

In April, 1797, Mr. Pearce attended a meeting of ministers at Arnsby. A person present has recorded that, "upon this occasion, he was previously expected to preach; but, as he did not arrive till the service was ready to commence, one of the brethren was engaged to supply his place. On the appearance of Mr. Pearce, however, the minister entreated to be excused; when he was thus addressed by that amiable man: 'My dear brother, I am fatigued with my journey, and unfit to preach: you complain of many fears besetting you, and know not that I am as timid and nervous as yourself; oftentimes, and especially since my nervous complaint, I have suffered to an agony in the prospect of such an exercise; but, on the principle of benevolence, to save you from those painful feelings, I will endeavor to encounter my own and comply with your request.'" Of the sermon he then preached, notes were taken from his lips at the time, by the friend referred to; and though, as the writer remarks, they are "extremely inadequate to convey a just idea of the discourse," since Mr. Pearce's impassioned enlargements on his principal ideas formed the peculiar excellence of his pulpit exercises, yet as excellent in themselves, and happily illustrating the text, it is conceived they will be found acceptable to the pious reader.

Rev. 7:9; "I beheld, and lo, a great multitude, which no man can number, of all nations, and kindred, and people, and tongues, stood before the throne, and before the Lamb."

Life is a journey; Christians are travelers; but the world to which we are going is to us unknown. Those who have gone thither have not returned to give us any information about it....The doctrine which Christ has left behind him, however, supplies us with all the information that is necessary to our happiness. Here life and immortality are brought to light. From his doctrine we learn what heaven is, and what its employments are. In general, we know that heaven is a place of society: when Lazarus died, he was carried to Abraham's bosom. And from the passage before us, we learn that it is a very large and blessed society.

I. Inquire, OF WHOM THE SOCIETY OF HEAVEN WILL CONSIST.

1. Jesus the Mediator......He is the sun that enlightens the world....He who shed his blood for your salvation....He whom your souls adore, and desire to see, and to enjoy.... "I go to prepare a place for you: I will come again, and receive you unto myself; that where I am, there ye may be also." "Father, I will that they also whom thou hast given me, be with me where I am; that they may behold my glory, which thou hast given me." We shall "stand before the throne, and before the Lamb."

2. The angels of God shall form a part of this society. They even now hold an uninterrupted intercourse with the church of God on earth; are continually "ascending and descending on the Son of man;"— are "sent forth to minister for those who shall be heirs of salvation;"—and at length shall lead us to the throne of God and the Lamb, and we shall dwell among them.

3. This society will comprehend all good men,—"a great multitude which no man can number, of all nations, and kindred, and people, and tongues."...There are three things which prevent the full society of good men on earth:—1. We are separated by distance of time. We have heard of Abel....of Enoch, who "walked with God,"....of Abraham....of Paul, and others eminent for piety; but we have never seen them. Could we but see and converse with these good men, they would teach us to walk with God too....Well, there we shall see them; there also, Jesus and his disciples!—2. Here we are separated by distance of place. Some good men live in Europe; a few in Africa; some in America; and Asia at least contains one good man,[17] with whom we have taken sweet counsel,......but we shall see his face no more!......Well, we shall meet again in glory, and part no more.—3. Good men are separated by difference of sentiment. Here they are divided into various classes, and distinguished by several peculiarities; and, as truth is the bond of union, we necessarily feel most attached to those whose principles and dispositions are most congenial with our own. But there shall be no dissensions......One blaze of light shall illuminate every heart!

II. Inquire, WHEREIN WILL CONSIST THE BLESSEDNESS OF THIS HEAVENLY SOCIETY.

1. There they shall be all holy. One reason why we do not rejoice more in the society of the godly here is, that we have so much sin amongst us, while the world around us is lying in wickedness. Very often, like Lot, our souls are "vexed with the filthy conversation of the wicked;" and, with the Psalmist, we are ready to say, "Wo unto us, that we sojourn in Mesech, and dwell in the tents of Kedar!"....Here, a good man feels his pleasure abated by the reflection that, perhaps, his nearest relations are farthest off from the kingdom of heaven, and his house is not so with

---

[17] The preacher here made a most pathetic (passionate) allusion to Mr. Carey.

God....But none of these things are found in heaven: there we shall never behold sinners, nor be grieved with their conduct any more: "there shall in no wise enter into it any thing that defileth, neither whatsoever worketh abomination or maketh a lie; but they who are written in the Lamb's book of life."

2. Not only all shall be holy, but they shall be *eminently* so. When we meet with good men, we rejoice in their society, and feel a oneness of heart with them: but alas! we soon discover so many defects; in some a little pride, in others a little covetousness....like the spots in the sun, which, though they do not obscure its rays, yet become a blemish. But there every subject shall be as righteous as his Lord, and every disciple as holy as his Master.

3. There they shall be completely happy, as well as holy. Many of our sorrows in this world arise from sympathy; and religion not only allows, but teaches us "to weep with those that weep; to bear each other's burdens, and so fulfill the law of Christ." We have some happiness in our religious friends; but often have to say, 'Lord, he whom thou lovest is sick.' Here, a dear friend is called to lament the loss of an affectionate wife, a faithful husband, an only child, or a tender parent....there, a beloved friend is involved in some worldly difficulties or temptations. These diminish the happiness of society....But, in heaven, the tears shall be wiped from all faces, sorrow and sighing shall flee away, and each shall be as happy as his capacity will admit.

4. Perfect union in our religious sentiments, affections, and worship, will form an essential part of the felicity of heaven. The want of such an agreement diminishes the aggregate of social happiness, and evil passions both produce and are produced by it......In the exercise of public worship we feel our minds elevated and dignified; our hearts are more enlarged than in private duties: the latter may be more profitable, but the former are more joyful......Here, however, our pleasures are abated by the limitation of our society; there, the society will be abundantly large, consisting of "a great multitude which no man can number;" and they shall be "all of one heart and of one soul."

5. This society shall be blessed with permanence and perpetuity. Fellowship with Christian brethren on earth is sweet, and, while engaged in acts of social worship, we feel the endearing bands sweetly drawn around us; but soon we are called to part, and parting divides our joy.....Our social pleasures are often damped by the

necessity of exclusion from the church,—by the death of valuable friends....But there shall be no exclusion from that society; no more death; "neither shall the inhabitants say any more, I am sick."

From hence we may learn, 1. What must be our qualifications for heaven. John, 3:5. 2. To be reconciled to bereaving providences, and to our own death: such as die in the Lord are gone to this blessed society. 3. To endeavor to render our intercourse with Christians on earth more like that above.

To the above may be added a few extracts of letters which he addressed to his friends in 1797 and 1798.

To Dr. Ryland.
"March, 1797.

"During the last three weeks I have, at times, been very poorly, with colds, &c. Am better now, and have been all along assisted in going through my public duties. Let us continue to pray for each other till death makes it a needless service. How uncertain is life, and what a blessing is death to a saint! I seem lately to feel a kind of *affection* for death. Methinks if it were visible I could embrace it. 'Welcome herald, that bids the prisoner be free; that announces the dawn of everlasting day; that bids the redeemed come to Zion with everlasting joy, to be beyond the reach of an erroneous judgment and a depraved heart.' To believe, to feel, to speak, to act *exactly* as God will have me; to be wholly absorbed and taken up with him; this, nothing short of this, can make my bliss complete. But *all this is mine.* Oh the height, the depth, the length, the breadth of redeeming love! It conquers my heart, and constrains me to yield myself a living sacrifice, acceptable to God, through Jesus Christ.— My dear brother, we have had many happy meetings on earth: the best is in reserve.

'No heart upon earth can conceive
The bliss that in heaven they share;
Then who this dark world would not leave,
And cheerfully die to be there?'

"Oh how full of love, and joy, and praise shall we be when that happy state is ours! Well, yet a little while, and He that shall come will come. Even so, come, Lord Jesus! My dear brother, forgive the hasty effusions of a heart that loves you in the bowels of Jesus, and is always happy in testifying itself to be affectionately yours,—S. P."

To Mr. Cave.[18]
On the falling away of some who had promised fair in religion.
"March, 1797.

"I thank you, my dear brother, for the confidence you repose in me, the affection you have for me, and the freedom with which you write to me. Assure yourself that I sincerely sympathize in the cutting events which you have lately experienced. Trying indeed! Your heart must bleed. Yet be not discouraged in your work. The more *Satan* opposes *Christ,* the more let us oppose *him.* He comes with great violence because his time is short. His kingdom is on the decline; his strong holds are besieged, and he knows they must soon be taken. Whilst it lasts, he is making desperate sallies on the armies of the Lamb. It is no great wonder that he fights and wounds a raw recruit now and then, who strays from the camp, and, thoughtless of the danger, keeps not close by the Captain's tent. I hope our glorious Leader will heal the wounded, and rescue the captive. He is sure to make reprisals. Christ will have ten to one. You will yet see his arm made bare. He shall go forth like a man of war. The prisoners shall be redeemed, and the old tyrant shall be cast into the bottomless pit. Be of good cheer, my fellow soldier. The cause is not ours, but God's. Let us endure hardness, and still fight the good fight of faith. At last we shall come off conquerors through him who hath loved us.

"I hope you have some causes for joy as well as grief. I trust though one, or two, or three fall, the tens and the twenties stand their ground. Oh do what you can to cheer them under the common trial. Let them not see a faint heart in *you.* Fight manfully still. Tell them to watch the more; to pray the harder; to walk the closer with God. So out of the eater shall come forth meat, and sweetness out of the strong.   S.P."

---

[18] Mr. Cave was a young man, licensed to the ministry by Mr. Pearce's church, and became the immediate successor of Mr. Carey, at Leicester. His life was highly honorable to the cause of Jesus Christ, though he was never very popular as a preacher. For many years before his death he taught a respectable school at Birmingham, and occasionally supplied the pulpits of his brethren. In the early part of the present year [1844] he was found dead in his bed, at the age of more than seventy years.

To Mr. Bates and Mrs. Barnes,
who had been burnt out of their residence.

"The many expressions of Christian friendship which I received
from you, and your affectionate families, during my late visit to
London, will often excite grateful recollection in future, as they
have almost daily since I parted from you; and though I do not write
this avowedly as a mere letter of acknowledgment, yet I wish it to
assure you that I am not forgetful of my friends, nor unthankful for
their kindness. May all the favour you show to the servants of our
common Lord, for his sake, be amply recompensed in present peace,
and future felicity, when the promise of Him who cannot lie shall be
fulfilled,— 'A cup of cold water given to a disciple, in the name of
a disciple, shall not lose its reward.'

"But whilst you, my dear friends, live 'in hope of the glory' that
remains 'to be revealed,' I am persuaded that you expect *all* as the
fruit of sovereign mercy, which first forms us to the mind of Christ,
then accepts, and then rewards. Truly, if sinners be rewarded, it
must be 'of grace, and not of debt.' Yet it is a mercy of unspeakable
magnitude that grace should establish a connection between
obedience and enjoyment, such a connection as at once insures joy
to the believer, and glory to Christ.

"Oh that our thoughts, our affections, our desires, may be much
in heaven! *Here,* you have been taught, is 'no continuing city,' no
certain place of abode; and though you have been taught it awfully
in flames, yet if you learn it effectually, the terror of the means will
be conquered by the excellency and glory of the consequences. Yes,
my friends, 'in heaven we have a better and enduring substance:' the
apartments there are more spacious; the society more sweet; the
enjoyments more perfect; and all to last for ever. Well may
Christians 'rejoice in hope of the glory of God!'"

To Mr. Carey
"Birmingham, Sept. 8, 1797.

"My very dear Brother,

"It might be wrong to compare the pleasure which any of your
letters from India to Europe give, with that which between the same
friends is derived from European letters to India. Your want of
Christian society may make Christian correspondence sweeter than

we, who are surrounded with affectionate brethren in the Lord, can conceive; otherwise I should have referred you to your own feelings when you hear from us, for an idea of the pleasure I derive from your brotherly epistles. Indeed, my dear brother, neither distance nor absence abates the ardent attachment my soul bears to yours; on the contrary, I feel it grow year by year, and I sometimes derive greater joy in the prospect of heaven itself, from the expectation of meeting with my beloved Carey there. I can hardly refrain from repeating, what I have so often told you before, that I long to meet you on earth, and to join you in your labors of love among the poor dear brethren: yes, would my Lord bid me so, I should with transport obey the summons, and take a joyful farewell of the land that bare me, though it were for ever; but I must confess that the path of duty appears to me clearer than before to be at home, at least for the present: not that I think my connections in England a sufficient argument, but that I am somewhat necessary to the mission itself, and shall be as long as money is wanted, and our number of active friends does not increase. Brother Fuller and myself have the whole of the collecting business on our hands; and, though there are many others about us who exceed me in grace and gifts, yet their other engagements forbid, or their peculiar turn of mind disqualifies them for that kind of service. I wish, however, to be thankful, if our dear Lord will but employ me as a foot in the body. I consider myself as united to the hands, and eyes, and mouth, and heart, and all; and, when the body rejoices, I have my share of gladness with the other members.

"At this moment I rejoice, though it be with trembling. Your communications respecting Sookmun, and Yardee, and Doorgotteea, and the other whose name you forgot, more than repay every painful step; but do they hold on their way? O, my brother, be not discouraged if you cannot say they do; nor will we be discouraged, should future letters terminate our pleasing hope respecting them. If they are not effectually called, God will call others, and yet set up his empire and make his name glorious in Hindoostan. Should they still appear to be really the sons of God by faith in Christ Jesus, tell them there is one in Birmingham who loves them in the bowels of Jesus Christ—a poor sinner, by nature as bad as they, but who, like them, is looking for the mercy of the Lord Jesus Christ unto eternal life; tell them he remembers them by name in prayer to their Father and his Father, to their God and his God;

tell them he hopes to meet them in glory, and to join them eternally, singing to the Lamb that was slain for both, glory in the highest.

"I am glad that at last you have received most of my letters, and I hope, should any considerable time elapse in future without your hearing from English friends, you will set it down to the account of a precarious conveyance, and not to our neglect of you: like the comforts of the holy man of Uz, they may be delayed for a season, to crowd upon you in greater abundance in the end.

"I have considerably affected my spirits by night-reading on mission history during the last winter, so that I had hardly fortitude enough to enter my own pulpit, or sometimes to engage in family prayer; but through mercy I am much recovered, having been more regular in going to bed, and taking more exercise by day, although I am still incapable of close thinking or much writing, without pain in my head, followed with an almost stupefaction for a time.

"Our church is in very favorable circumstances. I have baptized several lately, and many more are in a very hopeful state. We are at present strangers to all discord; we live in peace and much affection. God grant it may abide and abound!

"A society has lately been formed in London for preaching to the Jews: very few attended; but a Jew of some consequence lately told one of the supporters of that lecture that it had occasioned some consideration – that the men of influence deterred the poorer sort from attending; 'but (said he) I would have you print some small tracts upon the subject – we may read when we durst not hear.' Hence we fondly hope the ice is broken: I rejoice in every step that is taking: it will do good to Christians, if not to the posterity of Abraham.

"I think in one of your letters you hint a suspicion that 'the ten tribes yet exist in India.' Have you pursued the inquiry? What is the result?

"I have had with me this afternoon a blind woman from the workhouse, the eyes of whose mind the Lord appears to have truly enlightened. She reminds me of brother Thomas's blind Brahmin. O that he may be enabled to behold the Lamb of God, and see the glory of God in him!

"May my dear brother enjoy much of God in his own soul, and see his power and his glory displayed in Hindoostan more than he ever did in a British sanctuary.

"I am, dear brother, more than I can express, your affectionate brother,   S.P."

To Mr. and Mrs. Bowyer, Pall Mall.

"Nov. 17, 1797.

"Blessed be 'the Preserver of men' for all his goodness to dear Mr. and Mrs. B——. With theirs shall my gratitude also ascend, whilst separated from their society; and with theirs shall it more warmly and permanently ascend, when we meet to form a part of the 'general assembly, and church of the first-born.'

"I do not return to London this autumn, but I mean to visit Portsmouth. I must be indebted to you for my directions. We shall be very happy to see you at Luke Street; but Wales I suppose will be the vortex that will swallow up much of your time. Well, so *you* are happy, we must be disinterested enough to be satisfied, although we be denied a personal participation.

"Let us not forget that we are Christians; and Christians profess a hope of a better country than *Cambria* contains. *There* we all belong. Already citizens by privilege, we shall be so by possession soon.

'Roll swiftly round, ye wheels of time,
And bring the welcome day!'

"In hope of greeting you both in that good land, I remain most affectionately yours,—S. P."

To Dr. Ryland.

"Nov. 17, 1797.

"I feel much for you in relation both to the duties and trials of your present situation; at the same time I bless God who fixed you in it, because I am persuaded that it will be for his glory in the churches of Christ. And though none but those whose hands are full of religious concerns can guess at your difficulties, yet our blessed Redeemer knows them all. O my brother, you are travailing for him who redeemed you by his blood, who sympathizes with you, and who will graciously crown you at last. Small as my trials are, I would turn smith, and work at the anvil and the forge, rather than bear them for any other master than *Christ*. Yet, were they ten thousand times as many as they are, the thought of their being for Him, I trust, would sweeten them all.

"I have reason to be very thankful for much pleasure of late, both as a Christian and a minister. I have never felt so deeply my need of a Divine Redeemer, and seldom possessed such solid confidence that he is mine. I want more and more to become a little child, to dwindle into nothing in my own esteem, to renounce my own wisdom, power, and goodness, and simply look to and live upon Jesus for all. I am ashamed that I have so much pride, so much self-will. O my Saviour! make me 'meek and lowly in heart;' in this alone I find 'rest to my soul.'

"I could say much of what Immanuel has done for my soul; but I fear lest even this should savour of vanity. When shall I be like my Lord? Oh welcome death, when I have nothing more to do for Christ! To him, till then, may I live every day and every hour. Rather may I be annihilated than not live to him.

"You will rejoice with me to hear that we have a pleasing prospect as a church. Several very hopeful and some very valuable characters are about to join us. Lord, carry on thy work!"

A few weeks after, he writes to Dr. Carey: "A spirit for village preaching prevails much in England and Scotland. I have pleasing prospects of settled congregations in two neighboring villages, to the first of which I went but little more than twelve months since. On Lord's Day about thirty of our members go in turn and pray, exhort, read sermons, &c. which the Lord has greatly blessed."

To Mrs. Pearce, on the dangerous illness of one of the children.

"Portsmouth, Jan. 29, 1798.

"Ignorant of the circumstances of our dear child, how shall I address myself to her dearer mother? With a fluttering heart, and a trembling hand, I, in this uncertainty, resume my pen. One consideration tranquillizes my mind,—I and mine are in the hands of *God;* the wise, the good, the indulgent Parent of mankind! Whatever *he* does is best. I am prepared for all his will, and hope that I shall never have a feeling whose language is not, 'Thy will be done.'

"I am most kindly entertained here by Mr. and Mrs. Shoveller; and, except my dear Sarah's presence, feel myself at home. *They* have had greater trials than *we* can at present know. They have attended *seven* children to the gloomy tomb; they have been supported beneath their loss by Him who hath said, 'As thy days, so shall thy strength be.' Mrs. S. tells me she 'blessed God for all.' May my dear Sarah be enabled to do the same, whatever the result may prove. Tomorrow I expect another letter from you; yet, lest you should too much feel my absence, I will not delay forwarding this a single post. Oh that it may prove in some degree a messenger of consolation!

"Yesterday I preached three times: God was very good. I received your letter before the first service: you may be assured that I bore you on my heart in the presence of my Lord and yours; nor shall I pray in vain: He will either restore the child, or support you under the loss of it. I dare not pray with importunity for *any earthly good;* for 'who knoweth what is good for man in this life, all the days of his vain life, which he spendeth as a shadow?' But *strength* to bear the loss of earthly comforts he has *promised:* for *that* I importune; and *that, I* doubt not, will be granted.

"In a house directly opposite to the window before which I now write, a *wife, a mother, is* just departed! Why am I not a bereaved husband? Why are not my children motherless? When we compare our condition with our wishes, we often complain; but if we compare it with that of many around us, our complaints will be exchanged for gratitude and praise."

To Mr. Carey.

Portsmouth, Feb. 5, 1798.

"I am here, my dear brother, on the same errand which took you from Europe to India, seeking the salvation of the heathen: but how differently am I situated from my dear friends in Bengal! They are laboring in the midst of idolatrous strangers: I am reposing in the bosom of Christian friendship. Blessed be God, we shall find one resting place at last; and soon shall we be reposing there. O how short the space which in this world we can employ for God! Surely whatever our hands find to do, we should do with all our might.

"I am stimulated to new exertions at home by my dear brother's activity abroad. I bless God who inspired you with such a zeal in such a cause, and who still adds fuel to the precious flame. Long may your heart be preserved, glowing with the same ardor for Immanuel's honor and the salvation of poor heathens!

"The people here are very liberal to the mission. I have been here a little more than a week, and have already raised £78. Could I stay through this week, I suppose it would be made £100; but my dear wife writes me that our eldest child (just six years old) is dying in a fever, so that I must return as soon as I can. The Lord support the mother and myself!

"Had I time, I would write to brethren Tomas and Fountain also. I have written them both twice lately. You will give my warmest Christian love to them, and to all that love our Lord Jesus in Bengal. Your frequent correspondence will always rejoice the heart of your friends, among whom assure yourself none is more heartily yours in our dear Jesus than   S.P."

To R. Bowyer, Esq.

"Feb. 14, 1798.

"Not a day has hurried by, since I parted with my dear friends in Pall Mall, but they have been in my affectionate remembrance; but, not being able to speak with any satisfaction respecting our dear child, I have withheld myself from imparting new anxieties to bosoms already alive to painful sensibility.

"At length, however, a gracious God puts it in my power to say that there is hope. After languishing between life and death for many days, she now seems to amend. We flatter ourselves that she has passed the crisis, and will yet be restored to our arms; but parental fears forbid too strong a confidence. It may be that our most merciful God saw that the shock of a sudden removal would be too strong for the tender feelings of a mother; and so by degrees prepares for the stroke which must fall at last. However, she is in the best hands, and we are, I hope, preparing for submission to whatever may be the blessed will of God.

"I was brought home in safety, and feel myself in much better health in consequence of my journey. Oh that it may be all consecrated to my Redeemer's praise!

"Happy should I be if I could oftener enjoy your friendly society; but we must wait for the full accomplishment of our social wishes till we come to that better world for which Divine grace is preparing *us.—There* our best, our brightest hopes, and there our warmest affections must be found. Could we have all we want below, we should be reluctant to ascend, when Jesus calls us home. No, this is not our rest; it is polluted with sin, and dashed with sorrow: but though our pains in themselves are evil, yet our God turns the curse into a blessing, and makes all that we meet with accomplish our good.

"What better can I wish, my friends, than the humble place of Mary, or the happy rest of John! Faith can enjoy them both, till actually we fall at the Saviour's feet, and lean upon his bosom, when we see him as he is.

'Oh the delights, the heavenly joys,
The glories of the place,

Where Jesus sheds the brightest beams
Of his o'erflowing grace!'"

To Mr. Carey

"Birmingham, Sept. 26, 1798.

"My dear Brother,

"It is impossible for me to give you a just idea of the effect your last affectionate letter produced on my feelings. What regret did I feel that, for so long a time, you had received nothing from me: though the recollection that, whatever had become of my letters, I had neither forgotten nor neglected you, somewhat relieved me. I hope long ere now you have had abundant proof of this; and I am really mistaken if I have not been your most voluminous correspondent.

"But how kind it was in you to give me credit for the continuance of my friendship, even when the expected evidences of it were wanting! This I deeply feel, and for this I most affectionately thank you, as well as for all those glowing expressions of Christian attachment which overwhelmed my heart, and drowned me, and many more who heard them, in a flood of tears. O could I be indulged with the enjoyment of your society once more in the flesh, to renew all the sweet intercourse we have had together at Leicester, at Northampton, at Kettering, at Walgrave, at Birmingham, at London, &c. and to give full vent to all those strong emotions which have been now nearly six years kindling and strengthening whilst seas and continents have separated us! Methinks a greater gratification my heart has never conceived; and, might I be allowed the choice, INDIA should be the spot,—there would I hasten on the wings of the wind, and, whilst I gratified my inclination, perpetuate my joy, till He, whose love to us is the sole cause of our love to each other, should call one of us from the stage of action, and leave the other for a little longer season, to finish the work that was given him to do.

"But how wild my wishes run! Am I not fixed in my present station by the Lord Jesus, who has fixed you in yours? Has he not, by his servants at least, forbidden my removal? Does he not prosper me where I am, and honor me with opportunities of doing something for his cause among the heathen, although I am not, like you, called to visit and immediately instruct them? Is not the period of continuance here extremely short? and, when I leave this world, will it not be in the sure and certain hope of meeting my dear brother in glory? I confess these considerations ought to satisfy me, and I hope they have their influence.

> 'Obedient to my Head,
> Where he appoints I'd go;
> And still in Jesus' footsteps tread,
> And do his work below.'

"I have still reason to rejoice in the Lord's goodness to us at Birmingham. We have had some pleasing additions lately, and next ordinance day we expect from eight to twelve more. Through great mercy we have long enjoyed perfect peace, but we longed after closer union than on the usual plan it was possible for a church of nearly 400 members to expect. We therefore agreed to adopt two new measures, and, if we judge of the issue by the beginning, they seem to promise the fulfillment of our wishes.

"First, instead of a public lecture after the ordinance, we have a church-meeting for the following purposes:

"1. Let every brother be called upon in his turn to pray, four or five might engage on an evening; but let none exceed four or five minutes.

"2. Let the minister, and every other member who has, during the last month, received any intelligence respecting the state of religion in our own town, in the kingdom, in Europe, in the world, communicate it: and for this purpose let our brethren who travel on business, or otherwise, make a point of inquiring into the state of religion in the places through which they pass, and make a report on their return, whilst others enlarge their correspondence as they have opportunity.

"3. Let every brother be at liberty to give exhortations to the church on any practical subject.

"4. Should these exercises, on any evening, not occupy the whole of the allotted time, let there be some profitable question always on the table, for friendly and serious discussion.

"Secondly, we have agreed to divide the whole church into districts of ten families in each, selected according to the nearness of their residence. A brother in each district to visit ever member in his district for one month; then let the visitor give his roll to the next brother on the list, and so on monthly; and at the end of each month let all visitors meet and report to the disciples and the minister the state of all and each member in the church; whilst a committee is formed to maintain a regular correspondence with every member whom Providence has called to another place of residence.

"The first of these plans we put in practice about six months ago; and we found it very profitable. But the novelty excited suspicion that we met for political discussion, and we thought it prudent to decline. However, we have now resumed our meeting, admitting strangers into the gallery. It has had a blessed effect in promoting our acquaintance and union, and I ardently hope will increase in its advantages.

"My dearest brother, we deeply sympathize with you in all your afflictions; and if I say but little on your trials, assure yourself it is not because I am insensible to their weight, but because I fear to probe your wounded heart, lest it should unnecessarily make it bleed afresh. If my poor prayers may aught avail, they are not, nor shall be wanting on your behalf. May He who was himself "a man of sorrows, tempted in all points like as we are," succor, comfort, and, if it is his blessed will, deliver you. Yet who knoweth what is good for a man, all his vain life, which he passeth as a shadow?—no doubt there is a need-be that we should endure heaviness through these self-same afflictions. I have lately been much led to realize the existing, actual, universal government of God; and I feel myself constrained to subdue every wish but for holiness, and to check every complaint but for the evils of my heart. Yes, my brother, surrounded with troubles—personal, domestic, religious, or civil—we will still shout 'Hallelujah, for the Lord God Omnipotent reigneth.'

"Most affectionately yours in Jesus   S.P."

CHAPTER IV

AN ACCOUNT OF HIS LAST AFFLICTION, AND THE HOLY AND HAPPY EXERCISES OF HIS MIND UNDER IT.

Early in October, 1798, Mr. Pearce attended at the Kettering ministers' meeting, and preached from Psalm 90:16,17, "Let thy work appear unto thy servants, and thy glory unto their children. And let the beauty of the Lord our God be upon us: and establish thou the work of our hands upon us; yea, the work of our hands establish thou it." He was observed to be singularly solemn and affectionate in that discourse. If he had known it to be the last time that he should address his brethren in that part of the country, he could scarcely have felt or spoken in a more interesting manner. It was a discourse full of instruction, full of a holy unction, and that seemed to breathe an apostolical ardour. On his return he preached at Market-Harborough; and riding home the next day in company with his friend Mr. Summers, of London, they were overtaken with rain. Mr. Pearce was wet through his clothes, and towards evening complained of a chilliness. A slight hoarseness followed. He preached several times after this, which brought on an inflammation, and issued in a consumption. It is probable that if his constitution had not been previously impaired, such effects might not have followed in this instance. His own ideas on this subject are expressed in a letter to Dr. Ryland, dated Dec. 4, 1798; and in another to Mr. King, dated from Bristol, on his way to Plymouth, March 30, 1799. In the former, he says, "Ever since my Christmas journey last year to Sheepshead, Nottingham, and Leicester, on the mission business, I have found my constitution greatly debilitated, in consequence of a cold caught after the unusual exertions which circumstances then demanded: so that, from a frame that could endure any weather, I have since been too tender to encounter a single shower without danger; and the duties of the Lord's Day, which, as far as bodily strength went, I could perform with little fatigue, have since frequently overcome me. But the severe cold I caught in my return from the last Kettering ministers' meeting has affected me so much that I have sometimes concluded I must give up preaching entirely; for though my head and spirits are better than for two years past, yet my stomach is so very weak that I cannot pray in my family without frequent pauses for breath, and in the pulpit it is labour and agony which must be felt to be conceived of. I have however made shift to preach sometimes thrice, but mostly only twice on a Lord's Day, till the last, when the morning sermon only, though I delivered it with great pleasure of mind, and with as much caution as to my voice as possible, yet cost me so much labour as threw me into a fever till the next day, and prevented my sleeping all night."—In the latter,—he thus writes:— "Should my life be spared, I and my family, and all my connections, will stand indebted, under God, to you. Unsuspecting of danger myself, I believe I should have gone on with my exertions, till the grave had received me. Your attention sent Mr. B. (the apothecary) to me, and then I first learned what I have since been increasingly convinced of—*that I* was *rapidly destroying the vital principle.* And the kind interest you have taken in my welfare ever since, has often drawn the grateful tear from my eye. May the God of heaven and earth reward your kindness to his unworthy servant, and save you from all the evils from which your distinguished friendship would have saved me."

Such were his ideas. His labours were certainly abundant; perhaps too great for his constitution: but it is probable that nothing was more injurious to his health than a frequent exposure to night air, and an inattention to the necessity of changing damp clothes.

Hitherto we have seen in Mr. Pearce the active, assiduous, and laborious servant of Jesus Christ; but now we see him laid aside from his work, wasting away by slow degrees, patiently enduring the will of God, and cheerfully waiting for his dissolution. And as here is but little to narrate, I shall content myself with copying his letters, or extracts from them, to his friends, in the order of time in which they were written, only now and then dropping a few hints to furnish the reader with the occasions of some of them.

To Dr. Ryland.

"Birmingham, Oct. 8, 1798.

"O my dear brother, your letter of the 5th, which I received this morning, has made me thankful for all *my pulpit agonies,* as they enable me to weep with a weeping brother. They have been of use to me in other respects; particularly in teaching me the importance of attaining and maintaining that spirituality and pious ardour in which I have found the most effectual relief; so that on the whole I must try to 'glory in tribulations also.' I trust I often can when the conflict is past; but to glory 'in' them, especially in mental distress—*hic labor, hoc opus est* – this is the labor, this is the work.

"But how often has it been found that when ministers have felt themselves most embarrassed, the most effectual good has been done to the people! Oh for hearts entirely resigned to the will of God!

"How happy should I be could I always enjoy the sympathies of a brother who is tried in these points as I of late have been!"

To Mr. Fuller.

"Birmingham, Oct. 29, 1798.

"I caught a violent cold in returning from our last committee-meeting, from which I have not yet recovered. A little thing now affects my constitution, which I once judged would be weather and labour proof for at least thirty years, if I lived so long. I thank God that I am not debilitated by iniquity. I have lately met with an occurrence which occasioned me much pain and perplexity . . . . Trials soften our hearts, and make us more fully prize the dear few into whose faithful, sympathizing bosoms we can with confidence pour our sorrows. I think I should bless God for my afflictions, if they produced no other fruit than these—the tenderness they inspire, and the friendships they capacitate us to enjoy. Pray, my dear brother, for yours affectionately,—S. P."

To a young man (Mr. Matthew Griffiths) who had applied to him for advice how he should best improve his time, previous to his going to the Bristol Academy:

Birmingham, Nov. 13, 1798.

"My Dear M.,

"I can only confess my regret at not replying to yours at a much earlier period, and assure you that the delay has been accidental, and not designed. I felt the importance of your request for advice—I was sensible it deserved some consideration before it was answered.—I was full of business at the moment—I put it by, and it was forgotten; and now it is too late. The time of your going to Bristol draws nigh. If, instead of an opinion respecting the best way of occupying your time before you go, you will accept a little counsel during your continuance there, I shall be happy at any time to contribute such a mite as my experience and observation have put in my power.

"At present, the following rules appear of so much moment, that, were I to resume a place in any literary establishment, I would religiously adopt them as the standard of my conduct:—First, I would cultivate a spirit of habitual devotion. Warm piety connected with my studies, especially at my entrance upon them, would not only assist me in forming a judgment on their respective importance, and secure the blessing of God upon them; but would so cement the religious feeling with the literary pursuit, as that it might abide with me for life. The habit of uniting these, being once formed, would, I hope, be never lost; and I am sure that, without this, I shall both pursue trivial and unworthy objects, and those that are worthy I shall pursue for a wrong end.—Secondly, I would determine on a uniform submission to the instructions of my preceptor, and study those things which would give him pleasure. If he be not wiser than I am, for what purpose do I come under his care? I accepted the pecuniary help of the Society on condition of conforming to its will; and it is the Society's will that my tutor should govern me. My example will have influence: let me not, by a single act of disobedience, or by a word that implicates dissatisfaction, sow the seeds of discord in the bosoms of my companions.—Thirdly, I would pray and strive for the power of *self-government*, to form no plan, to utter not a word, to take no step, under the mere influence of passion. Let my judgment be often asked, and let me always give it time to answer. Let me always guard against a light or trifling spirit; and particularly as I shall be amongst a number of youths whose years will incline them all to the same frailty.—Fourthly, I would in all my weekly and daily pursuits observe the strictest *order*. Always let me act by a plan. Let every hour have its proper pursuit; from which let nothing but a settled conviction that I can employ it to better advantage ever cause me to deviate. Let me have fixed time for prayer, meditation, reading, languages, correspondence, recreation, sleep, &c.—Fifthly, I would not only assign to every hour its proper pursuit; but what I did I would try to do with all my might. The hours at such a place are precious beyond conception, till the student enters on life's busy scenes. Let me set the best of my class ever before me, and strive to be better than they. In humility and diligence, let me aim to be the first.—Sixthly, I would particularly avoid a *versatile habit*. In all things I would persevere. Without this, I may be a gaudy butterfly; but never, like the bee, will my hive bear examining. Whatever I take in hand, let me first be sure I understand it, then duly consider it, and, if it be good, let me adopt and use it.

"To these, my dear brother, let me add three or four things more minute, but which, I am persuaded, will help you much.—*Guard against a large acquaintance while you are a student.* Bristol friendship, while you sustain that character, will prove a vile thief, and rob you of many an invaluable hour.—Get *two or three of the students, whose piety you most approve, to meet for one hour in a week for experimental conversation and mutual prayer.* I found this highly beneficial, though, strange to tell, by some we were persecuted for our practice!—*Keep a diary.* Once a week at farthest call yourself to an account as to what advances you have made in your different studies; in divinity, history, language, natural philosophy, style, arrangement, and, amidst all, *do* not forget to inquire, Am I more fit to *serve* and to *enjoy* God than I was last week?

On Dec. 2, 1798, he delivered his last sermon. The subject was taken from Dan. 10.19, "O man, greatly beloved, fear not; peace be unto thee, be strong, yea, be strong. And when he had spoken unto me, I was strengthened, and said, Let my lord speak; for thou hast strengthened me."— "Amongst all the Old Testament saints," said he, in his introduction to that discourse, "there is not one whose virtues were more, and whose imperfections were fewer, than those of Daniel. By the history given of him in this book, which yet seems not to be complete, he appears to have excelled among the excellent." Doubtless, no one was further from his thoughts than himself: several of his friends, however, could not help applying it to him, and that with a painful apprehension of what followed soon after.

To Mr. Cave, Leicester.
"Birmingham, Dec. 4, 1798.
".....Blessed be God, my mind is calm; and though my body be weakness itself, my spirits are good, and I can write as well as ever,

though I can hardly speak two sentences without a pause. All is well, brother! all is well, for time and eternity. My soul rejoices in the everlasting covenant ordered in all things and sure. Peace from our dear Lord Jesus be with your spirit, as it is (yea, more also) with

"Your affectionate brother—S. P."

To Dr. Ryland.

"Birmingham, Dec. 9, 1798.
Lord's Day evening

"My dear Brother,

"After a Sabbath—such a one I never knew before—spent in an entire seclusion from the house and ordinances of my God, I seek Christian converse with you in a way in which I am yet permitted to have intercourse with my brethren. The day after I wrote to you last, my medical attendant laid me under the strictest injunctions not to speak again in public for one month at least. He says that my stomach is become so irritable, through repeated inflammations, that conversation, unless managed with great caution, would be dangerous;—that he does not think my present condition alarming, provided I take rest; but, without that, he intimated my life was in great danger. He forbids my exposing myself to the evening air on any account, and going out of doors, or to the door, unless when the air is dry and clear; so that I am, during the weather we now have in Birmingham, (very foggy,) a complete prisoner; and the repeated cautions from my dear and affectionate friends, whose solicitude, I conceive, far exceeds the danger, compel me to a rigid observance of the doctor's rules.

"This morning brother Pope took my place; and in the afternoon Mr. Brewer (who has discovered uncommon tenderness and respect for me and the people since he knew my state) preached a very affectionate sermon from I Sam. 3:18—'it is the Lord, let him do what seemeth him good.' By what I hear, his sympathizing observations, in relation to the event which occasioned his being then in my pulpit, drew more tears from the people's eyes than a dozen such poor creatures as their pastor could deserve. But I have, blessed be God, long had the satisfaction of finding myself embosomed in friendship........the friendship of the people of my charge: though I lament their love should occasion them a pang....but thus it is....our Heavenly Father sees that, for our mixed characters, a mixed state is best.

"I anticipated a day of gloom: but I had unexpected reason to rejoice that the shadow of death was turned into the joy of the morning; and though I said, with perhaps unequaled feeling, how amiable are thy tabernacles!' yet I found the God of Zion does not neglect the dwellings of Jacob. My poor wife was much affected at so novel a thing as leaving me behind her, and so it was a dewy morning; but the Sun of Righteousness soon arose, and shed such ineffable delight throughout my soul, that I could say, 'it is good to be here.' Motive to resignation and gratitude also crowded upon motive, till my judgment was convinced that I ought to rejoice in the Lord exceedingly, and so my whole soul took its fill of joy. May I, if it be my Savior's will, feel as happy when I come to die! When my poor Sarah lay at the point of death for some days after the birth of her first child, toward the close of them I enjoyed such support, and felt my will so entirely bowed down to that of God, that I said in my heart, 'I shall never fear another trial....He that sustained me amidst this flame, will defend me from every spark!' And this confidence I long enjoyed. But that was nearly six years ago, and I had almost forgotten the land of the Hermonites and the hill Mizar. But the Lord has prepared me to receive a fresh display of his fatherly care, and his (shall I call it?) punctilious veracity. If I should be raised up again, I shall be able to preach on the faithfulness of God more experimentally than ever. Perhaps some trial is coming on, and I am to be instrumental in preparing them for it; or if not, if I am to depart hence to be no more seen, I know the Lord can carry on his work as well without me as with me. He who redeemed the sheep with his blood, will never suffer them to perish for want of a shepherd, especially since he himself is the Chief Shepherd of souls. But my family! Ah, there I find my faith, but still imperfect. However, I do not think the Lord will ever take me away till he helps to leave my fatherless children in his hands and trust my widow also with him. 'His love in times past,' and I may add in times present too, 'forbids me to think he will leave me, at last, in trouble to sink.' Whilst my weakness was gaining ground, I used to ask myself how I could bear to be laid by. I have dreamed that this was the case; and, both awake and asleep, I felt as though it were an evil that could not be born: - but now I find the Lord can fit the back to the burden; and, though I think I love the thought of serving Christ at this moment better than ever, yet he has made me willing to be......nothing, if he please to have it so; and now my happy heart 'could sing itself away to everlasting bliss.'

"O what a mercy that I have not brought on my affliction by serving the devil! What a mercy that I have so many dear sympathizing friends! What a mercy that I have so much dear domestic comfort! What a mercy that I am in no violent bodily pain! What a mercy that I can read and write without doing myself an injury! What a mercy that my animal spirits have, all the time this has been coming on, (ever since the last Kettering meeting of ministers,) been vigorous—free from dejection! And, which I reckon among the greatest of this day's privileges, what a mercy that I have been able to employ myself for Christ and his dear cause to-day; as I have been almost wholly occupied in the concerns of the (I hope) reviving church at Bromsgrove, and the infant church at Cradley! O, my dear brother, it is all mercy; is it not? O help me then in his praise, for he is good, for his mercy endureth forever.

"Ought I to apologize for this experimental chat with you, who have concerns to transact of so much more importance than any that are confined to an individual? Forgive me if I have intruded too much on your time—but do not forget to praise, on my behalf, a faithful God. I shall now leave room against I have some business to write about—till then, adieu—but let us not forget that this God is our God forever and ever, and will be our guide even unto death. Amen—amen. We shall soon meet in heaven.   S.B."

To Mr. Nichols, Nottingham.
"Birmingham, Dec. 10, 1798.

"I am now quite laid by from preaching, and am so reduced in my internal strength that I can hardly converse with a friend for five minutes without losing my breath. Indeed, I have been so ill that I thought the next ascent would be, not to a pulpit, but to a throne— the throne of glory. Yes, indeed, my friend, the religion of Jesus will support when flesh and heart fail; and, in my worst state of body, my soul was filled with joy. I am now getting a little better, though but very slowly. But fast or slow, or as it may, the Lord doth all things well."

To R. Bowyer, Esq.

"....I have overdone myself in preaching. I am now ordered to lie by, and not even to *converse,* without great care; nor indeed, till today, have I for some time been able to utter a sentence without a painful effort. Blessed be God! I have been filled all through my affliction with peace and joy in believing; and at one time, when I thought I was entering the valley of death, the prospect beyond was so full of glory, that, but for the sorrow it would have occasioned to some who would be left behind, I should have longed that moment to have mounted to the skies. O my friend, what a mercy that I am not receiving the wages of sin; that my health has not been impaired by vice; but that, on the contrary, I am *bearing in my body the marks of the Lord Jesus!* To him be all the praise! Truly, I have proved that God is faithful; and most cheerfully would I take double the affliction for one half of the joy and sweetness which have attended it."

To a Minister.

"Dear Mr. W.,

"Be so good as to accept the enclosed sermon.[19]   Though I publish, I can no longer preach. My Master has no need of me just now, or he would not silence me; but I am in good hands; and in the midst of my imprisonment can shout, with joy unspeakable, 'Hallelujah, for the Lord God reigneth.' So wise, so just, so good is he in whose hands my breath is, and whose are all my ways, that I am perfectly satisfied with all his blessed will; nor would I have it otherwise, were an alteration in my power, so long as my Father sees it best to continue the heavenly discipline.   During my affliction I have tasted much of the sweetness of the promises, and my soul has been fed as with marrow and fatness. I have sometimes hesitated in encouraging my people to rely on the fullness of the promises in all cases, because I feared that if the Lord should lay me by as a broken vessel, my revolting heart would be dissatisfied and complain; but, verily, now I know that God can render submission as happy as exertion, and call forth the passive graces to as good purpose, for the joy of his people and the glory of this grace, as the more active ones.

"'O sweet affliction! sweet affliction!' I could not but frequently exclaim, when my health was at the lowest ebb, and at the moment when I thought I should never see my dear people again, till I met them on the hill of Zion. Yes, where my Lord Jesus is, there are, there must be, peace, and joy, and confidence; and whether it be in

---

[19] The last but one he ever preached, entitled, MOTIVES TO GRATITUDE. It was delivered on the day of national thanksgiving, and printed at the request of his own congregation.

the sanctuary of praise, or on the bed of languishing, ''tis heaven to see his smiling face;' he can make a dying bed feel 'soft as downy pillows are.' I would not have been without this trial for the Indies; it has taught me more of my Bible and my God than seven years' mere study could have done. 'O trust in the Lord, ye his saints, for there is no want to them that fear him.'

"I consider now, though I am young, that my best days are over; but I cannot describe to you what a solid satisfaction I feel in reflecting that my best days have not been devoted to the work of the devil, but to the service of my blessed Jesus. O what a mercy that he called me in early life, and so saved me from those distressing recollections which must attend the solitary and afflicting hours of those who are permitted to waste their prime in the practice of sin and forgetfulness of God.

> 'He shall have all the praise, for he
> Hath loved, and lived, and died for me.'

"Affectionately yours,   S.P."

To Mr. Bates and Mrs. Barnes, Minories.
"Birmingham, Dec. 14, 1798.
"I could tell you much of the Lord's goodness during my affliction. Truly 'his right hand hath been under my head, and his left embraced me.' And when I was at the worst, especially, and expected ere long to have done with time, even *then,* such holy joy, such ineffable sweetness filled my soul, that I would not have exchanged that situation for any besides heaven itself.

"O my dear friends, let us live to *Christ,* and lay ourselves wholly out for him whilst we live; and then, when health and life forsake us, he will be the strength of our heart, and our portion for ever."

About this time the congregation at Cannon Street was supplied for several months by Mr. Ward, who has since gone as a missionary to India. Here that amiable young man became intimately acquainted with Mr. Pearce, and conceived a most affectionate esteem for him. In a letter to a friend, dated Jan. 5, 1799, he writes as follows:

"I am happy in the company of dear brother Pearce. I have seen more of God in him than in any other person I ever knew. Oh how happy should I be to live and die with him![20] When well, he preaches three times on a Lord's Day, and two or three times in the week besides. He instructs the young people in the principles of religion, natural philosophy, astronomy, &c. They have a benevolent society, from the funds of which they distribute forty or fifty pounds a year to the poor of the congregation. They have a sick society for visiting the afflicted in general; a book society at chapel; a Lord's Day school, at which more than two hundred children are instructed. Add to this, missionary business, visiting the people, an extensive correspondence, two volumes of mission history preparing for the press, &c.; and then you will see something of the soul of Pearce. He is every where venerated, though but a young man; and all the kind, tender, gentle affections make him as a little child at the feet of his Saviour.—W.W."

In February, he rode to the opening of a Baptist meeting-house at Bedworth; but did not engage in any of the services. Here several of his brethren saw him for the last time. Soon afterwards, writing to the compiler of these Memoirs, he says,—"The Lord's Day after I came home I tried to speak a little after sermon. It inflamed my lungs afresh, produced phlegm, coughing, and spitting of blood. Perhaps I may never preach more. Well, the Lord's will be done. I thank him that he ever took me into his service; and now, if he sees fit to give me a discharge, I submit."

---

[20] How sincerely that affectionate esteem was returned, is evident by the following extract of a letter form Mr. Pearce to Mr. Carey, dated March, 1799:

"In Cannon-street we have been remarkably happy. Peace has been enjoyed without interruption, and the leaven has appeared to be diffusing itself, though by unequal degrees, throughout the mass of the congregation. The Lord has been very gracious to us since I have been unable to preach, in inclining the heart of dear brother Ward to spend that time in Birmingham which he had otherwise spent at Ewood Hall. He has been here ten weeks, and I suppose will stay till near the time of his embarking for India. I indeed rejoice in the prospect of your having so amiable an addition to your number. I feel a pang at every thought of parting with him, and would much rather, were such the will of the Lord, go with him than stay behind. His labors here have been generally acceptable, and in some instances, I trust, useful both to saints and sinners. He loves village preaching, and the villagers are particularly attached to him; they send from the respective neighborhoods where he has preached, and beg that he will come once more before he leaves the country; and it has given me heartfelt pleasure that not in one instance have I discovered the smallest backwardness in him to these primitive labors. When he goes, I know not where we shall look for a successor."

During the above meeting a word was dropped by one of his brethren which he took as a reflection, though nothing was further from the intention of the speaker. It wrought upon his mind; and in a few days he wrote as follows:—"Do you remember what passed at B—? Had I not been accustomed to receive *plain, friendly* remarks from you, I should have thought you meant to insinuate a reproof. If you did, tell me plainly. If you did not, it is all at an end. You will not take my naming it unkindly, although I should be mistaken; such affectionate explanations are necessary, when suspicions arise, to the preservation of friendship; and I need not say that I hold the preservation of your friendship in no small account."

The above is copied, not only to set forth the spirit and conduct of Mr. Pearce in a case wherein he felt himself aggrieved, but to show in how easy and amiable a manner thousands of mistakes might be rectified, and differences prevented, by a frank and timely explanation.

To a Friend.
(Occasioned by an instance of hopeful conversion.)
"Birmingham, March 4, 1799.

"My dear Friend,

"Thanks be to God! thanks to you, thanks to your family, my dear friend, for restoring one who had been given up for lost! Is it true that _____, though dead, is alive again; though lost, is found? O that the happy change may prove as sincere and permanent as it is truly pleasing! May divine goodness help you to fix those salutary convictions, and render them immutable to the day of death!

"I am sure the whole family will feel a new sensation at the mention of ____ now. Even we, who loved it well before, now think of it with an energy of joy, and regard it as we should a tomb, from whence a corrupting body had revivified to become an important blessing to all its connections.

"We are not without affliction; but we have so much to be thankful for, that it would be criminal to complain. Complain! Not whilst every dispensation is mixed with paternal love, and comes with a Father's benediction. S.P."

To Mr. Comfield, Northampton.
"Birmingham, March 4, 1799.

"I could wish my sympathies to be as extensive as human—I was going to say (and why not?) as animal misery. The very limited comprehension of the human intelligence forbids this indeed, and whilst I am attempting to participate as far as the news of affliction reaches me, I find the same events do not often produce equal feelings. We measure our sympathies, not by the causes of sorrow, but by the sensibilities of the sorrowful; hence I abound in feeling on *your* account. The situation of your family must have given distress to a man of any character; but in you it must have produced agonies. I know the tenderness of your heart: your feelings are delicately strong. You must feel much, or nothing; and he that knows you, and does not feel much when you feel, must be a brute.

"May the fountain of mercy supply you with the cheering stream! May your sorrow be turned into joy!

"I am sure that I ought to value more than ever your friendship for me. You have remembered me, not merely in my affliction, but in your own. Our friendship, our benevolence, must never be compared with that of Jesus; but it is truly delightful to see the disciple treading, though at a humble distance, in the footsteps of a Master, who, amidst the tortures of crucifixion, exercised forgiveness to his murderers, and the tenderness of filial piety to a disconsolate mother! When we realize the scene, how much do our imaginations embrace—the persons—the circumstances—the words—'Woman behold thy son! John, behold thy mother!'"

By the above letter, the reader will perceive that, while deeply afflicted himself, he felt in the tenderest manner for the afflictions of others.

In the month of March Mr. Pearce wrote several letters to Mr. Carey, from which the following are extracts. They furnish additional proofs of the happy state of his mind, the warmth of his love to the brethren, and his enlarged desires for the salvation of souls.

"On my return from the last Kettering mission meeting I took a violent cold, which being neglected, grew worse; and, thinking that pulpit sweats would effect a cure, I remitted none of my labors either at home or among the villagers; on the contrary, after walking several miles, I sometimes preached an extra sermon. This was imprudent: my lungs became inflamed, and at length were so exceedingly irritable that I could not even converse in private for two minutes without pain and danger. The doctor ordered me to keep myself undisturbed and unemployed; saying that if it were the end of March instead of November, he could give me better hope of recovery, for he thought that either a warmer climate or a warmer season was absolutely necessary. Do you think, my dear brother, that, when the doctor mentioned a warmer climate, I was without thoughts of Mudnabatty? Ah! thought I, had the society sent me there when I so earnestly entreated them, I had not now been shut out from all service for God and enjoyment of his people for want of a warmer climate. For some time a discharge of blood, a pain in my side, a loss of appetite, soreness in my breast, and an irregular pulse, led me to apprehend that death was fast approaching. Sweet were the thoughts of dying; and, although I could not but regret that I should leave this world without having made one effort for the salvation of 'the sinners of the Gentiles,' personally among them, yet that I had, indirectly at least, endeavored the accomplishment of that most desirable object, was a matter of inexpressible satisfaction and delight. I greatly accused myself of inactivity in the Redeemer's cause. I saw that my zeal had been tardy, unequal, and perhaps often ineffectual for want of being more ardent and persevering. Yet the thought that the Lord had ever employed me, that I had not been quite idle, that some good had been done, some portions of divine truth propagated, some daring sinners reclaimed, some broken hearts bound up and comforted, some additions made to the church of the Lord Jesus Christ, and some improvement in knowledge, devotion, and virtue among his people – these were occasions of grateful delight; so that, with all my numberless infirmities and crimes, I was enabled to say, I have not lived nor run in vain. These considerations, joined to the opening prospects of celestial blessings, constrained me to exclaim, 'O it is good to be here!'

"We rejoice in all your joy, and especially I am delighted with what you say respecting the light of Christianity extending where your personal labors had never reached. 'Fly abroad, thou blessed Gospel!'

"Thus indeed may the Lord be preparing his way among the Indian heathen, and after the outward light may come the inward life. Even so, Lord Jesus!

"I received your letter to the dear departed Swartz, and the reply of Gericke, with vast satisfaction, not so much for the news contained, but for its authenticity. I have been more or less conversant with the German accounts every week for about twelve months past. Mr. Grant lent them to me; they begin where Niecamp's Latin quarto leaves off, and, as I don't read the German language myself, I have gotten, as oft as I could, a young gentleman of the town to come for one or two hours in the day and read them to me in English, whilst I write down whatever strikes me as memorable. The tediousness of the writers, and the irregularity of my translator, has long detained me on this part of my Mission History, a work to which, I think I told you before, I have for some years devoted my leisure hours; though my nervous complaint the last two years, my late affliction, and my constant run of pastoral duties and extensive correspondence, leave a mind, naturally indolent, too plausible an excuse for reposing when it ought to be at work, and hence I proceed by slow degrees.

"With regard to the admission of the Hindoos, &c. to baptism and the Lord's Supper, with the permission given them to retain their former distinctions of caste, as it seems our Danish brethren do, I greatly hesitate, unless these distinctions are regarded and acknowledged as perfectly civil, and having nothing religious in them; because, 1. It would be an acknowledgement of a false religion, and so having fellowship with idols. 2. All religious distinctions, even those which the divinely instituted economy of Moses formed, are expressly said to be abolished in the equalizing religion of Jesus Christ, in whom there is neither Greek nor Jew, &c. If it be said that the Jews were tolerated in a separate worship from the Gentiles for a time, it may be replied that there appears no toleration of the Gentiles in willingly declining communion with the Jews. The Jews were not wrong in their idea of the divine authority of a separate worship; their only mistake was concerning the prolonging that separation beyond the time when it ought to have ceased. The Jews also, though they preserved a distinction in their worship at the first, nevertheless worshipped the true God. But if there be any religious acknowledgment in the preservation of caste, &c. it is an idolatrous one. Adieu, my dear brethren: love to brethren Thomas and Fountain.

"You will find in the Evangelical Magazine some modern information, respecting the Languedoc and its vicinity that gives occasion for Christian pleasure. I contemplate a mission to France, when the way to visit it shall be opened, with pleasurable hopes. I have been endeavoring for some years to get five of our ministers to agree that they will apply themselves to the French language with this express object in view; then we might spend two months annually in that country, and at least satisfy ourselves that Christianity was not lost in France for want of a fair experiment in its favor: and who can tell what God might do?

"The mass of the people in Ireland, as you know, are Catholics; ignorant—bigoted—cruel. The Lord has a few there, however, who weep over the state of the land. I have received a very affectionate and pressing invitation to visit that country again this year, but my health forbids, else I should rejoice among Irish sinners again to publish the unsearchable riches of Christ. I have also been pleased with another letter from Rahue, in which a gentleman presses me to procure an itinerant to settle in that country, engaging to bear his expenses, to board him, to find him a horse for his journey, and to add twenty-five guineas per annum for his private use. O Lord! how do we want laborers in thy harvest! Would to God I could find a suitable man! but our congregations increase so rapidly in England, that we cannot get ministers enough for them. Yet I hope the Lord will provide for that benighted island. The civil state of that country, indeed, rather discourages present efforts: all about Connaught they seem up in arms, expecting another visit from France; and it is positively reported that there is a powerful armament now fitting out at Brest on purpose for another descent upon Ireland. Should they succeed, England may begin to tremble: but our hope is in God, who, let what may come upon us as *Britons,* hath promised that all shall work for good to us as *Christians.* Should any awful convulsions produce general infidelity in Europe, how delightful is the thought that the Lord is gathering a church in Asia! Who can tell, but that as the evangelic stream flowed from the Asiatic fountain through countries barbarous and uncultivated, whose inhabitants, having adopted the Christian theory, associated therewith their former savage manners, and thus polluted the immaculate waters; so from Asia the same pure stream shall again meander through the nations, whose manners having been rendered gentle and kind by the experience of many cruel ages, and by the operation of wise, humane, and salutary laws at length established, shall no longer tinge this sacred stream with blood, nor render it corrupt by any other vicious association, so that it shall bring on its bosom the ardors of devotion, to perfect the already cultivated virtue of the European world.

"Ah! this is what we want. A Catholic may be devout; a deist may be victorious; but, in him who is a genuine disciple of Jesus, virtue gives the ornament to devotion, and devotion imparts dignity to virtue. And the above scene always opens on my view when I apply my perspective to future ages. Enough for a volume is here, and it is well my paper is nearly filled, or I should tire you with an essay on the beautiful union of love to God with love to man, or devotion and virtue.

"Ever, ever yours, S.P."

He was now setting out for Plymouth; and after observing, in a letter to Mr. Fuller, dated March 23, 1799, the great danger he was supposed to be in, with respect to a consumption, he adds,— "But thanks be to God, who giveth my heart the victory, let my poor body be consumed, or preserved. In the thought of *leaving,* I feel a momentary gloom; but in the thought of *going,* a heavenly triumph.

'Oh to grace how great a debtor!'

"Praise God with me, and for me, my dear brother, and let us not mind dying any more than sleeping. No, no; let every Christian sing the loudest as he gets the nearest to the presence of his God. Eternally yours in Him who hath washed us both in his blood,—S. P."

To Mr. Medley, London.
"March 23, 1799.
"My affliction has been rendered sweet by the supports and smiles of Him whom I have served in the gospel of his Son. He hath delivered, he doth deliver, and I trust that he will yet deliver. Living or dying, all is well for ever. Oh what shall I render to the Lord?"

It seems that, in order to avoid wounding Mrs. P.'s feelings, he deferred the settlement of his affairs till he arrived at Bristol; whence he wrote to his friend, Mr. King, requesting him to become an executor. Receiving a favourable answer, he replied as follows:

"Bristol, April 6, 1799.
"Your letter, just received, affected me too much with feelings both of sympathy and gratitude, to remain unanswered a single post. Most heartily do I thank you for accepting a service which friendship alone can render agreeable in the most simple cases. Should that service demand your activities at an early period, may no unforeseen occurrence increase the necessary care! But may the Father of the fatherless, and Judge of the widows, send you a recompense into your own bosom, equal to all that friendship to

which, under God, I have been so much indebted in life, and reposing on whose bosom, even death itself loses a part of its gloom. In you, my children will find another father—in you, my wife another husband. Your tenderness will sympathize with the one, under the most distressing sensibilities; and your prudent counsels be a guide to the others, through the unknown mazes of inexperienced youth. Enough—blessed God! my soul prostrates, and adores thee for such a friend."

To Mr. Fuller.

"Plymouth, April 18, 1799.

"The last time that I wrote to you was at the close of a letter sent to you by brother Ryland. I did not like that postscript form; it looked so card-like as to make me fear that you would deem it unbrotherly. After all, perhaps, you thought nothing about it; and my anxieties might arise only from my weakness, which seems to be constantly increasing my sensibilities. If ever I felt love in its tenderness for my friends, it has been since my affliction. This, in a great measure, is no more than the love of 'publicans and harlots, who love those that love them.' I never conceived myself by a hundred degrees so interested in the regards of my friends, as this season of affliction has manifested I was; and therefore, so far from claiming any 'reward' for loving them in return, I should account myself a monster of ingratitude were it otherwise. Yet there is something in affliction itself, which, by increasing the delicacy of our feelings, and detaching our thoughts from the usual round of objects which present themselves to the mind when in a state of health, may be easily conceived to make us susceptible of stronger and more permanent impressions of an affectionate nature.

"I heard at Bristol that you and your friends had remembered me in your prayers, at Kettering. Whether the Lord whom we serve may see fit to answer your petitions on my account, or not, may they at least be returned into your own bosoms.

"For the sake of others I should be happy could I assure you that my health was improving. As to myself, I thank God that I am not without a desire to depart, and to be with Christ, which is far better. I find that neither in sickness, nor in health, I can be so much as I wish like Him whom I love. 'To die is gain:' oh to gain that state, those feelings, that character, which perfectly accord with the mind of Christ, and are attended with the full persuasion of his complete and everlasting approbation! I want no heaven but this; and, to gain this, most gladly would I this moment expire. But if to abide in the flesh be more needful for an individual of my fellow men,—Lord, let thy will be done; only let Christ be magnified by me, whether in life or death!

"The weather has been so wet and windy since I have been at Plymouth, that I could not reasonably expect to be much better; and I cannot say that I am much worse. All the future is uncertain. Professional men encourage me; but frequent returns appear, and occasional discharges of blood check my expectations. If I speak but for two minutes, my breast feels as sore as though it were scraped with a rough-edged razor; so that I am mute all the day long, and have actually learned to converse with my sister by means of our fingers.

"I thank you for yours of April 4th, which I did not receive till the 12th, the day that I arrived at Plymouth. On the 16th, a copy of yours to brother Ryland came to hand, to which I should have replied yesterday, but had not leisure. I am happy and thankful for your success. May the Lord himself pilot the 'Criterion' safely to Calcutta River!

"Unless the Lord work a miracle for me, I am sure that I shall not be able to attend the Olney meeting. It is to my feelings a severe anticipation; but how can I be a Christian, and not submit to God?"

To Mr. Wm. Ward
"Plymouth, April 22, 1799.
"Most affectionately do I thank you for your letter, so full of information and of friendship. To our common Friend, who is gone into heaven, where he ever sitteth at the right hand of God for us, I commend you. Whether I die, or live, God will take care of you till he has ripened you for the common salvation. Then shall I meet my dear brother Ward again; and who can tell how much more interesting our intercourse in heaven will be made by the scenes that most distress our poor spirits here? Oh, had I none to live for, I had rather die than live, that I may be at once like Him whom I love. But while he insures me grace, why should I regret the delay of glory? No: I will wait his will who performeth all things for me.

"My dear brother, had I strength I should rejoice to acquaint you with the wrestlings and the victories, the hopes and the fears, the pleasures and the pangs, which I have lately experienced. But I must forbear. All I can now say is that God hath done me much good by all, and made me very thankful for all he has done.

"Alas! I shall see you no more. I cannot be at Olney on the 7th of May. The journey would be my death. But the Lord whom you serve will be with you then, and for ever. My love to all the dear assembled saints, who will give you their benedictions at that solemn season."

"Ever yours, &c.S.P."

To Mr. King.

"Plymouth, April 23, 1799.

"My dear Friend and Brother,

"I have the satisfaction to inform you that at length my complaint appears to be removed, and that I am by degrees returning to my usual diet, by which, with divine blessing, I hope to be again strengthened for the discharge of the duties and the enjoyment of the pleasures which await me among the dear people of my charge.

"I am indeed informed, by a medical attendant here, that I shall never be equal to the labors of my past years, and that my return to moderate efforts must be made by slow degrees. As the path of duty, I desire to submit; but, after so long a suspension from serving the Redeemer in his church, my soul pants for usefulness more extensive than ever, and I long to become an apostle to the world. I do not think I ever prized the ministerial work so much as I now do. Two questions have been long before me. The first, shall I live or die? The second, if I live, how will my life be spent? With regard to the former, my heart answered, 'It is no matter—all is well; for my own sake, I need not be taught that it is best to be with Christ; but, for the sake of others, it may be best to abide in the body. I am in the Lord's hands; let him do by me as seemeth him best for me and mine, and for his cause and honor in the world! But, as to the second question, I could hardly reconcile myself to the thought of living, unless it were to promote the interests of my Lord; and, if my disorder should so far weaken me as to render me incapable of the ministry, nothing then appeared before me but gloom and darkness. However, I will hope in the Lord; and, though he hath chastened me sorely, yet, since he has not given me over unto death, sparing mercy will be followed with strength, that I may show forth his praise in the land of the living.

"I am still exceedingly weak, more so than at any period before I left home, except the first week of my lying by; but I am getting strength, though slowly. It is impossible at present to fix any time for my return. It grieves me that the patience of the dear people should be so long tried; but the trial is as great on my part as it can be on theirs, and we must pity and pray for one another. It is now a task for me to write at all, or this should have been longer.   S.P."

To Dr. Ryland.

"Plymouth, April 24, 1799.

"Very Dear Brother,

"My health is in much the same state as when I wrote last, excepting that my muscular strength rather increases, and my powers of speaking seem less and less every week. I have, for the most part, spoken only in whispers for several days past; and even these seem too much for my irritable lungs. My father asked me a question to-day; he did not understand me when I whispered; so I was obliged to utter *one word,* and one word *only,* a little louder, and that brought on a soreness, which I expect to feel till bed-time.

"I am still looking out for fine weather; all here is cold and rainy. We have had but two or three fair and warm days since I have been here; then I felt better. I am perfectly at a loss even to guess what the Lord means to do with me; but I desire to commit my ways to him, and be at peace. I am going today about five miles into the country, (to Tamerton,) where I shall await the will of God concerning me.

"I knew not of any committee-meeting of our Society to be held respecting Mr. Marshman and his wife. I have therefore sent no vote, and, indeed, it is my happiness that I have full confidence in my brethren, at this important crisis, since close thinking, or much writing, always increases my fever, and promotes my complaint.

"My dear brother, I hope you will correspond much with Kettering. I used to be a medium; but God has put me out of the way. I could weep that I can serve him no more; and yet I fear some would be tears of pride. O for perfect likeness to my humble Lord!"

To Mr. King.

"Tamerton, May 2, 1799.

".... Give my love to all the dear people at Cannon Street. O pray that He who afflicts would give me patience to endure. Indeed, the state of suspense in which I have been kept so long requires much of it; and I often exclaim, ere I am aware, O my dear people! O my dear family! when shall I be restored to you again? The Lord forgive all the sin of my desires! At times I feel a sweet and perfect calm, and wish ever to live under the influence of a belief in the *goodness* of God, and of all his plans, and all his works."

The reader has seen how much he regretted being absent from the solemn designation of the missionaries at Olney. He, however, addressed the following lines to Mr. Fuller, which were read at the close of that meeting, to the dissolving of nearly the whole assembly in tears:

"Tamerton, May 2, 1799.

" . . . . Oh that the Lord, who is unconfined by place or condition, may copiously pour out upon you all the rich effusions of his Holy Spirit on the approaching day! My most hearty love to each missionary who may then encircle the throne of grace. Happy men! Happy women! You are going to be fellow labourers with Christ himself! I congratulate—I almost envy you; yet I love you, and can scarcely now forbear dropping a tear of love as each of your names passes across my mind. Oh what promises are yours; and what a reward! Surely heaven is filled with double joy, and resounds with unusual acclamations, at the arrival of each missionary there. O be faithful, my dear brethren, my dear sisters, be faithful unto death, and all this joy is yours! Long as I live, my imagination will be hovering over you in Bengal; and, should I die, if separate spirits be allowed a visit to the world they have left, methinks mine would soon be at Mudnabatty, watching your labours, your conflicts, and your pleasures, whilst you are always abounding in the work of the Lord."

To Dr. Ryland.

"Plymouth, May 14, 1799.

"My Dear Brother,

"Yours of the 11th instant I have just received, and thank you for your continued concern for your poor unworthy brother.

"I have suffered much in my health since I wrote to you last, by the increase of my feverish complaint, which filled me with heat and horror all night, and in the day sometimes almost suffocated me with the violence of its paroxysms. I am extremely weak; and now that warm weather, which I came into Devon to seek, I dread as much as the cold, because it excites the fever. I am happy however in the Lord. I have not a wish to live or die, but as he pleases. I truly enjoy the gospel of our Lord Jesus Christ, and would not be without his Divine atonement, whereon to rest my soul, for ten thousand worlds. I feel quite weaned from earth, and all things in it. Death has lost his sting, the grave its horrors, and the attractions of heaven, I had almost said, are sometimes violent.

'Oh to grace how great a debtor!'

"But I am wearied. May all grace abound towards my dear brother, and his affectionate—S. P."

To Mr. Pope.
"Plymouth, May 24, 1799

"I cannot write much – this I believe is the only letter I have written (except to my wife) since I wrote you last. My complaint has issued in a confirmed slow nervous fever, which has wasted my spirits and strength, and taken a great part of the little flesh I had when in health away from me. The symptoms have been very threatening, and I have repeatedly thought that, let the physician do what he will, he cannot keep me long from those heavenly joys for which, blessed be God, I have lately been much longing; and, were it not for my dear people and family, I should have earnestly prayed for leave to depart, and to be with Christ, which is so much better than to abide in this vain, suffering, sinning world.

"The doctors, however, now pronounce my case very hopeful – say there is little or no danger – but that all these complaints require a great deal of time to get rid of. I still feel myself on precarious ground, but quite resigned to the will of Him who, unworthy as I am, continues daily to 'fill my soul with joy and peace in believing.' Yes, my dear friend! now my soul feels the value of a free, full, and everlasting salvation; and, what is more, I do enjoy that salvation while I rest all my hope on the Son of God in human nature dying on the cross for me. To me, now, health or sickness, pain or ease, life or death, are things indifferent. I feel so happy in being in the hands of infinite love, that, when the severest strokes are laid upon me, I receive them with pleasure, because they come from my heavenly Father's hands!

'O, to grace how great a debtor!' &c.   S.P"

To the Church in Cannon-street.

"Plymouth, May 31, *1799.*

"To the dear people of my charge, the flock of Christ, assembling in Cannon Street, Birmingham, their afflicted but affectionate pastor, presents his love in Christ Jesus, the great Shepherd of the sheep.

"MY DEAREST, DEAREST FRIENDS AND BRETHREN,

"Separated as I have been a long time from you, and during that time of separation having suffered much both in body and mind, yet my heart has still been with you, participating in your sorrows, uniting in your prayers, and rejoicing with you in the hope of that glory to which Divine faithfulness has engaged to bring us, and for which our heavenly Father, by all his providences and by every operation of his Holy Spirit, is daily preparing us.

"Never, my dear brethren, did I so much rejoice in our being made 'partakers of the heavenly calling' as during my late afflictions. The sweet thoughts of glory, where I shall meet my dear Lord Jesus, with all his redeemed ones, perfectly freed from all that sin which now burdens us and makes us groan from day to day,—this transports my soul, whilst out of weakness I am made strong, and at times am enabled to glory even in my bodily infirmities, that the power of Christ, in supporting when flesh and heart fail, may the more evidently rest upon me. O my dear brethren and sisters, let me, as one alive almost from the dead, let me exhort you to stand fast in that blessed gospel which for ten years I have now preached among you— the gospel of the grace of God; the gospel of God; the gospel of free, full, everlasting salvation, founded on the sufferings and death of *God manifest in the flesh.* Look much at this all-amazing scene!

'Behold! a God descends and dies
To save my soul from gaping hell;'

and then say, whether any poor broken-hearted sinner need be afraid to venture his hopes of salvation on such a sacrifice; especially since He who is thus 'mighty to save' hath said that 'whosoever cometh to him he will in no wise cast out.' You, beloved, who have found the peace-speaking virtue of this blood of atonement, must not be satisfied with what you have already known or enjoyed. The only way to be constantly happy, and constantly prepared for the most awful changes which we must all experience, is, to be constantly *looking* and *coming* to a dying Saviour; renouncing all our own worthiness; cleaving to the loving Jesus as our all in all; giving up every thing, however valuable to our worldly interests, that clashes with our fidelity to Christ; begging that of his fullness we may receive 'grace upon grace,' whilst our faith actually *relies on* his power and faithfulness, for the full accomplishment of every promise in his word that we plead with him; and guarding against every thing that might for a moment bring distance and darkness between your souls and your precious Lord. If you *thus live,* (and oh that you may daily receive fresh life from Christ so to do!) 'the peace of God will keep your hearts and minds,' and you will be filled with 'joy unspeakable and full of glory.'

"As a *church,* you cannot conceive what pleasure I have enjoyed in hearing that you are in peace, that you attend prayer-meetings, that you seem to be stirred up of late for the honour and prosperity of religion. Go on in these good ways, my beloved friends, and assuredly the God of peace will be with you. Yes, if after all I should be taken entirely from you, yet God will surely visit you, and never leave you, nor forsake you.

"As to my health, I seem on the whole to be still mending, though but *very* slowly. The fever troubles me often, both by day and night, but my strength increases. I long to see your faces in the flesh; yea, when I thought myself near the gates of the grave, I wished, if it were the Lord's will, to depart among those whom I so much loved, But I am in good hands, and all must be right.

"I thank both you and the congregation most affectionately for all the kindness you have shown respecting me and my family during my absence. The Lord return it a thousand-fold! My love to every one, both old and young, rich and poor, as though named. The Lord bless to your edification the occasional ministry which you enjoy. I hope you regularly attend upon it, and keep together, as 'the horses in Pharaoh's chariot.' I pray much for you; pray, still pray, for your very affectionate, though unworthy, pastor."

In a postscript to Mr. King, he says, "I have made an effort to write this letter: my affections would take no denial; but it has brought on the fever."

Towards the latter end of May, when Mr. Ward and his companions were just ready to set sail, a consultation concerning Mr. Pearce was held on board the Criterion, in which all the missionaries and some of the members of the Baptist Missionary Society were present. It was well known that he had for several years been engaged in preparing materials for a "History of Missions," to be comprised in two volumes octavo; and as the sending of the gospel amongst the heathen had so deeply occupied his heart, considerable expectations had been formed by religious people of his producing an interesting work on the subject. The question now was, Could not this performance be finished by other hands, and the profits of it be appropriated to the benefit of Mr. Pearce's family? It was admitted by all that this work would, partly from its own merits, and partly from the great interest which the author justly possessed in the public esteem, be very productive; and that it would be a delicate and proper method of enabling the religious public, by subscribing liberally to it, to afford substantial assistance to the family of this excellent man. The result was, that one of the members of the Society addressed a letter to Mr. Pearce's relations at Plymouth, requesting them to consult him, as he should be able to bear it, respecting the state of his manuscripts, and to inquire whether they were in a condition to admit of being finished by another hand; desiring them also to assure him, for his present relief concerning his dear family, that whatever the hand of friendship could effect on their behalf should be accomplished. The answer, though it left no manner of hope as to the accomplishment of the object, yet is so expressive of the reigning dispositions of the writer's heart, as an affectionate husband, a tender father, a grateful friend, and a sincere Christian, that it cannot be uninteresting to the reader:

"Tamerton, June 24, 1799.
"To use the common introduction of 'dear brother' would fall so far short of my feelings towards a friend whose uniform conduct has ever laid so great claim to my affection and gratitude, but whose recent kindness—kindness in adversity—kindness to my *wife*— kindness to my *children*—kindness that would go far to 'smooth the bed of death,' has overwhelmed my whole soul in tender thankfulness, and engaged my everlasting esteem. I know not how to begin .... 'Thought is poor, and poor expression.' The *only* thing that lay heavy on my heart, when in the nearest prospect of eternity, was the future situation of my family. I had but a comparatively small portion to leave behind me, and yet that little was the *all* that an amiable woman,—delicately brought up, and, through mercy, for the most part comfortably provided for since she entered on domestic life,—with five babes to feed, clothe, and educate, had to subsist on. Ah, what a prospect! Hard and long I strove to realize the

promises made to the widows and the fatherless; but *these alone* I could not fully rest on and enjoy. For my own part, God was indeed very gracious. I was willing, I hope, to linger in suffering, if I might thereby most glorify him; and death was an angel whom I longed to come and embrace me, 'cold' as his embraces are; but how could I leave those who were dearest to my heart in the midst of a world in which although thousands now professed friendship for me, and, on my account, for mine; yet, after my decease, would, with few exceptions, soon forget my widow and my children, among the crowds of the needy and distressed.—It was at this moment of painful sensibility that *your heart* meditated a plan to remove my anxieties—a plan too that would involve much personal labour before it could be accomplished. 'Blessed be God who put it into thy heart, and blessed be thou.' May the blessing of the widow and the fatherless rest on you and yours for ever. Amen and amen!

"You will regret perhaps that I have taken up so much respecting yourself; but I have scarcely gratified the shadow of my wishes. Excuse then, on the one hand, that I have said so much; and accept, on the other, what remains unexpressed.

"My affections and desires are among my dear people at Birmingham; and, unless I find my strength increase here, I purpose to set out for that place in the course of a fortnight, or at most a month. The journey, performed by short stages, may do me good; if not, I expect when the winter comes to sleep in peace; and it will delight my soul to see them once more before I die. Besides, I have many little arrangements to make among my books and papers, to prevent confusion after my decease. Indeed, till I get home, I cannot fully answer your kind letter; but I fear that my materials consist so much in references which none but myself would understand, that a second person could not take it up and prosecute it. I am still equally indebted to you for a proposal so generous, so laborious.

"Rejoice with me that the blessed gospel still 'bears my spirits up.' I am become familiar with the thoughts of dying. I have taken my leave often of the world, and, thanks be to God, I do it *always* with *tranquility,* and *often* with *rapture.* Oh what grace, what grace it was that ever called me to be a Christian! What would have been my present feelings if I were going to meet God with all the filth and load of my sin about me! But God in my nature has put my sin away, taught me to love him, and long for his appearing. O my dear brother, how consonant is *everlasting praise* with such a great salvation!"

After this, another letter was addressed to Mr. Pearce by Mr. Fuller, informing him more particularly that the above proposal did not originate with an individual, but with several of the brethren who dearly loved him, and had consulted on the business; and that it was no more than an act of justice to one who had spent his life in serving the public; also requesting him to give directions by which his manuscripts might be found and examined, lest he should be taken away before his arrival at Birmingham. To this he answered as follows:

Plymouth, July 6, 1799.

"I need not repeat the growing sense I have of your kindness, and yet I know not how to forbear.

"I cannot direct Mr. K—to *all* my papers, as many of them are in books from which I was making extracts; and if I could, I am persuaded that they are in a state too confused, incorrect, and unfinished, to suffer you or any other friend to realize your kind intentions.

"I have possessed a tenacious memory. I have begun one part of the history; read the necessary books; reflected; arranged; written perhaps the introduction, and then trusting to my recollection, with a revisal of the books as I should want them, have employed myself in getting materials for another part, &c. Thus, till my illness, the volumes existed in my head—my books were at hand, and I was on the eve of writing them out, when it pleased God to make me pause; and as close thinking has been strongly forbidden me, I dare say that were I again restored to health, I should find it necessary to go over much of my former reading to refresh my memory.

"It is now Saturday. On Monday next we purpose setting out on our return. May the Lord prosper our way! Accept the sincere affection, and the ten thousand thanks, of your brother in the Lord,—S. P."

As the manuscripts were found to be in such a state that no person, except the author himself, could finish them, the design was necessarily dropped. The public mind, however, was deeply impressed with Mr. Pearce's worth; and that which the friendship of a few could not effect, has since been amply accomplished by the liberal exertions of many.

To Dr. Ryland.

"Birmingham, July 20, 1799

"My very dear Brother,

"Your friendly anxieties on my behalf demand the earliest satisfaction. We had a pleasant ride to Newport on the afternoon we left you, and the next day, without much fatigue, reached Tewkesbury; but the road was so rough, from Tewkesbury to Evesham, that it wearied and injured me more than all the jolting we had before put together. However, we reached Alcester on Wednesday evening, stopped there a day to rest, and last night (Friday) were brought safely hither, blessed be God!

"I find myself getting weaker and weaker, and so my Lord instructs me in his pleasure to remove me soon. You say well, my dear brother, that at such a prospect I 'cannot complain.' No, blessed be His dear name who shed his blood for me, he helps me to rejoice at times with joy unspeakable. Now I see the value of the religion of the cross. It is a religion for a dying sinner. It is all the most guilty, the most wretched can desire. Yes, I taste its sweetness, and enjoy its fullness, with all the gloom of a dying bed before me. And far rather would I be the poor emaciated and emaciating creature that I am, than be an emperor, with every earthly good about him—but without a God!

"I was delighted the other day, in re-perusing the *Pilgrim's Progress,* to observe that, when Christian came to the top of the hill Difficulty, he was put to sleep in a chamber called Peace. 'Why how good is the Lord of the way to me!' said I. I have not reached the summit of the hill yet, but, notwithstanding, he puts me to sleep in the chamber of Peace every night.....True, it is often a chamber of pain; but, let pain be as formidable as it may, it has never yet been able to expel that peace which the great Guardian of Israel has appointed to keep my heart and mind through Christ Jesus.

"I have been laboring lately to exercise most love to God when I have been suffering most severely,—but what shall I say? Alas! too often the sense of pain absorbs every other thought. Yet there have been seasons when I have been affected with such a delightful sense of the loveliness of God as to ravish my soul and give predominance to the sacred passion. It was never till to-day that I got any personal instruction from our Lord's telling Peter by what death he should glorify God. O what a satisfying thought it is, that God appoints those means of dissolution whereby he gets most glory to himself! It was the very thing I needed; for, of all the ways of dying, that which I most dreaded was by a consumption, in which it is now highly probable my disorder will issue. But, O my dear Lord, if by this death I can most glorify thee, I prefer it to all others; and thank thee that by this means thou art hastening my fuller enjoyment of thee in a purer world.

"A sinless state! 'Oh, 'tis a heaven worth dying for!' I cannot realize any thing about heaven but the presence of Christ and his people, and a perfect deliverance from sin——and I want no more—— I am sick of sinning——soon I shall be beyond its power.

'O glorious hour! O blest abode!
I shall be near, and like my God!'

"I only thought of filling one side—and now have not left room to thank you and dear Mrs. Ryland for the minute, affectionate, and constant attentions you paid us in Bristol. May the Lord reward you! Our hearty love to all around, till we meet in heaven.
  "Eternally yours in Christ.   S.P."

To Mr. Birt.
"Birmingham, July 26, 1799.
  "It is not with common feelings that I begin a letter to you. Your name brings so many interesting circumstances of my life before me, in which your friendship has been so uniformly and eminently displayed, that now, amidst the imbecilities of sickness, and the serious prospect of another world, my heart is overwhelmed with gratitude, whilst it glows with affection,—an affection which eternity shall not annihilate, but improve.
  "We reached Bristol on the Friday after we parted from you, having suited our progress to my strength and spirits. We staid with Bristol friends till Monday, when we pursued our journey, and went comfortably on till the uncommonly rough road from Tewkesbury to Evesham quite jaded me; and I have not yet quite recovered from the excessive fatigue of that miserable ride. At Alcester we rested a day and a half; and, through the abundant goodness of God, we safely arrived at Birmingham on Friday evening, the 19th of July.
  "I feel an undisturbed tranquility of soul, and am cheerfully waiting the will of God. My voice is gone, so that I cannot whisper without pain; and of this circumstance I am at times most ready to complain. For, to see my dear and amiable Sarah look at *me,* and then at the *children,* and at length bathe her face in tears, without my being able to say one kind word of comfort,—Oh!! .... Yet the Lord supports me under this also; and I trust will support me to the end."

To Mr. Rock.

"July 28, 1799.

". . I am now to all appearance within a few steps of eternity. In Christ I am safe. In him I am happy. I trust we shall meet in heaven."

To R. Bowyer, Esq.

"Birmingham, Aug. 1, 1799.

"Much disappointed that I am not released from this world of sin, and put in possession of the pleasures enjoyed by the spirits of just men made perfect, I once more address my dear fellow heirs of that glory which, ere long, shall be revealed to us all.

"We returned from Devon last Friday week. I was exceedingly weak, and for several days afterwards got rapidly worse. My friends compelled me to try another physician. I am still told that I shall recover. Be that as it may, I wish to have my own will annihilated, that the will of the Lord may be done. Through his abundant grace, I have been, and still am, happy in my soul; and I trust my prevailing desire is that, living or dying, I may be the Lord's."

To Dr. Ryland.

"Birmingham, Aug. 4, 1799.

Lord's–Day evening

"My very dear Brother.

"Still, I trust, hastening to the land 'where there shall be no more curse,' I take this opportunity of talking a little with you on the road; for we are fellow travelers, and a little conversation by the way will not lose me the privilege of getting first to the end of my journey.

"It is seventeen years, within about a week, since I first actually set out on my pilgrimage; and, when I review the many dangers to which during that time I have been exposed, I am filled with conviction that I have all along been the care of omnipotent love. Ah how many Pliables, and Timorouses, and Talkatives have I seen, while my quivering heart said, 'Alas! I shall soon follow these sons of apostasy, prove a disgrace to religion, and have my portion with hypocrites at last.'

"These fears may have had their uses—may have made me more cautious, more distrustful of myself, and kept me more dependent on the Lord.

"With what intricacy to our view, and yet with what actual skill and goodness, does the Lord draw his plans and mark out our path!

Here we wonder and complain. Soon we shall all agree that it was a right path to the city of habitation; and what we now most deeply regret shall become the subject of our warmest praises.

"I am afraid to come back again to life. Oh, how many dangers await me!—Perhaps I may be overcome of some fleshly lust—perhaps I may get proud and indolent, and be more of the priest than of the evangelist—surely I rejoice in feeling my outward man decay, and having the sentence of death in myself. O what prospects are before me in the blessed world whither I am going! To be holy as God is holy—to have nothing but holiness in my nature—to be assured, without a doubt, and eternally to carry about this assurance with me, that the pure God looks on me with constant complacency, for ever blesses me, and says, as at the first creation— 'It is very good.' I am happy now in hoping in the divine purposes towards me; but I know, and the thought is my constant burden, that the Being I love best always sees something in me which he infinitely hates. 'Oh, wretched, wretched man that I am!' The thought even now makes weep: and who can help it, that seriously reflects he never comes to God to pray or praise, but he brings what his God detests along with him, carries it with him wherever he goes, and can never get rid of it as long as he lives! Come, my dear brother, will you not share my joy and help my praise, that soon I shall leave this body of sin and death behind, to enter on the perfection of my spiritual nature, and patiently to wait till this natural body shall become a spiritual body, and so be a fit vehicle for my immortal and happy spirit.

"But I must forbear—I have been very unwell all day: but this evening God has kindly given me a respite—my fever is low and my spirits are cheerful, so I have indulged myself in unbosoming my feelings to my dear friend.   S.P."

To R.. Bowyer, Esq. on his having sent him a print of Mr. Schwartz, the missionary on the Malabar coast.

"Birmingham, Aug. 16, 1799.
"On three accounts was your last parcel highly acceptable. It represented a man whom I have long been in the habit of loving and revering; and whose character and labours I intended, if the Lord had not laid his hand upon me *by my present illness*, to have presented to the public in Europe, as he himself presented them to the millions of

Asia.—The execution, bearing so strong a likeness to the original, heightened its value. And then the hand from whence it came, and the friendship it was intended to express, add to its worth."

To Mr. Fuller.

"Birmingham, Aug. 19, 1799.

"The doctor has been making me worse and weaker for three weeks. In the middle of last week he spoke confidently of my recovery; but today he has seen fit to alter his plans; and if I do not find a speedy alteration for the better, I must have done with all physicians but Him who 'healeth the broken in heart.'

"For some time after I came home, I was led to believe my case to be consumptive; and then, thinking myself of a certainty near the kingdom of heaven, I rejoiced hourly in the delightful prospect.

"Since then I have been told that I am not in a dangerous way; and though I give very little credit to such assertions in this case, yet I have found my mind so taken up with earth again, that I seem as though I had another soul. My spiritual pleasures are greatly interrupted, and some of the most plaintive parts of the most plaintive psalms seem the only true language of my heart. Yet, 'Thy will be done,' I trust, prevails; and if it be the Lord's will that I linger long, and suffer much, O let him give me the patience of hope, and still, his will be done!—I can write no more. This is a whole day's work; for it is only after tea that, for a few minutes, I can sit up, and attend to any thing.   S.P."

From the latter end of August, and all through the month of September, to the 10th of October, *the day on which he died,* he seems to have been unable to write. He did not, however, lose the exercise of his mental powers; and though, in the last of the above letters, he complains of darkness, it appears that he soon recovered that peace and joy in God by which his affliction, and even his life, were distinguished.

A little before he died, he was visited by Mr. Medley, of London, with whom he had been particularly intimate on his first coming to Birmingham. Mr. Pearce was much affected at the sight of his friend, and continued silently weeping for nearly ten minutes, holding and pressing his hand. After this, he spoke, or rather whispered, as follows:— "This sick bed is a Bethel to me; it is none other than the house of God, and the gate of heaven. I can scarcely express the pleasures that I have enjoyed in this affliction. The nearer I draw to my dissolution, the happier I am. It scarcely can be called an affliction, it is so counterbalanced with joy. You have lost your pious father; tell me how it was."—Here Mr. Medley informed him of particulars. He wept much at the recital, and especially at hearing of his last words,—"Home, home!"—Mr. Medley telling him of some temptations he had lately met with, he charged him to keep near to God. "Keep close to God," said he, "and nothing will hurt you!"

In a paper addressed to Mrs. P. containing his last wishes as to the disposal of his property, and written apparently when his lungs were too much afflicted to allow him to speak, he writes thus:

"Forgive me, my dearest Sarah, if I have in the smallest degree been 'severe.' I saw that your tender heart was overwhelmed. I could not see it without anguish. I realized your prospects, and did not wonder that you felt as a creature; but I feared you did not make use of your privilege as a Christian.

"I long to lead your mind for comfort to an immortal source; to a God who is both able and willing to do far more abundantly for you than you can ask or think. You are able to think on and ask for much. You can think of being supported under the trial which is now before you, but God can do more; he can make you happy under it, and thankful for it. The second year of our marriage it seemed as though you were to be taken from me. O how my heart was torn at the prospect! and yet, in the midst of it, the Lord was so pleased to calm my mind and to reconcile me to his blessed will that I had not a wish for your life, if he saw fit to take it! He can, and he will, I trust, do the same by you. Only cast your burden upon him, and he hath said, 'I will sustain thee.'"

The following memoranda were taken down occasionally by Mrs. Pearce, within four or five weeks of Mr. Pearce's death.

He once said, "I have been in darkness two or three days, crying, 'Oh when wilt thou comfort me?' But last night the mist was taken from me, and the Lord shone in upon my soul. Oh that I could speak? I would tell a world to trust a faithful God. Sweet affliction, now it worketh glory, glory!"

Mrs. P. having told him the various exercises of her mind, he replied,—"O trust the Lord; if he lifts up the light of his countenance upon you, as he has done upon me this day, all your mountains will become molehills. I feel your situation, I feel your sorrows; but he who takes care of sparrows will care for you and my dear children."

When scorching with burning fever, he said, "Hot and happy."—One Lord's Day morning he said, "Cheer up, my dear, think how much will be said today of the faithfulness of God. Though *we* are called to separate, *he* will never separate from you. I wish I could tell the world what a good and gracious God he is. Never need they who trust in him be afraid of trials. He has promised to give strength for the day; that is his promise. Oh what a lovely God! and he is *my* God and *yours.* He will never leave us nor forsake us, no never! I have been thinking that this and that medicine will do me good, but what have I to do with it? It is in my Jesus' hands; he will do it all, and there I leave it. What a mercy is it I have a good bed to lie upon; you, my dear Sarah, to wait upon me, and friends to pray for me! Oh how thankful should I be for all my pains! I want for nothing; all my wishes are anticipated. Oh I have felt the force of those words of David,—'Unless thy law (my gracious God!) had been my delight, I should have perished in mine affliction.' Though I am too weak to read it, or hear it, I can think upon it, and oh how good it is! I am in the best hands I could be in; in the hands of my dear Lord and Saviour, and he will do all things well. Yes, yes, he cannot do wrong."

One morning Mrs. P. asked him how he felt.—"Very ill, but unspeakably happy in the Lord, and *my* dear *Lord Jesus.*" Once beholding her grieving, he said, "O my dear Sarah, do not be so anxious, but leave me entirely in the hands of Jesus, and think, if you were as wise as he, you would do the same by me. If he takes me, I shall not be lost; I shall only go a little before: we shall meet again never to part."

After a violent fit of coughing he said, "It is all well. Oh what a good God is he! It is done by him, and it must be well.—If I ever recover, I shall pity the sick more than ever; and if I do not, I shall go to sing delivering love; so you see it will be all well. Oh for more patience! Well, my God is the God of patience, and he will give me all I need. I rejoice it is in my Jesus' hands to communicate, and it cannot be in better. It is my God who gives me patience to bear all his will."

When, after a restless night, Mrs. P. asked him what she should do for him—"You can do nothing but pray for me, that I may have patience to bear all my Lord's will."—After taking a medicine he said, "If it be the Lord's will to bless it, for your sake, and for the sake of the dear children . . . . but the Lord's will be done. Oh I fear I sin, I dishonour God by impatience; but I would not for a thousand worlds sin in a thought if I could avoid it." Mrs. P. replied, she trusted the Lord would still keep him; seeing he had brought him thus far, he would not desert him at last. "No, no," he said, "I hope he will not. 'As a father pitieth his children, so the Lord pitieth them that fear him.' Why do I complain? My dear Jesus' sufferings were much sorer and more bitter than mine. 'And did he thus suffer, and shall I repine?' No; I will cheerfully suffer my Father's will."

One morning, after being asked how he felt, he replied, "I have but one severe pain about me; what a mercy! Oh how good a God to afford some intervals amidst so much pain! He is altogether good. Jesus lives, my dear, and that must be our consolation." After taking a medicine which operated very powerfully, he said, "This will make me so much lower; well, let it be. Multiply my pains, thou good God; so thou art but glorified, I care not what I suffer: all is right."

Being asked how he felt after a restless night, he replied, "I have so much weakness and pain, I have not had much enjoyment; but I have a full persuasion that the Lord is doing all things well. If it were not for strong confidence in a lovely God, I must sink; but all is well. O blessed God, I would not love thee less. O support a sinking worm! Oh what a mercy to be assured that all things are working together for good!"

Mrs. P. saying, 'If we must part, I trust the separation will not be for ever.'

"Oh, no," he replied, "we sorrow not as those who have no hope." She said, 'Then you can leave me and your dear children with resignation, can you?' He answered, "My heart was pierced through with many sorrows, before I could give you and the dear children up; but the Lord has heard me say, Thy will be done; and I now can say (blessed be his dear name!) I have none of my own."

His last day, October 10th, was very happy. Mrs. P. repeated this verse,

> 'Since all that I meet shall work for my good,
> The bitter is sweet, the medicine is food;
> Though painful at present, 'twill cease before long,
> And then, oh how pleasant the conqueror's song!"

He repeated, with an inexpressible smile, the last line, *"The conqueror's song."*

He said once, "O my dear! what shall I do? But why do I complain? He makes all my bed in my sickness." She then repeated those lines,

> 'Jesus can make a dying bed,
> Feel soft as downy pillows are.''

"Yes," he replied, "he can, he does, I feel it."

CHAPTER V

GENERAL OUTLINES OF HIS CHARACTER.

To develop the character of any person, it is necessary to determine what was his governing principle. If this can be clearly ascertained, we shall easily account for the tenor of his conduct.

The governing principle in Mr. Pearce, beyond all doubt, was HOLY LOVE.

To mention this is sufficient to prove it to all who knew him. His friends have often compared him to "that disciple whom Jesus loved." His religion was that of the heart. Almost every thing that he saw, or heard, or read, or studied, was converted to the feeding of this divine flame. Every subject that passed through his hands seemed to have been cast into this mould. Things that to a merely speculative mind would have furnished matter only for curiosity, to him afforded materials for devotion. His sermons were generally the effusions of his heart, and invariably aimed at the hearts of his hearers.

For the justness of the above remarks I might appeal, not only to the letters which he addressed to his friends, but to those which his friends addressed to him. It is worthy of notice how much we are influenced in our correspondence by the turn of mind of the person we address. If we write to a humorous character, we shall generally find that what we write, perhaps without being conscious of it, will be interspersed with pleasantries; or if to one of a very serious cast, our letters will be more serious than usual. On this principle it has been thought we may form some judgment of our own spirit by the spirit in which our friends address us. These remarks will apply with singular propriety to the correspondence of Mr. Pearce. In looking over the first volume of "Periodical Accounts of the Baptist Mission," the reader will easily perceive the most affectionate letters from the missionaries are those which are addressed to him.

It is not enough to say of this affectionate spirit, that it formed a prominent feature in his character; it was rather the life-blood that animated the whole system. He seemed, as one of his friends observed, to be baptized in it. It was holy love that gave the tone to his general deportment: as a son, a subject, a neighbour, a Christian, a minister, a pastor, a friend, a husband, and a father, he was manifestly governed by this principle; and this it was that produced in him that lovely uniformity of character which constitutes the true *beauty of holiness*.

By the grace of God he was what he was; and to the honour of grace, and not the glory of a sinful worm, be it recorded. Like all other men, he was the subject of a depraved nature. He felt it, and lamented it, and longed to depart that he might be freed from it; but certainly we have seldom seen a character, taking him altogether, "whose excellences were so many and so uniform, and whose imperfections were so few." We have seen men rise high in contemplation, who have abounded but little in action.— We have seen zeal mingled with bitterness, and candour degenerate into indifference: experimental religion mixed with a large portion of enthusiasm; and what is called rational religion void of every thing that interests the heart of man.—We have seen splendid talents tarnished with insufferable pride; seriousness with melancholy; cheerfulness with levity; and great attainments in religion with uncharitable censoriousness towards men of low degree: but we have not seen these things in our brother Pearce.

There have been few men in whom has been united a greater portion of the contemplative and the active—holy zeal and genuine candour—spirituality and rationality—talents that attracted almost universal applause, and yet the most unaffected modesty—faithfulness in bearing testimony against evil, with the tenderest compassion to the soul of the evil doer—fortitude that would encounter any difficulty in the way of duty, without any thing boisterous, noisy, or overbearing—deep seriousness, with habitual cheerfulness—and a constant aim to promote the highest degrees of piety in himself and others, with a readiness to hope the best of the lowest; not "breaking the bruised reed," nor "quenching the smoking flax."

He loved the Divine character as revealed in the Scriptures.—
To adore God, to contemplate his glorious perfections, to enjoy
his favour, and to submit to his disposal, were his highest delight.
"I felt," says he, "when contemplating the hardships of a
missionary life, that were the universe destroyed, and I the only
being in it besides God, he is fully adequate to my complete
happiness; and had I been in an African wood, surrounded with
venomous serpents, devouring beasts, and savage men, in such a
frame, I should be the subject of perfect peace and exalted joy.
Yes, O my God! thou hast taught me that THOU ALONE art worthy
of my confidence; and, with this sentiment fixed in my heart, I
am freed from all solicitude about my temporal concerns. If thy
presence be enjoyed, poverty shall be riches, darkness light,
affliction prosperity, reproach my honour, and fatigue my rest!"

He loved the gospel.—The truths which he believed and taught
dwelt richly in him, in all wisdom and spiritual understanding.
The reader will recollect how he went over the great principles of
Christianity, examining the grounds on which he rested, in the
first of those days which he devoted to solemn fasting and prayer
in reference to his becoming a missionary;[21] and with what ardent
affection he set his seal anew to every part of Divine truth as he
went along.

If salvation had been of works, few men, according to our
way of estimating characters, had a fairer claim; but, as he
himself has related, he could not meet the king of terrors in this
armour.[22] So far was he from placing any dependence on his own
works, that the more he did for God, the less he thought of it in
such a way. "All the satisfaction I wish for here," says he, "is to
be doing my heavenly Father's will. I hope I have found it my
meat and drink to do his work; and can set to my seal that the
purest pleasures of human life spring from the humble obedience
of faith. It is a good saying, 'We cannot do too much for God,
nor trust in what we do too little.' I find a growing conviction of
the necessity of a free salvation. The more I do for God, the less I
think of it; and am progressively ashamed that I do no more."

---

[21] See Chapter II, p. 39 of this volume
[22] Chapter I, p. 21 of this volume

Christ crucified was his darling theme, from first to last.[23] This was the subject on which he dwelt at the outset of his ministry among the Coleford colliers, when "he could scarcely speak for weeping, nor they hear for interrupting sighs and sobs." This was the burden of the song, when addressing the more polished and crowded audiences at Birmingham, London, and Dublin; this was the grand motive exhibited in sermons for the promotion of public charities; and this was the rock on which he rested all his hopes, in the prospect of death. It is true, as we have seen, he was shaken for a time, by the writings of a *Whitby,* and of a *Priestley;* but this transient hesitation, by the overruling grace of God, tended only to establish him more firmly in the end. "Blessed be his dear name," says he, under his last affliction, "who shed his blood for me. He helps me to rejoice at times with joy unspeakable. Now I see the value of the religion of the cross. It is a religion for a dying sinner. It is all the most guilty and the most wretched can desire. Yes, I taste its sweetness, and enjoy its fullness, with all the gloom of a dying bed before me; and far rather would I be the poor emaciated and emaciating creature that I am, than be an emperor with every earthly good about him, but without a God."

Notwithstanding this, however, there were those in Birmingham, and other places, who would not allow that *he preached the gospel.* And if by the gospel were meant the doctrine taught by Mr. *Huntington,* Mr. *Bradford,* and others who followed hard after them, it must be granted he did not. If the fill and depravity of man operate to destroy his accountableness to his Creator—if his inability to obey the law, or comply with the gospel, be of such a nature as to excuse him in the neglect of either—or, if not, yet if Christ's coming under the law frees believers from all obligations to obey its precepts—if gospel invitations are addressed only to the regenerate—if the illuminating influences of the Holy Spirit consist in revealing to

---

[23] Mr. P. being one week-day evening in London, and not engaged to preach, asked his friend Mr. S. where he could hear a good sermon. Mr. S. mentioned two places. "Well," said Mr. P. "tell me the character of the preachers, that I may choose." "Mr. D." said his friend, "exhibits the orator, and is much admired for his eloquence." "Well," said Mr. P. "and what is the other?" "Why, I hardly know what to say of Mr. C.; he always throws himself in the background, and you see his Master only." "That's the man for me then," said the amiable Pearce: "let us go and hear him."

us the secret purposes of God concerning us, or impressing us with the idea that we are the favourites of heaven—if believing such impressions be Christian faith, and doubting of their validity unbelief—if there be no such thing as progressive sanctification, nor any sanctification inherent, except that of the illumination before described—if wicked men are not obliged to do any thing beyond what they can find in their hearts to do, nor good men to be holy beyond what they actually are—and if these things constitute the *gospel,* Mr. Pearce certainly *did not* preach it. But if a man, whatever be his depravity, be necessarily a free agent, and accountable for all his dispositions and actions—if gospel invitations be addressed to men, not as elect nor as non-elect, but as sinners exposed to the righteous displeasure of God—it Christ's obedience and death rather increase than diminish our obligations to love God and one another—if faith in Christ be a falling in with God's way of salvation, and unbelief a falling out with it—if sanctification be a progressive work, and so essential a branch of our salvation as that without it no man shall see the Lord—if the Holy Spirit instruct us in nothing by his illuminating influences but what was already revealed in the Scriptures, and which we should have perceived but for that we loved darkness rather than light—and if he incline us to nothing but what was antecedently right, or to such a spirit as every intelligent creature ought at all times to have possessed—then Mr. Pearce *did* preach the gospel; and that which his accusers call by this name is *another gospel,* and not the gospel of Christ.

Moreover, if the doctrine taught by Mr. Pearce be not the gospel of Christ, and that which is taught by the above writers and their adherents be, it may be expected that the effects produced will in some degree correspond with this representation. And is it evident to all men who are acquainted with both, and who judge impartially, that the doctrine taught by Mr. Pearce is productive of "hatred, variance, emulations, wrath, strife, railings, evil surmisings, and perverse disputings;" that it renders those who embrace it, "lovers of their own selves, covetous, boasters, proud, false accusers, fierce, despisers of those that are good;" while that of his adversaries promotes "love, joy, peace, long-suffering, gentleness, goodness, faith, meekness, and temperance? .... "*why even of yourselves judge ye not what is right? .... ye shall know them by their fruits.*"

Mr. Pearce's ideas of preaching *human obligation* may be seen in the following extract from a letter addressed to a young minister who was sent out of the church of which he was a pastor. "You request my thoughts how a minister should preach *human obligation.* I would reply, do it *extensively,* do it *constantly;* but, withal, do it *affectionately,* and *evangelically.* I think, considering the general character of our hearers, and the state of their mental improvement, it would be time lost to argue much from the data of natural religion. The best way is perhaps to express duties in Scripture language, and enforce them by evangelical motives; as the example of Christ—the end of his sufferings and death—the consciousness of his approbation—the assistance he has promised—the influence of a holy conversation on God's people, and on the people of the world—the small returns we at best can make for the love of Jesus—and the hope of eternal holiness. These form a body of arguments which the most simple may understand, and the most dull may feel. Yet I would not neglect on *some occasions* to show the obligations of man to love his Creator—the reasonableness of the Divine law—and the natural tendency of its commands to promote our own comfort, the good of society, and the glory of God. These will serve to *illuminate,* but, after all, it is 'the gospel of the grace of God' that will most effectually *animate,* and impel to action."

Mr. Pearce's affection to the doctrine of the cross was not merely, nor principally, on account of its being a system which secured his own safety. Had this been the case, he might, like others whose religion originates and terminates in self-love, have been delighted with the idea of the grace of the Son; but it would have been at the expense of all complacency in the righteous government of the Father. He might have admired something which he accounted the gospel, as saving him from misery; but he could have discerned no loveliness in the Divine law as being holy, just, and good, nor in the mediation of Christ as doing honour to it. That which in his view constituted the glory of the gospel was, that God is therein revealed as the just God and the Saviour—just, and the justifier of him that believeth in Jesus.

He was a lover of good men.—He was never more in his element than when joining with them in spiritual conversation, prayer, and praise. His heart was tenderly attached to the people of his charge; and it was one of the bitterest ingredients in his cup during his long affliction to be cut off from their society. When in the neighbourhood of Plymouth, he thus writes to Mr. King, one of the deacons, "Give my love to all the dear people. O pray that He who afflicts would give me patience to endure. Indeed the state of suspense in which I have been kept so long requires much of it; and I often exclaim, ere I am aware, O my dear people! O my dear family, when shall I return to you again?" He conscientiously dissented from the Church of England, and from every other national establishment of religion, as inconsistent with what he judged the Scriptural account of the nature of Christ's kingdom; nor was he less conscientious in his rejection of infant baptism, considering it has having no foundation in the Holy Scriptures, and as tending to confound the church and the world: yet he embraced with brotherly affection great numbers of godly men both in and out of the establishment. His spirit was truly catholic: he loved all who loved our Lord Jesus Christ in sincerity. "Let us pray," said he in a letter to a friend, "for the peace of Jerusalem: they shall prosper who love—not this part, or the other, but who love her—that is, the whole body of Christ."[24]

He bore good-will to all mankind.—It was from this principle that he so ardently desired to go and preach the gospel among the heathen. And even under his long affliction, when at times he entertained hopes of recovery, he would say, "My soul pants for usefulness more extensive than ever: I long to become an apostle to the world!" The errors and sins of men wrought much in him in a way of pity. He knew that they were culpable in the sight of God; but he knew also that he himself was a sinner, and felt that they were entitled to his compassion. His zeal for the Divinity and atonement of his Saviour never appeared to have operated in

---

[24] The following anecdote will illustrate the tender respect with which he uniformly treated the feelings of those from whom he conscientiously differed in sentiment or practice.

He one day heard that Mr. Richard Cecil was in Birmingham, and had preached two Wednesday evenings at St. Mary's Chapel. Mr. P. arranged his time to hear him one evening; but an unexpected occurrence detained him so late that, when he came to the chapel, the prayers were nearly concluded. He remarks that, in these circumstances, he thought it best not to enter, lest, being a public character, his doing so should be construed into a designed contempt for the church service.

a way of unchristian bitterness against those who rejected these important doctrines; and though he was shamefully traduced by professors of another description as a mere legal preacher, and his ministry held up as affording no food for the souls of believers—and though he could not but feel the injury of such misrepresentations, yet he does not appear to have cherished unchristian resentment, but would at any time have laid himself out for the good of his worst enemies. It was his constant endeavour to promote as good an understanding between the different congregations in the town as the nature of their different religious sentiments would admit. The cruel bitterness of many people against Dr. Priestley and his friends, at and after the Birmingham riots, was affecting to his mind. Such methods of opposing error he abhorred. His regard to mankind made him lament the consequences of war; but while he wished and prayed for peace to the nations, and especially to his native country, he had no idea of turbulently contending for it. Though friendly to civil and religious liberty, he stood aloof from the fire of political contention. In an excellent Circular Letter to the churches of the midland association in 1794, of which he was the writer, he thus expresses himself:—"Have as little as possible to do with the world. Meddle not with political controversies. An inordinate pursuit of these, we are sorry to observe, has been as a canker-worm at the root of vital piety; and caused the love of many, formerly zealous professors, to wax cold. 'The Lord reigneth;' it is our place to 'rejoice in his government, and quietly wait for the salvation of God.' The establishment of his kingdom will be the ultimate end of all those national commotions which terrify the earth. 'The wrath of man shall praise him; and the remainder of wrath he will restrain.'" From this time, more than ever, he turned his whole attention to the promoting of the kingdom of Christ, cherishing and recommending a spirit of contentment and gratitude for the civil and religious advantages that we enjoyed. Such were the sentiments inculcated in the last sermon that he printed, and the last but one that he preached. His dear young friends who are gone to India will never forget how earnestly he charged them by letter, when confined at Plymouth, to conduct themselves in all civil matters as peaceable and obedient subjects to the government under which they lived, in whatever country it might be their lot to reside.

It was love that tempered his faithfulness with so large a portion of tender concern for the good of those whose conduct he was obliged to censure.—He could not bear them that were evil; but would set himself against them with the greatest firmness; yet it was easy to discover the pain of mind with which this necessary part of duty was discharged. It is well remembered how he conducted himself towards certain preachers in the neighbourhood, who, wandering from place to place, corrupted and embroiled the churches; whose conduct he knew to be as dishonourable as their principles were loose and unscriptural; and, when requested to recite, particulars in his own defence, his fear and tenderness for character, his modest reluctance to accuse persons older than himself, and his deep concern that men engaged in the Christian ministry should render such accusations necessary, were each conspicuous, and proved to all present that the work of an accuser was to him *a strange work.*

It was love that expanded his heart, and prompted him to labour in season and out of season for the salvation of sinners.—This was the spring of that constant stream of activity by which his life was distinguished. His conscience would not suffer him to decline what appeared to be right. "I dare not refuse," he would say, "lest I should shrink from duty. Unjustifiable ease is worse than the most difficult labours to which duty calls." To persons who never entered into his views and feelings, some parts of his conduct, especially those which relate to his desire of quitting his country that he might preach the gospel to the heathen, will appear extravagant; but no man could with greater propriety have adopted the language of the apostle, "Whether we be beside ourselves, it is to God; or whether we be sober, it is for your cause; for the love of Christ constraineth us."

He was frequently told that his exercises were too great for his strength; but such was the ardour of his heart, "He could not die in a better work." When he went up into the pulpit to deliver his last sermon, he thought he should not have been able to get through; but when he got a little warm, he felt relieved, and forgot his indisposition, preaching with equal fervour and freedom as when in perfect health. While he was laid aside he could not forbear hoping that he should some time resume his delightful work; and, knowing the strength of his feelings to be such that it would be unsafe to trust himself, he proposed for a time to write his discourses, that his mind might not be at liberty to overdo his debilitated frame.

All his counsels, cautions, and reproofs, appear to have been the effect of love.—It was a rule dictated by his heart, no less than by his judgment, to discourage all evil speaking; nor would he approve of just censure unless some good and necessary end were to be answered by it. Two of his distant friends being at his house together, one of them, during the absence of the other, suggested something to his disadvantage. He put a stop to the conversation by answering, "He is here, take him aside, and tell him of it by himself: you may do him good."

If he perceived any of his acquaintance bewildered in fruitless speculations, he would in an affectionate manner endeavour to draw off their attention from the mazes of confusion to the simple doctrines of the cross. A specimen of this kind of treatment will be seen in the letter, No. 1, which follows this chapter.

He was affectionate to all, but especially towards the *rising generation.* The youth of his own congregation, of London, and of Dublin, have not forgot his melting discourses, which were particularly addressed to them. He took much delight in speaking to the children, and would adapt himself to their capacities, and expostulate with them on the things which belonged to their everlasting peace. While at Plymouth, he wrote thus to one of his friends, "Oh how should I rejoice, were there a speedy prospect of my returning to my great and *little* congregations!" Nor was it by preaching only that he sought their eternal welfare: several of his letters are addressed to young persons.—See Nos. II, III, and IV after the close of this chapter.

With what joy did he congratulate one of his most intimate friends, on hearing that three of the younger branches of his family had apparently been brought to take the Redeemer's yoke upon them!— "Thanks, thanks be to God," said he, "for the enrapturing prospects before you as *a father,* as a *Christian father* especially. What, *three* of a family! and these three at once! Oh the heights and depths, and lengths and breadths of his unfathomable grace! My soul feels joy unspeakable at the blessed news. Three immortal souls secured for eternal life! Three rational spirits preparing to grace Immanuel's triumphs, and sing his praise! Three examples of virtue and goodness, exhibiting the genuine influence of the true religion of Jesus before the world!—Perhaps three mothers training up to lead three future families in the way to heaven. Oh what a train of blessings do I see in this event! Most sincerely do I participate with my dear friend in his pleasures, and in his gratitude."

Towards the close of life, writing to the same friend, he thus concludes his letter: "Present our love to dear Mrs._____,and the family, especially those whose hearts are engaged to seek the Lord and his goodness. O tell them they will find him good all their lives, supremely good on dying beds, and best of all in glory."

In his visits to the sick he was singularly useful. His sympathetic conversation, affectionate prayers, and endearing manner of recommending to them a compassionate Saviour, frequently operated as a cordial to their troubled hearts. A young man of his congregation was dangerously ill. His father living at a distance was anxious to hear from him; and Mr. Pearce, in a letter to the minister on whose preaching the father attended, wrote as follows: "I feel for the anxiety of Mr. V — , and am happy in being at this time a Barnabas to him. I was not seriously alarmed for his son till last Tuesday, when I expected from every symptom, and the language of his apothecary, that he was nigh unto death. But, to our astonishment and joy, a surprising change has since taken place. I saw him yesterday apparently in a fair way of recovery. His mind for the first part of his illness was sometimes joyful, and almost constantly calm: but, when at the worst, suspicions crowded his mind; he feared he had been a hypocrite. I talked, and prayed, and wept with him. One scene was very affecting: both he and his wife appeared like persons newly awakened. They never felt *so strongly* the importance of religion before. He conversed about the tenderness of Jesus to broken-hearted sinners; and, whilst we spoke, it seemed as though he came and began to heal the wound. It did me good, and I trust was not unavailing to them. They have since been for the most part happy; and a very pleasant interview I had with them on the past day."

Every man must have his seasons of relaxation. In his earlier years he would take strong bodily exercise. Of late he occasionally employed himself with the microscope, and in making a few philosophical experiments.

"We will amuse ourselves with philosophy," said he to a philosophical friend, "but Jesus shall be our teacher." In all these exercises he seems never to have lost sight of God; but would be discovering something in his works that should furnish matter for praise and admiration. His mind did not appear to have been unfitted, but rather assisted by such pursuits, for the discharge of the more spiritual exercises, into which he would fall at a proper season, as into his native element. If in company with his friends, and the conversation turned upon the works of nature, or art, or any other subject of science, he would cheerfully take a part in it, and when occasion required, by some easy and pleasant transition, direct it into another channel. An ingenious friend once showed him a model of a machine which he thought of constructing, and by which he hoped to be able to produce a perpetual motion. Mr. Pearce, having patiently inspected it, discovered where the operation would stop, and pointed it out. His friend was convinced, and felt, as may be supposed, rather unpleasant at his disappointment. He consoled him; and, a prayer-meeting being at hand, said to this effect, "We may learn from hence our own insufficiency, and the glory of that Being who is 'wonderful in counsel, and excellent in working:' let us go and worship Him."

His mind and gentle disposition, not apt to give or take offence, often won upon persons in matters wherein at first they have shown themselves averse. When collecting for the Baptist mission, a gentleman, who had no knowledge of him, or of the conductors of that undertaking, made some objections on the ground that the Baptists had little or nothing to say to the unconverted. This objection Mr. Pearce attempted to remove, by alleging that the parties concerned in this business were entirely of another mind. "I am glad to hear it," said the gentleman; "but I have my fears." "Then pray, sir," said Mr. Pearce, "do not give till you are satisfied." "Why, I assure you," replied the other, "I think the Methodists more likely to succeed than you; and should feel more pleasure in giving them ten guineas, than you one." "If you give them twenty guineas, sir," said Mr. Pearce, "we shall rejoice in their success; and if you give us one, I hope it will not be misapplied." The gentleman smiled, and gave him four.

His figure, to a superficial observer, would, at first sight, convey nothing very interesting; but, on close inspection, his countenance would be acknowledged to be a faithful index to his soul. Calm, placid, and, when in the pulpit especially, full of animation, his appearance was not a little expressive of the interest he felt in the eternal welfare of his audience; his eyes beaming benignity, and speaking in the most impressive language his willingness to *impart not only the gospel of God, but his own soul also.*

His imagination was vivid, and his judgment clear. He relished the elegances of science, and felt alive to the most delicate and refined sentiments; yet these were things on account of which he does not appear to have valued himself. They were rather his amusements than his employment.

His address was easy and insinuating; his voice pleasant, but sometimes overstrained in the course of his sermon; his language chaste, flowing, and inclining to the florid: this last, however, abated as his judgment ripened. His delivery was rather slow than rapid; his attitude graceful; and his countenance, in almost all his discourses, approaching to an affectionate smile. He never appears, however, to have studied what are called the graces of pulpit action; and whatever he had read concerning them, it was manifest that he thought nothing of them, or of any other of the ornaments of speech, at the time. Both his action and language were the genuine expressions of an ardent mind, affected, and sometimes deeply, with his subject. Being rather below the common stature, and disregarding, or rather, I might say, disapproving every thing pompous in his appearance, he has upon some occasions been prejudged to his disadvantage; but the song of the nightingale is not the less melodious for his not appearing in a gaudy plumage. His manner of preparing for the pulpit may be seen in a letter addressed to Mr. C — , of L — , who was sent out of his church, and which may be of use to others in a similar situation. See Letter No. V. which follows the close of this chapter.

His ministry was highly acceptable to persons of education; but he appears to have been most in his element when preaching to the poor. The feelings which he himself expresses, when instructing the colliers, appear to have continued with him through life. It was his delight to carry the glad tidings of salvation into the villages wherever he could find access and opportunity. And as he sought the good of their souls, so he both laboured and suffered to relieve their temporal wants; living himself in a style of frugality and self-denial, that he might have whereof to give to them that needed.

Finally, *he possessed a large portion of real happiness.*—There are few characters whose enjoyments, both natural and spiritual, have risen to so great a height. He dwelt in love; and "he that dwelleth in love dwelleth in God, and God in him." Such a life must needs be happy. If his religion had originated and terminated in self-love, as some contend the whole of religion does, his joys had been not only of a different nature, but far less extensive than they were. His interest was bound up with that of his Lord and Saviour. Its afflictions were his affliction, and its joys his joy. The grand object of his desire was to "see the good of God's chosen, to rejoice in the gladness of his nation, and to glory with his inheritance." "What pleasures do those lose," says he, "who have no interest in God's gracious and holy cause!"[25]

If an object of joy presented itself to his mind, he would delight in multiplying it by its probable or possible consequences. Thus it was, as we have seen, in his congratulating his friend on the conversion of three of his children; and thus it was when speaking of a people who divided into two congregations, not from discord, but from an increase of numbers; and who generously united in erecting a new and additional place of worship:—"These liberal souls are subscribing," said he, "in order to support a religion which, as far as it truly prevails, will render others as liberal as themselves."

His heart was so much formed for social enjoyment, that he seems to have contemplated the heavenly state under this idea with peculiar advantage. This was the leading theme of a discourse from Rev. 5:9-12, which he delivered at a meeting of ministers at Arnsby, April 18, 1797; and of which his brethren retain a lively remembrance. On this pleasing subject he dwells also in a letter to his dear friend Birt.— "I had much pleasure, a few days since, in meditating on the affectionate language of our Lord to his sorrowful disciples:— 'I go to prepare a place for you.' What a plenitude of consolation do these words contain! what a sweet view of heaven as a place of *society!* It is *one place* for us all; that place where his glorified body is, there all his followers shall assemble, to part no more. Where he is, there we shall be also. O blessed anticipation! There shall be Abel, and all the martyrs; Abraham, and all the patriarchs; Isaiah, and all the prophets; Paul, and all the apostles; Gabriel, and all the angels; and, above all, Jesus, and all his

---

[25] See the Letter to Dr. Ryland, May 30, 1796.

ransomed people! Oh to be amongst the number! My dear brother, let us be strong in the Lord. Let us realize the bliss before us. Let our faith bring heaven itself near, and feast, and live upon the scene. Oh what a commanding influence would it have upon our thoughts, passions, comforts, sorrows, words, ministry, prayers, praises, and conduct. What manner of persons should we be in all holy conversation and godliness!"

In many persons the pleasures imparted by religion are counteracted by a gloomy constitution; but it was not so in him. In his disposition they met with a friendly soil. Cheerfulness was as natural to him as breathing; and this spirit, sanctified by the grace of God, gave a tincture to all his thoughts, conversation, and preaching. He was seldom heard without tears; but they were frequently tears of pleasure. No levity, no attempts at wit, no aiming to excite the risibility of an audience, ever disgraced his sermons. Religion in him was habitual seriousness, mingled with sacred pleasure, frequently rising into sublime delight, and occasionally overflowing with transporting joy.

LETTERS REFERRED TO IN THE PREVIOUS CHAPTER

Letter No. I

To a young man whose mind he perceived was bewildered with fruitless speculations.

"The conversation we had on our way to _____ so far interested me in your religious feelings, that I find it impossible to satisfy my mind till I have expressed my ardent wishes for the happy termination of your late exercises, and contributed my mite to the promotion of your joy in the Lord. A disposition more or less to 'skepticism,' I believe, is common to our nature, in proportion as opposite systems and jarring opinions, each supported by a plausibility of argument, are presented to our minds; and with some qualification, I admit Robinson's remark, 'That he who never doubted never believed.' While examining the grounds of persuasion, it is right for the mind to hesitate. Opinions ought not to be prejudged, any more than criminals. Every objection ought to have its weight; and the more numerous and forcible objections are, the more cause shall we finally have for the triumph, *'Magna est veritas et prevalcbit;'* but there are two or three considerations which have no small weight with me in relation to religious controversies.

"The first is, the importance of truth. It would be endless to write on truth in general. I confine my views to what I deem the leading truth in the New Testament,—*the atonement made on behalf of sinners by the Son of God; the doctrine of the cross; Jesus Christ and him crucified.* It surely cannot be a matter of small concern whether the Creator of all things, out of mere love to rebellious men, exchanged a throne for a cross, and thereby reconciled a ruined world to God. If this be not true, how can we respect the Bible as an inspired book, which so plainly attributes our salvation to the grace of God, 'through the redemption, which is in Christ Jesus?' And if we discard the Bible, what can we do with prophecies, miracles, and all the power of evidence on which, as on adamantine pillars, its authority abides? Surely the infidel has more to reject than the believer to embrace. That book then which we receive, not as the word of man, but as the word of God, not as the religion of our ancestors, but on the invincible conviction which attends an impartial investigation of its evidences—that book reveals a truth of the highest importance to man, consonant to the opinions of the earliest ages and the most enlightened nations, perfectly consistent with the Jewish economy as to its spirit and design, altogether adapted to unite the equitable and merciful perfections of the Deity in the sinner's salvation, and above all things calculated to beget the most established peace, to inspire with the liveliest hope, and to engage the heart and life in habitual devotedness to the interest of morality and piety. Such a doctrine I cannot but venerate; and to the *author* of such a doctrine my whole soul labours to exhaust itself in praise.

> 'Oh the sweet wonders of the cross,
> Where God my Saviour loved and died!'

Forgive, my friend, forgive the transport of a soul compelled to feel where it attempts only to explore. I cannot on *this* subject control my passions by the laws of logic. 'God forbid that I should glory, save in the cross of Christ Jesus my Lord!'

"Secondly, I consider man as a depraved creature, so depraved that his judgment is as dark as his appetites are sensual, wholly dependent on God, therefore, for religious light as well as true devotion, yet such a dupe to pride as to reject every thing which the narrow limits of his comprehension cannot embrace, and such a slave to his passions as to admit no law but self-interest for his government. With these views of human nature I am persuaded we ought to suspect our own decisions, whenever they oppose truths too sublime for our understandings, or too pure for our lusts. To err on this side, indeed, 'is human;' wherefore the wise man saith, 'He that trusteth to his own heart is a fool.' Should therefore the evidence be only equal on the side of the gospel of Christ, I should think with this allowance we should do well to admit it.

"Thirdly, if the gospel of Christ be true, it should be heartily embraced. We should yield ourselves to its influence without reserve. We must come to a point, and resolve to be either infidels or Christians. To know the power of the sun we should expose ourselves to his rays; to know the sweetness of honey we must bring it to our palates. Speculations will not do in either of these cases; much less will it in matters of religion. 'My son,' saith God, 'give me thine heart!'

"Fourthly, a humble admission of the light we already have is the most effectual way to a full conviction of the truth of the doctrine of Christ. ' If any man will *do* his will, he shall know of his doctrine whether it be of God.' If we honour God as far as we know his will, he will honour us with further discoveries of it. Thus shall we know if we follow on to know the Lord; thus, thus shall you, my dear friend, become assured that there is salvation in no other name than that of Jesus Christ: and thus, from an inward experience of the quickening influences of his Holy Spirit, you will join the admiring church, and say of Jesus, 'This is my Beloved, this is my Friend; he is the chiefest among ten thousand, he is altogether lovely.' Yes, I yet hope—I expect—to see you rejoicing in Christ Jesus; and appearing as a living witness that he is faithful who hath said—'Seek, and ye shall find; ask, and receive, that your joy may be full.'"   S.P.

In another letter to the same correspondent, after congratulating himself that he had discovered such a mode of killing noxious insects as should put them to the least pain, and which was characteristic of the tenderness of his heart, he proceeds as follows: "But enough of nature. How is my brother *as a Christian?* We have had some interesting moments in conversation on the methods of grace, that grace whose influence reaches to the day of adversity and the hour of death; seasons when of every thing else it may be said, 'Miserable comforters are they all!' My dear friend, we will amuse ourselves with philosophy, but Christ shall be our teacher; Christ shall be our glory; Christ shall be our portion. Oh that we may be enabled 'to comprehend the heights, and depths, and lengths, and breadths, and to know the love of Christ, which passeth knowledge!'"

Affectionately yours, S.P.

Letter No. II

To a young gentleman of his acquaintance, who was then studying physic at Edinburgh.

"Did my dear friend P— know with what sincere affection and serious concern I almost daily think of him, he would need no other evidence of the effect which his last visit and his subsequent letters have produced. Indeed there is not a young man in the world, in earlier life than myself, for whose universal prosperity I am so deeply interested. Many circumstances I can trace, on a review of the past fourteen years, which have contributed to beget and augment affection and esteem; and I can assure you that *every interview* and *every letter* still tends to consolidate my regard.

"Happy should I be if my ability to serve you at this important crisis of human life were equal to your wishes or my own. Your situation demands all the aids which the wisdom and prudence of your friends can afford, that you may be directed not only to the most worthy objects of pursuit, but also to the most effectual means for obtaining them. In your professional character it is impossible for me to give you any assistance. If any general observations I can make should prove at all useful, I shall be richly rewarded for the time I employ in their communication.

"I thank you sincerely for the freedom wherewith you have disclosed the peculiarities of your situation, and the views and resolutions wherewith they have inspired you. I can recommend nothing better, my dear friend, than *a determined adherence* to the purposes you have already formed respecting the intimacies you contract and the associates you choose. In such a place as Edinburgh, it may be supposed, no description of persons will be wanting. Some so notoriously vicious that their atrocity of character will have no small tendency to confirm your morals, from the odious contrast which their practices present to your view. Against these therefore I need not caution you. You will flee them as so many serpents, in whose breath is venom and destruction. More danger may be apprehended from those mixed characters, who blend the profession of philosophical refinement with the secret indulgence of those sensual gratifications which at once exhaust the pocket, destroy the health, and debase the character.

"That morality is friendly to individual happiness and to social order, no man who respects his own conscience or character will have the effrontery to deny. Its avenues cannot, therefore, be too sacredly guarded, nor those principles which support a virtuous practice be too seriously maintained. But morality derives, it is true, its best, its only support from the principles of religion. 'The fear of the Lord,' said the wise man, 'is to hate evil.' He therefore who endeavours to weaken the sanctions of religion, to induce a sceptical habit, to detach my thoughts from an *ever-present God.* and my hopes from a futurity of holy enjoyment, he is a worse enemy than the man who meets me with the pistol and the dagger. Should my dear friend then fall into the company of those whose friendship cannot be purchased but by the sacrifice of revelation, I hope he will ever think such a price too great for the good opinion of men who blaspheme piety and dishonour God. Deism is indeed the fashion of the day, and, to be in the mode, you must quit the good old path of devotion, as too antiquated for any but monks and hermits: so as you laugh at religion, that is enough to secure to you the company and the applause of the sons of politeness. Oh that God may be a buckler and a shield to defend you from their assaults! Let but their private morals be inquired into, and, if they may have a hearing, I dare engage they will not bear a favourable testimony to the good tendency of scepticism; and it may be regarded as an indisputable axiom, that what is unfriendly to virtue is unfriendly to man.

"Were I to argue *a posteriori* in favour of truth, I should contend that those principles must be true which, first, corresponded with general observation—secondly, tended to general happiness—thirdly, preserved a uniform connexion between cause and effect, evil and remedy, in all situations.

"I would then apply these data to the principles held on the one side by the deists, and on the other by the believers in revelation. In the application of the *first,* I would refer to the state of human nature. The deist contends for its purity and powers. Revelation declares its depravity and weakness. I compare these opposite declarations with the facts that fall under constant observation. Do I not see that there is a larger portion of vice in the world than of virtue; that no man needs solicitation to evil, but every man a guard against it: and that thousands bewail their subjection to lusts which they have not power to subdue, whilst they live in moral slavery, and cannot burst the chain? Which principle then shall I admit'? Will observation countenance the *deistical?* I am convinced to the contrary, and must say, I cannot be a deist without becoming a fool; and, to exalt my reason, I must deny my senses.

"I take the *second* datum, and inquire which tends most to general happiness? To secure happiness, three things are necessary: —*objects, means,* and *motives.* The question is, which points out the *true source* of happiness, which directs to the *best means* for attaining it, and which furnishes me with the most *powerful motives* to induce my pursuit of it? If I take a deist for my tutor, he tells me that *fame* is the object, universal *accommodation of manners to interest* the means, and *self-love* the spring of action. Sordid teacher! From him I turn to *Jesus. His* better voice informs me that the source of felicity is the *friendship of my God;* that *love to my Maker,* and *love to man,* expressed in all the noble and amiable effusions of devotion and benevolence, are the means; and that *the glory of God,* and *the happiness of the universe,* must be my motives. Blessed Instructor; thy dictates approve themselves to every illuminated conscience, to every pious heart! Do they not, my dear P—, approve themselves to yours?

"But I will not tire your patience by pursuing these remarks. Little did I think of such amplification when I first took up my pen. Oh that I may have the joy of finding that these (at least well meant) endeavours to establish your piety have not been ungraciously received, nor wholly unprofitable to your mind! I am encouraged to these effusions of friendship by that amiable *self-distrust* which your letter expresses,—a temper not only becoming the earlier stages of life, but graceful in all its advancing periods.

"Unspeakable satisfaction does it afford me to find that you are conscious of the necessity of 'first' seeking assistance from heaven. Retain, my dear friend, this honourable, this equitable sentiment. 'In all thy ways acknowledge God, and he shall direct thy paths.'

"I hope you will still be cautious in your intimacies. You will gain more by a half-hour's intercourse with God than the friendship of the whole college can impart. Too much acquaintance would be followed with a waste of that precious time on the present improvement of which your future usefulness and respectability in your profession depend. Like the bee, you may do best by sipping the sweets of every flower; but remember the sweetest blossom is not the *hive*.

"P. S. So many books have been published on the same subject as the manuscript which you helped me to copy, that I have not sent it to the press."[24]

Letter No. III

To a young lady at school, Miss A. H., a daughter of one of the members of his church.

"I cannot deny myself the pleasure which this opportunity affords me of expressing the concern I feel for your happiness, arising from the sincerest friendship,—a friendship which the many amiable qualities you possess, together with the innumerable opportunities I have had of seeing them displayed, have taught me to form and perpetuate.

"It affords me inexpressible pleasure to hear that you are so happy in your present situation—a situation in which I rejoice to see you placed, because it is not merely calculated to embellish the manners, but to profit the soul. I hope that my dear Ann, amidst the various pursuits of an ornamental or scientific nature which she may adopt, will not omit that first, that great concern, the dedication of her heart to God. To this, my dear girl, every thing invites you that is worthy of your attention. The dignity of a rational and immortal soul, the condition of human nature, the gracious truths and promises of God, the sweetness and usefulness of religion, the comfort it yields in affliction, the security it affords in temptation, the supports it gives in death, and the prospects it opens of life everlasting; all these considerations, backed with the

---

[24] The compiler believes this was an answer to Mr. Peter Edwards's *Candid Reasons for Renouncing the Principles of Anti-Paedobaptism.* He knows Mr. Pearce did write an answer to that performance. By the imposing air of the writer he has acknowledged he was at first a little stunned; but, upon examining his arguments, found it no very difficult undertaking to point out their fallacy.

uncertainty of life, the solemnity of judgment, the terrors of hell, and the calls of conscience and of God,—all demand your heart for the *blessed Jehovah.* This, and nothing short of this, is true religion. You have often heard, and often *written* on religion: it is time you should FEEL it now. Oh what a blessedness will attend your hearty surrender of yourself to the God and Father of men! Methinks I see all the angels of God *rejoicing* at the sight; all the saints in heaven partaking of their joy; Jesus himself, who died for sinners, gazing on you with delight; your own heart filled with peace and joy in believing; and a thousand streams of goodness flowing from your renovated soul to refresh the aged saint, and to encourage your fellow youth to seek first the kingdom of heaven, and press on to God. But oh, should I be mistaken! Alas, alas, I cannot bear the thought. O thou Saviour of sinners, and God of love, take captive the heart of my dear young friend, and make her truly willing to be wholly thine!

"If you can find freedom, do oblige me with a letter on the state of religion in your soul, and be assured of every sympathy or advice that I am capable of feeling or giving."

Letter No. IV

To a young gentleman in Dublin, written soon after Mr. P.'s return from that city.

"Dear Master B.

"Your letter of the 21st of July gave me no small degree of pleasure, and should have been answered long before now, had not my numerous engagements at home compelled me to suspend my correspondence abroad. Except one letter, which I sent to Dublin to inform my friends of my safe return, this is the first day in which I have found time to write to Ireland since I left it. You will not, therefore, think me forgetful of you, or unconcerned about your prosperity: believe me, from the first conversation I had with you to the present moment, I have felt no small degree of solicitude for your eternal interests. Happy, indeed, shall I be to find that you continue anxious to secure them; for what are all the honors, the pleasures, or the wealth of this world, when compared with the spiritual and abiding blessings of religion? Could we insure all that is esteemed by men, and enjoy it uninterruptedly for a thousand ages, yet, when those ages have passed how miserable should we be without religion! But life is short, and the pleasures of it are embittered by many crosses and trials, so that our earthly comforts yield but little good, 'nor yield that little long.' It is, therefore, most blessed advice that our Savior gives, John, 6: 27: 'Labor not for the bread which perisheth, but for that bread which endureth to everlasting life,' &c. Observe, my dear young friend, what our Savior teaches you in these words.

"1. That religion is to the soul what bread is to the body: it feeds, nourishes, and strengthens the mind. 2. This heavenly bread affords abiding comfort and support: it 'endures to everlasting life.' 3. The enjoyment of this sacred food deserves our most earnest pursuit. 'Labor' for it. Let your whole heart and soul be in this great business of religion. If it be not sought and secured, how tremendous the consequences! the soul is lost—lost —lost for ever! O seek, therefore, my dear youth, 'seek the Lord while he may be found, call upon him while he is near,' 'draw nigh to him, and he will draw nigh to you.' 4. It must be received, not as the reward of any good thing in you, or for any good thing to be done by you: 'The Son of man will give it to you.' Yes, were we to have nothing; but what we deserve, our best portion would be hell; but, 'of his mercy he saves us, according to his own purpose and grace, which was given us in Christ before the world began.' 2 Tim. 1: 9. From the mercy of Christ you must receive every thing. Here you must apply for pardon. Here you must come for wisdom. Here you must receive strength and comfort. 'All is in Christ, who of God is made unto us wisdom, and righteousness, and sanctification, and redemption.' 1 Cor. 1: 30. S.P."

Letter No. V

To a young Minister, Mr. Cave, of Leicester, on preparation for the pulpit.

"MY DEAR BROTHER,

"Your first letter gave me much pleasure. I hoped you would learn some useful lesson from the first Sabbath disappointment. Every thing is good that leads us to depend more simply on the Lord. Could I choose my frames, I would say respecting industry in preparation for public work, as is frequently said respecting Christian obedience—I would apply as close as though I expected no help from the Lord, whilst I would depend upon the Lord for assistance as though I had never made any preparation at all.

"I rejoice much in every thing that affords you ground for solid pleasure. The account of the affection borne you by the people of God was therefore a matter of joy to my heart, especially as I learnt from the person who brought your letter that the friendship seemed pretty general.

"Your last has occasioned me some pain on your account, because it informs me that you have been 'exceedingly tried in the pulpit;' but I receive satisfaction again from considering that the gloom of midnight precedes the rising day, not only in the natural world, but frequently also in the Christian minister's experience. Do not be discouraged, my dear brother; those whose labours God has been pleased most eminently to bless, have generally had their days of prosperity ushered in with clouds and storms. You are in the sieve; but the sieve is in our Saviour's hands; and he will not suffer any thing but the chaff to fall through, let him winnow us as often as he may. No one at times, I think I may say, has been worse tried than myself in the same manner as you express; though I must be thankful it has not been often.

"You ask direction of me, my dear brother. I am too inexperienced myself to be capable of directing others; yet if the little time I have been employed for God has furnished me with any thing worthy of communication, it will be imparted to no one with more readiness than to you.

"I should advise you, when you have been distressed by hesitation, to reflect whether it arose from an inability to recollect your ideas, or to obtain words suited to convey them.—If the former, I think these two directions may be serviceable: First, Endeavour to think *in a train.* Let one idea depend upon another in your discourses, as one link does upon another in a chain. For this end I have found it necessary to arrange my subjects in the order of time. Thus, for instance,—If speaking of the promises, I would begin with those which were suited to the earliest inquiries of a convinced soul; as pardon, assistance in prayer, wisdom, &c.; then go to those parts of Christian experience which are usually subsequent to the former; as promises of support in afflictions, deliverance from temptations, and perseverance in grace; closing with a review of those which speak of support in death, and final glory. Then all the varieties of description respecting the glory of heaven will follow in natural order; as, the enlargement of the understanding, purification of the affections, intercourse with saints, angels, and even Christ himself, which will be *eternal:* thus beginning with the lowest marks of grace, and ascending step by step, you arrive at last in the fruition of faith. This mode is most natural, and most pleasing to the hearers, as well as assisting to the preacher; for one idea gives birth to another, and he can hardly help going forward regularly and easily.

"Secondly, labour to *render your ideas transparent to yourself.* Never offer to introduce a thought which you cannot *see through* before you enter the pulpit.—You have read in *Claude* that the best preparative to preach from a subject is to understand it; and I think Bishop Burnet says, 'No man properly understands any thing who cannot at *any time* represent it to others.'

"If your hesitation proceeds from a want of words, I should advise you—1. *To read good and easy authors; Dr. Watts especially.—To write a great part of your sermons,* and for a while get at least the leading ideas of every head of discourse by heart, enlarging only at the close of every thought.—3. Sometimes, as in the end of sermons, or when you preach in villages, *start of in preaching beyond all you have premeditated.* Fasten on some leading ideas; as the solemnity of death, the awfulness of judgment, the necessity of a change of heart, the willingness of Christ to save,

&c. Never mind how far you ramble from the point, so as you do not lose sight of it; and if your heart be any way warm, you will find some expressions then fall from your lips which your imagination could not produce in an age of studious application.— 4. *Divest yourself of all fear.* If *you* should break the rules of grammar, or put in or leave out a word, and recollect at the end of the sentence the impropriety, unless it makes nonsense, or bad divinity, never try to mend it, but let it pass. If so, perhaps only a few would notice it; but if you stammer in trying to mend it, you will expose yourself to all the congregation.

"In addition to all I have said, you know where to look, and from whom to seek that wisdom and strength which only God can give. To him I recommend you, my dear brother, assuring you of my real esteem for you, and requesting you will not fail to pray for the least of saints, but yours affectionately,   S. P."

CONCLUDING REFLECTIONS

The great ends of Christian biography are instruction and example. By faithfully describing the lives of men eminent for godliness, we not only embalm their memory, but furnish ourselves with fresh materials and motives for a holy life. It is abundantly more impressive to view the religion of Jesus as operating in a living character than to contemplate it abstractedly. For this reason, we may suppose the Lord the Spirit has condescended to exhibit, first and principally, the life of Christ; and, after his, that of many of his eminent followers. And for this reason he by his holy influences still furnishes the church with now and then a singular example of godliness, which it is our duty to notice and record. There can be no reasonable doubt that the life of Mr. Pearce ought to be considered as one of these examples. May that same Divine Spirit who had manifestly so great a hand in forming his character teach us to derive from it both instruction and edification!

First, in him we may see *the holy efficacy,* and by consequence, *the truth, of the Christian religion.*—It was long since asked, "Who is he that overcometh the world, but he who believeth that Jesus is the Son of God?" This question contained a challenge to men of all religions who were then upon the earth. Idolatry had a great diversity of species, every nation worshipping its own gods, and in modes peculiar to itself: philosophers also were divided into numerous sects, each flattering itself that it had found the truth: even the Jews had their divisions; their Pharisees, Sadducees, and Essenes: but, great as many of them were in deeds of divers kinds, an apostle could look them all in the face, and ask, "Who is he that overcometh the world?" The same question might be safely asked in every succeeding age. The various kinds of religion that still prevail, the pagan, Mohammedan, Jewish, papal, or protestant, may form the exteriors of man according to their respective models; but where is the man amongst them, save the true believer in Jesus, that overcometh the world? Men may cease from particular evils, and assume a very different character; may lay aside their drunkenness, blasphemies, or debaucheries, and take up with a kind of monkish austerity, and yet all may amount to nothing more than an exchange of vices. The lusts of the flesh will on many occasions give place to those of the mind; but to overcome the world is another thing. By embracing the doctrine of the cross, to feel not merely a dread of the consequences of sin, but a holy abhorrence of its nature—and, by conversing with invisible realities, to become regardless of the best, and fearless of the worst, that this world has to dispense—this is the effect of genuine Christianity, and this is a standing proof of its Divine original. Let the most inveterate enemy of revelation have witnessed the disinterested benevolence of a Paul, a Peter, or a John, and, whether he would own it or not, his conscience must have borne testimony that this is true religion. The same may be said of Samuel Pearce: whether the doctrine he preached found a place in the *hearts* of his hearers, or not, his spirit and life must have approved themselves to their *consciences*.

Secondly, In him we see *how much may be done for God in a little time*.—If his death had been foreknown by his friends, some might have hesitated whether it was worth while for him to engage in the work of the ministry for so short a period; yet if we take a view of his labours, perhaps there are few lives productive of a greater portion of good. That life is not always the longest which is spun out to the greatest extent of days. The best of all lives amounted but to thirty-three years; and the most important works pertaining to that were wrought in the last three. There is undoubtedly a way of rendering a short life a long one, and a long life a short one, by filling or not filling it with proper materials. That time which is squandered away in sloth, or trifling pursuits, forms a kind of blank in human life: in looking it over there is nothing for the mind to rest upon; and a whole life so spent, whatever number of years it may contain, must appear upon reflection short and vacant, in comparison of one filled up with valuable acquisitions and holy actions. It is like the space between us and the sun, which though immensely greater than that which is traversed in a profitable journey, yet, being all empty space, the mind gets over it in much less time, and without any satisfaction. If "that life be long which answers life's great end," Mr. Pearce may assuredly be said to have come to his grave in a good old age. And might we not all do much more than we do, if our hearts were more in our work? Where this is wanting, or operates but in a small degree, difficulties are magnified into impossibilities; a lion is in the way of extraordinary exertion; or if we be induced to engage in something of this kind, it will be at the expense of a uniform attention to ordinary duties. But some will ask, 'How are our hearts to be in our work?' Mr. Pearce's heart was habitually in his; and that which kept alive the sacred flame in him appears to have been—the constant habit of conversing with Divine truth, and walking with God in private.

Thirdly, in him we see, in clear and strong colours, *to what a degree of solid peace and joy true religion will raise us, even in the present world.*—A little religion, it has been justly said, will make us miserable; but a great deal will make us happy. The one will do little more than keep the conscience alive, while our numerous defects and inconsistencies are perpetually furnishing it with materials to scourge us; the other keeps the heart alive, and leads us to drink deep at the fountain of joy. Hence it is, in a great degree, that so much of the spirit of bondage, and so little of the spirit of adoption, prevails amongst Christians. Religious enjoyments with us are rather occasional than habitual; or if in some instances it be otherwise, we are ready to suspect that it is supported in part by the strange fire of enthusiasm, and not by the pure flame of Scriptural devotion. But in Mr. Pearce we saw devotion ardent, steady, pure, and persevering: kindled, as we may say, at the altar of God, like the fire of the temple, it went not out by night nor by day. He seemed to have learnt that heavenly art, so conspicuous among the primitive Christians, of converting every thing he met with into materials for love, and joy, and praise. Hence he laboured, as he expresses it, "to exercise most love to God when suffering most severely;" and hence he so affectingly encountered the billows that overwhelmed his feeble frame, crying,

> "Sweet affliction! sweet affliction!
> Singing as I wade to heaven."

The constant happiness that he enjoyed in God was apparent in the effects of his sermons upon others. Whatever we feel ourselves we shall ordinarily communicate to our hearers; and it has been already noticed, that one of the most distinguishing properties of his discourses was—that they inspired the serious mind with the liveliest sensations of happiness. They descended upon the audience, not indeed like a transporting flood, but like a shower of dew, gently insinuating itself into the heart, insensibly dissipating its gloom, and gradually drawing forth the graces of faith, hope, love, and joy; while the countenance was brightened almost into a smile, tears of pleasure would rise, and glisten, and fall from the admiring eye.

What a practical confutation did his life afford of the slander so generally cast upon the religion of Jesus, that it fills the mind with gloom and misery! No; leaving futurity out of the question, the whole world of unbelievers might be challenged to produce a character from among them who possessed half his enjoyments.

Fourthly, from his example we are furnished with *the greatest encouragement, while pursuing the path of duty, to place our trust in God.*—The situation in which he left his family, we have seen already, was not owing to an indifference to their interest, or an improvident disposition, or the want of opportunity to have provided for them; but to a steady and determined obedience to do what he accounted the will of God. He felt deeply for them, and we all felt with him, and longed to be able to assure him before his departure that they would be amply provided for; but, owing to circumstances which have already been mentioned, this was more than we could do. This was a point in which he was called to *die in faith;* and indeed so he did. He appears to have had no idea of that flood of kindness which, immediately after his decease, flowed from the religious public; but he believed in God, and cheerfully left all with him. "Oh that I could speak!" said he to Mrs. Pearce a little before his death, "I would tell a world to trust a faithful God. Sweet affliction! now it worketh glory, glory!" And when she told him the workings of her mind, he answered, "O trust the Lord! If he lift up the light of his countenance upon you, as he has done upon me this day, all your mountains will become molehills. I feel your situation: I feel your sorrows: but he who takes care of sparrows will care for you and my dear children."

The liberal contributions which have since been made, though they do not warrant ministers in general to expect the same, and much less to neglect providing for their own families on such a presumption, yet they must needs be considered as a singular encouragement, when we are satisfied that we are in the path of duty, to be inordinately "careful for nothing, but in every thing by prayer and supplication, with thanksgiving, to let our requests be made known unto God."

Finally, in him we see that *the way to true excellence is not to affect eccentricity, nor to aspire after the performance of a few splendid actions; but to fill up our lives with a sober, modest, sincere, affectionate, assiduous, and uniform conduct.*—Real greatness attaches to character; and character arises from a course of action. The solid reputation of a merchant arises not from his having made his fortune by a few successful adventures; but from a course of wise economy and honourable industry, which gradually accumulating advances by pence to shillings, and by shillings to pounds. The most excellent philosophers are not those who have dealt chiefly in splendid speculation, and looked down upon the ordinary concerns of men as things beneath their notice; but those who have felt their interests united with the interests of mankind, and bent their principal attention to things of real and public utility. It is much the same in religion. We do not esteem a man for one, or two, or three good deeds, any further than as these deeds are indications of the real state of his mind. We do not estimate the character of Christ himself so much from his having given sight to the blind, or restored Lazarus from the grave, as from his going about continually doing good.

These single attempts at great things are frequently the efforts of a vain mind, which pants for fame and has not patience to wait for it, nor discernment to know the way in which it is obtained. One pursues the shade, and it flies from him; while another turns his back upon it, and it follows him. The one aims to climb the rock, but falls ere he reaches the summit; the other, in pursuit of a different object, ere he is aware, possesses it; seeking the approbation of his God, he finds with it that of his fellow Christians.

THE END

FUNERAL SERMON

Preached by Dr. John Ryland

Occasioned by the Death of

The Rev. SAMUEL PEARCE

"The Presence of Christ the Source of Consolation"

John 14:18

I WILL NOT LEAVE YOU COMFORTLESS,
I WILL COME UNTO YOU.

So deeply am I sensible of the loss sustained by this church in general, not to say by the nearest relative of my dear departed brother, that on a partial view of their circumstances (and our views, especially of afflictive events, are too commonly partial), I could not be surprised, were some now present ready to exclaim, "Is there any sorrow like unto our sorrow, wherewith the Lord has this day afflicted us?" But though I scarcely know where a church could sustain an equal loss, by the removal of so young a pastor; nor can I conceive, there exists a widow, whom death has plundered of a richer store of blessings, by taking from her and from her infant care, the guide of their youth; yet, on more mature consideration, we must admit that lamentation to be applicable, even to them that feel the most pungent grief in this assembly. The event which has occasioned our present meeting, must deeply affect even strangers, whose hearts know how to feel; but all the dearest friends of the deceased must acknowledge, that the days of tribulation, which preceded this mournful evening, were not the season of displaying the Lord's anger, but of the clear manifestation of his faithfulness and love: They were to him the days of heaven upon earth. Surely they who drank with him the deepest out of his cup of affliction, could find no savour of the curse, no, not at the bottom; nor could they drink the bitter, without tasting also of the sweet, which was not sparingly dropped into it, but copiously infused. And after such proofs and illustrations of the divine fidelity, I cannot but believe, that she who needs them most of all, shall find farther stores of consolation laid up for her relief: since God her Maker is her husband, who giveth songs in the night.

This church also must be reminded, that there was a church at Jerusalem, near eighteen centuries ago, which sustained a loss unspeakably greater than that which they now bewail; while yet the sorrow, which was *then* endured, was quickly turned into joy. And your affectionate pastor, who, both in health and in sickness, cared so much for your welfare, did not hesitate to recommend to your attention, the kind assurance which was given for *their* relief; as believing it to contain ground of encouragement, on which *you* also are authorized to depend. He who said to his dear disciples, "I will not leave *you* comfortless orphans, I will come unto *you,*" has the same respect to his whole church in every age; and you, my brethren, may as safely relay on his gracious promise, as his very apostles.

Yes, beloved, we are authorized to make a general application of this word of consolation; and must affirm, that the promised presence of the blessed Redeemer is the best source of comfort, to all his people, in every time of trouble.

In complying with the request of my dear deceased brother, I shall first consider the subject in reference to those, to whom it was immediately addressed, and then endeavour to apply it to the present occasion.

FIRST. Let us notice the immediate reference of this declaration, to our Lord's disciples, who were then favoured with his bodily presence.

You are well aware that the words I haw read were spoken by the blessed Jesus, to those who followed him in the days of his humiliation; and that when he thus addressed them, sorrow had filled their hearts, because he had just announced his approaching departure. He came from the Father, and was come intro the world, and though the world was made by him, yet the world knew him not; but he had made himself known to these his disciples, whom he had chosen out of the world; and now when he was about to leave them, and go unto the Father, though his stupid and ungrateful countrymen would rather rejoice at his leaving the earth, than bewail it, yet his disciples could not but weep and lament and be sorrowful and surely, well they might, at the thought of losing such an invaluable Friend!

Especially we might expect this to be the case, if we reflect on the manner in which he was to be removed from them. They were to see him falsely accused, unjustly condemned, and cruelly murdered; being nailed to the cross with wicked hands, suspended between two thieves, and while thus numbered with transgressors, insulted and derided in his last agonies. Yes, he would be treated as the object of national abhorrence and execration, and that by the only people upon earth, who professed to be the worshippers of the true God. And his disciples must either view this barbarous treatment of their blessed Lord, or hide themselves from the shocking scene, by forsaking him in the hour of distress. In the meanwhile, he was also apparently abandoned by God himself, the zeal of whose house had consumed him; the Lord was pleased to bruise him, and put him to grief; he was resolved to make his soul an offering for sin, and therefore he called on his sword to awake against him, who was their good Shepherd; though he was one in covenant, yea, one in nature with himself; who could without robbery claim equality with God. What could be more surprising, distressing and perplexing to his disciples, than such a series of events!

While Jesus was with them he had fed them, and kept them as a Shepherd doth his flock; he had laid them like lambs in his bosom, and led them on gradually in the paths of truth and righteousness, as they were able to bear it. He had been gentle among them, as a nursing father is gentle towards his little children; pitying their infirmities, rectifying their mistakes, supplying their wants, healing their maladies; manifesting to them his Father's will, and keeping them in his name: and mull they now lose his visible pretence, and see him no more?

He had been little more than *three and thirty years* in the world, and most of them had known him but a very small part of that period; they had, however, now beheld his glory, and were convinced that it was the glory of the only begotten of the Father, full of grace and truth. They were satisfied that he alone had the words of eternal life; they believed and knew that he was the Christ, the Son of the living God; though at present they understood but imperfectly that plan of redemption, which rendered it expedient and necessary, that that he should suffer all these things and then enter into glory. This remaining ignorance must abundantly enhance their grief, at the intimations given them of his departure being at hand.

But in these words, their gracious Lord suggests, that *they* had no occasion to sink under their sorrows. He would *not leave* them *comfortless*, like destitute *orphans*, who had no affectionate parent, no wise tutor, no faithful guardian, to supply their wants, sympathize with them, protect them from evil, or instruct them in the way of duty. No, he had promised them his Holy Spirit, to be their Comforter and Monitor; and here he engages also, to come again to them himself; *I will come unto you,* saith our Lord. This promise was fulfilled to them in several ways-

1. In his *repeated appearances* to them, after his resurrection. Thus, as he suggests in the next verse, although in a little while, the world should see him no more, yet they should see him; and that sight should be the pledge that his words should hold good, "Because I live, ye shall live also." Accordingly the Evangelists attest, that he "shewed himself alive after his passion, by many infallible proofs, unto the Apostles whom he had chosen, being seen of them forty days," before he was taken up into glory: for God who raised him up, the third day after his crucifixion, "shewed him openly, not to all the people, but unto witnesses chosen before of God, even to us," says Peter, "who did eat and drink with him after he rose from the dead; whom he commanded to preach unto the people, and to testify that he is appointed to be the Judge of the living and the dead; and that to him all the prophets gave witness, that through his name, whosoever believeth in him, shall receive remission of sins." Therefore, though he soon left them again, being carried up into heaven, yet their understandings having been opened by him, that they might understand the scriptures, and see how it behooved him to suffer, and to rise again, "they worshipped him, when he was parted from them, and returned to Jerusalem with great joy," where they waited to

be endued with power from on high, and received the promised effusion of the Spirit, not many days afterward. But,

2. It received a more permanent accomplishment, in the continued enjoyment of his spiritual presence and divine influence. We fully ascertain this privilege to be included in the text, by comparing this promise, *I will come unto you,* with those declarations, recorded by Matthew, which admit of no solution without the acknowledgment of Christ's proper divinity: *"Where two or three are gathered together in my name, there am I, in the midst of than. And, lo I am with you always to the end of the world. Amen."*

3. At the end of the world, it shall receive a farther fulfillment, by our Lord's coming again in that human nature, which *"it behooved heaven to receive,* until the times of the restitution of all the things of which God spake by the mouth of his holy prophets, since the world began." Then he who went to prepare a place for his disciples, and all his subsequent followers, will come again, and receive them to himself; that where he is, there they may be also. Then they who were troubled for their adherence to his cause, shall enter into rest; when the Lord Jesus shall be revealed from heaven. At that same period, will he take vengeance on them who know not God, and who obey not the gospel of our Lord Jesus Christ, and punish them with everlasting destruction; when he shall come to be glorified in his saints, and admired in all them who believe. For God will bring with him them who now sleep in Jesus, while the believers who remain, at that time, alive upon earth, shall feel a change pass upon their bodies, to render them like those who are newly raised from the dead, and all "shall be caught up together to meet the Lord in the air, and so shall we ever be with the Lord. Wherefore," says Paul, "comfort one another with these words." He who testified these things to his disciples, while he was yet with them, repeated his promise long afterwards, to his servant John, saying, "Surely, I come quickly." May we unite with that beloved disciple, in saying, "Amen. Even so come, Lord Jesus."

And now, my brethren, if this assurance was sufficient to relieve the minds of the Apostles, when they lost the bodily presence of their Divine Matter, may we not safely proceed

SECONDLY, To apply the same consolation to the relief of those who are most affected by the late bereaving providence.

This Church has lost a most diligent, faithful, affectionate and valuable Pastor; and far be it from me to make light of your loss. All those churches who knew him only by occasional visits, all good men who had any opportunity of appreciating his worth, must sympathize with you; while they grieve to think that they themselves, who saw his face so seldom, shall see it no more. His brethren in the ministry, who enjoyed the pleasure and advantage of his friendship and correspondence, feel a loss which they will ever deplore. How then must you regret his removal, who were, many of you, the seals of his ministry; who, all of you, hoped long to enjoy his constant labours; and for whose welfare he laid himself out, with such unremitting assiduity? The Pastor, whose absence you mourn, possessed such an assemblage of lovely graces and acceptable qualifications, as are found united but seldom, even in truly Christian ministers. He had the firmest attachment to evangelical truth, and the most constant regard to practical godliness; he united remarkable soundness of judgment, with uncommon warmth of affections. I never saw, at least in one of his years, such active, ardent zeal, conjoined with such gentleness, modesty and deep humility; so much of the little child, and so much of the Evangelist, I can scarcely forbear saying, of the Apostle of Jesus Christ. I know not how to flatter you, with the hope of obtaining another minister; or myself, with the expectation of finding another friend, in whom *all* these charming qualities shall be found, in an *equal* degree. He was, indeed, "a burning and a shining light, and we rejoiced in his light, for a season;" but now we must lament, that he shines no more on earth; though we doubt not, that he shines like the sun, in the kingdom of his Father.

While he abode among us, his affections were evidently and eminently in heaven; his work, his family, and his people, were the only objects of regard, which made him willing to forego the bliss of the eternal world. And when he perceived that it was the Lord's will he should depart, your welfare was still his chief concern. For your consolation and benefit, he wished this passage to be considered at his funeral. He once alluded to another scripture, but laying that aside, lest it should occasion too much being said of himself, he fixed upon this; remarking, "If *he* comes to you, all will be well, you need not regret *my* removal." So you see, brethren, the design of your dear Pastor was to encourage you to claim a share in the promised presence of the Redeemer; which he knew extended to all his churches, and to every individual believer. He perceived that he was going to leave you, *he* could not promise to come again to you, though it was his great consolation to hope that you, in succession, will follow him; and meanwhile, the presence of his great Master, as to his divine nature, and the increasing influence of his Spirit, would be a sufficient compensation for any loss you could sustain by his departure. The spiritual presence of Christ could make up for the want of his bodily presence, to those who knew what was to enjoy the latter; it must then assuredly be sufficient to supply the absence of any under-shepherd. With this thought my dear brother consoled himself, in the beginning of his illness "If," said he, in a letter written the first Lord's day that he was confined from public worship, "if I am to depart hence, to be no more seen, I know the Lord can carry on his cause as well without me as with me; he who redeemed the sheep with his blood, will never suffer them to perish for want of shepherding, especially, since He himself is the chief Shepherd of souls."

Let me therefore attempt to assist you by directing your attention to the grounds on which you may safely expel the fulfillment of the promise, the magnitude of the magnitude of the promise itself, and the consequent obligation under which you are laid by it.

1. Consider the *ground* on which you may safety build an *expectation* that our Lord Jesus will come unto you.

Our Lord's ability to make good such a promise must here be noticed. Not only had he an inherent power to lay down his life, and to take it up again, in consequence of which he spent forty days with his disciples, before his ascension; but he has power to perform his standing engagements with his whole church, of being *with them, alway, to the end of the world,* whenever, and wherever, *two or three are gathered together in his name;* which promises most be connected with the text to enable you to claim any part in the consolation it will administer. Some modern enthusiasts, (who can believe any thing which does not imply that they are so *guilty* as to need the incarnate Son of God to make an atonement for their sins, by his precious blood) have fancied that the body of Jesus, who, according to them, was a mere man like ourselves; ascended no higher than the atmosphere, which surrounds the earth, and that he occasionally descends from thence to this globe, to visit invisibly and one at a time, the various congregations of Christians. This idea, it has been said, "cannot possibly do us any harm;" but, alas! it can do us but little good. If the Saviour should thus visit all those who are called by his name, our turn to be so favoured may occur but once in a life-time; or whether they who have invented this solution of Matt. 18:20, would admit us, whom they represent as irrational idolaters, to enjoy any share in his visits, I know not. Nor would it be of consequence, whether it were granted or denied; a mere man surveying us invisibly, now and then, could impart to us no spiritual blessing. But, if our great High-Priest be indeed, in the most exalted sense, the Son of God, who is *"passed through"* (cf. Heb. 4:14; 7:26; Eph. 4:9,10) these lower heavens, and is *"made higher* than the heavens," having "ascended up *far above* all heavens, that he might *fill all things,"* (according to the passage which we heard explained this morning by Brother West) and, if *"all power* be given unto him, in heaven and in earth," *then,* my brethren, your faith stands upon a firm foundation. He who, when he was upon earth, as to his humanity, could speak of himself as being "in heaven;" can as easily grant you the presence of his Divinity, now his human nature is in the world above.

Let the extent of his regard to his church, be also remembered. In his last prayer with his disciples, he prayed not alone for them who were present, but for all who should believe through their word. And "he ever liveth, to make intercession for all them, who come unto God by him." In every age hath his church been the object of his gracious regard: and he has fulfilled the promise which he made in the days of Zechariah, "Lo, I come, and I will dwell in the midst of thee, saith Jehovah. And many nations shall be joined unto Jehovah, in that day, and shall be my people; and I will dwell in the midst of thee, and thou shalt know that Jehovah God of Hosts hath sent me unto thee."—To the primitive church under all the pagan persecutions, was this promise fulfilled; to the Waldenses and Albigenses in the darkest times of Popery; to the first reformers from Antichristian error, and to their faithful successors; whether conformists or non-conformists; in this Island, on the continent of Europe, or in the wilds of North America. And at this day, wherever two or three assemble in his name, at Birmingham or at Bristol, in London or at Edinburgh, in Old Holland or in New Holland, at Mudnabatty, or at Otaheite, at the Cape of Good Hope or in Kentucky, there may our distant brethren, as well as ourselves, expect our glorious Lord to fulfill his word, *I will come unto you.*

The *express promises* he has made, of which the text is one, and we have recited several others, forbid us to doubt of the bestowment of this invaluable blessing. Jesus is the "faithful and true Witness; the same yesterday, to-day and for ever. In him all the promises of God are yea, and in him Amen, unto the glory of God by us."—He assured his servant Paul, in a season of peculiar difficulty, *"My grace* is sufficient for thee;" and the grace which could suffice for him, who accounted himself the chief of sinners, and less than the least of saints, is sufficient for us also. His strength is displayed to the greatest advantage in our weakness. O remember how it was lately displayed in the weakness, the extreme weakness, of your dear dying Pastor, on whom the power of Christ so visibly relied. When his heart and flesh were failing, how did he rejoice in God his Saviour, as the strength of his heart, and his portion for ever! And is there a mourner present, so feeble, so disconsolate, so bereaved of every created source of bliss, as that this grace will not suffice for her support? Or will he, who kept his word with such "punctilious veracity" to the Husband, forget his promise to the Widow and the Fatherless? Assuredly he will not.

Remember, my brethren, *the readiness of the Redeemer to hear and answer prayer.*—Though Paul besought him thrice upon one subject, before he received an immediate reply, the promise was fulfilled even before it was pronounced; he, like one who lived long before him, and like myriads who have since made trial of the same resource, was "strengthened with strength in his soul," before the

Saviour expressly declared, "My strength is made perfect in weakness." Continue therefore instant in prayer. Remember the apparent rebuffs encountered at first by the woman of Canaan, and how amply her faith was answered at last. Did not Jesus inculcate this maxim, "that men ought always to pray, and not to faint;" and spake a parable to illustrate and enforce that duty? Rich blessings, I trust, are still in reserve for you, in answer to the many servant petitions, which your dear Pastor offered up on your behalf, from the time of his first acquaintance with this Church, and during better than nine years, (Pearce was ordained August, 1790) wherein he has more fully undertaken the oversight of you in the Lord. May you yourselves pray without ceasing, and plead with the Lord his own exceeding great and precious promises, which will be found to contain blessings fully proportioned to all your necessities.

It was doubtless in consequence of many comfortable *evidences,* that *God has a number spiritual worshippers* among you, that my dear brother was encouraged to expect this declaration would be certainly fulfilled in your present circumstances. But though I gladly indulge a similar confidence, yet neither I, whose personal knowledge of you is very confined, nor he, whose acquaintance was much more intimate and general, could answer for every professor among you. From what has taken place in all the large congregations I have known, I am afraid lest the hopes of your Pastor may be disappointed, as to some individuals, whom he never suspected, but whose future apostasy will indicate the superficial nature of their present possession, and ensure them a final portion with hypocrites and unbelievers. Greatly shall I rejoice, if not *one* such character should ever be found among you; but to render the consolation in the text more certain, in its personal application, I must exhort you to examine and prove your own selves, and to give all diligence to make your calling and election sure. Unless you are such of whom God disapproves, Christ is in you, the hope of glory; he dwells in your hearts by faith, and you begin to be conformed to his lovely image. You account mental nearness to God the chief good. You value communion with him above all the world. Is not this the case, my brethren? I trust you, can say with the Psalmist, "Whom have I in heaven but thee, and there is none upon earth that I desire besides thee." Fear not, that the Lord will frustrate the desires his own Spirit has excited, or abandon that soul, whose wishes centre wholly in himself.

In the meanwhile, to increase the intenseness of your desires after the presence of Christ, let us proceed to consider:

2. The magnitude of the promise.

Has Christ said, "I will come unto you?" and have you been told tonight that his presence can make up every loss? Well may you credit the assertion, if you consider what is intended by the promise in the text.

It imports that *he will manifest to you his glory.* And O how delightful the sight! "Lord!" said Jude, "how is it that thou wilt manifest thyself unto us, and not unto the world?" This exclamation might denote partial ignorance, as well as grateful surprise: but the secret was in great measure explained, when the Spirit was poured out from on high. Then Paul observed, "God, who commanded the light to shine out of darkness, hath shined into our hearts, to give the light of the knowledge of the glory of God, in the face of Jesus Christ:" so that while others have "their understandings darkened, being alienated from the life of God, through the ignorance which is in them, because of the blindness (or rather the callousness) of their hearts; we all, with open face, beholding, as in a mirror, the glory of the Lord, are changed into the same image, from glory to glory, as by the Spirit of the Lord."

If the Lord grant you his special presence, you will not only realize his essential and mediatorial glory, but be cheered also with *a lively sense of his love.* And what consolation can equal that which must result from such a source? "To know the love of Christ, which passeth knowledge," is a blessing which the Apostle considered as immediately connected with being "filled with all the fullness of God;" and the bestowment of which was a proof that he is "able to do exceeding abundantly above all that we ask or think." Unless we could conceive the *full extent* of the happiness produced by the redemption of Christ throughout the whole empire of God; unless we could comprehend the *length* of eternity, in which the felicity of the saved shall be forever increasing, as fast as God shall increase their capacity of enjoyment; unless we could measure the lowest *depths* of hell, from whence our Saviour has ransomed us, with the invaluable price of his blood and the *height* of glory, to which we shall be raised as the reward of Immanuel's obedience; it will be impossible fully to conceive the greatness of his love. However, enough may be known to convince us that his favour is better than life, and to fill us, even in the present state, amidst all our outward trials, and even our inward conflicts, with joy unspeakable and full of glory.

Reflect, that if Christ should come unto you, according to this gracious promise, *he will communicate unto you,* more largely, *the supply of his Spirit.* And shall not this fit you for every duty, support you under every pressure, and ensure you the victory over every spiritual enemy? Yes, my beloved, if you enjoy much of the presence of Jesus, it will make you active for God, and excite you to every good work. You will not be slothful in business, but fervent in spirit, serving the Lord. You will aim at the divine glory in every thing, even in all your civil employments. You will gladly consecrate the gain of your merchandize to the Lord, and honour him with your substance. It will rejoice your soul to think that you are "not your own," but "bought with a price," and you will feel yourselves bound to "glorify God, with your bodies and with your spirits, which are God's:" nor can you forbear to admit his claim to all which you possess; for "the silver is mine and the gold is mine," saith the Lord of Hosts, and your thankful hearts must say, Amen. You will wish to inscribe on all your property and on all your utensils that blessed motto, *Holiness to the Lord.* The presence of Christ will inspire you with ardour, resolution and zeal, to promote his kingdom among men. You will not let your *Lord's-day Schools* decline; nor will your contribution to the MISSION, in which you stood foremost so early, now be suffered to fall off, because that dear man is gone to glory, who first excited your attention to these good works; but you will remember that Christ himself is with you, who walks among his golden candlesticks, to notice how their light shineth before men, to the honour of their heavenly Father.—If you should meet with farther trials, the presence of Jesus will suffice to support you under the cross, as it did the Apostles, and primitive Christians. O brethren! I pray you may live as seeing Him who is invisible. Remember that Christ, when upon earth, could not do more for his first disciples, than he can now perform for you, by his divine presence. Ah . . . if he were here, in his glorified body, . . or even in the lowly form in which he appeared in the days of his humiliation, ... if he often called upon you, . . . or you could, at any time, resort to him . . . or if he lodged at your house, . . or came thither as often as he visited the house of Lazarus, at Bethany; . . . would you not then consult him in every thing; and always follow his good advice? and fear no consequences, when you complied with his directions? And do you believe the Divinity of Christ, and act otherwise now? O shameful inconsistency! Look unto Jesus. *Look off,* my brethren, from all other objects; from all false confidences, from all discouragements, from all the foaming billows, which threaten to swallow you up, *unto Jesus.* He is above, looking down upon you. He is at hand, ready to assist you. See, how he stretches forth his arm to support you, and keep you from sinking in the deep waters. Separate from him, you can do nothing; but the weakest can do all things, can bear all burdens, can conquer all the hosts of hell, through Christ strengthening him.

If you are thus authorized to expect the presence of Christ, will he not *take you under the care of his providence.* How sweet is the idea of an omnipresent God! Not a local Deity, as the gods of the heathen were supposed to be, even by their own worshippers. But a God *afar off*, as well as *at hand*. Present with his captive servants, to check the violence of the fire, and stop the mouths of lions, in favour of his exiles in Babylon, as surely as ever he had been ready to hear prayer in his temple at Jerusalem. A God in India, as well as in England. Who shewed himself to be present with his servant *Pearce* in Birmingham, to make all his bed in his sickness: and was at the same time present, though we knew not where, with his servant *Ward* and his companions; whether they are still traversing the mighty ocean, or whether the *Criterion* has reached its desired haven. Perhaps, they have already met with *Carey*, and *Thomas*, and *Fountain*, and Jesus is in the midst of them, while they are praying for us in Bengal. Yes, Asia was long ago reminded, that "the eyes of JEHOVAH run to and fro throughout the whole earth, that he may shew himself strong in the behalf of them whose hearts are perfect towards him." And how comfortable is it to reflect, that this attribute of Deity, and every other, belongs to God the Son, as well as to God the Father. The husband of the church is the God of the whole earth. Jesus has all power on earth as well as in heaven. They, therefore, who "seek first the kingdom of God, and his righteousness," shall find "all things added unto them." "My God," (said Paul to the Philippians) "shall supply all your need, according to his riches in glory, by Christ Jesus." Cast on him, therefore, all your care: he careth for all his churches; and though you know not which way to look, he can find another pastor for this church, to repair the breach that death has made. He can raise up friends for the widow and the children of his departed servant; yea, he himself will be their guardian and defence. A father to the fatherless, and the patron of the widow, is God in his holy habitation; he will never fail them, nor forsake them.

FINALLY, The presence of Christ, with his people on earth, shall *prepare* them *for the uninterrupted enjoyment of his presence in the celestial world.* He himself will be with you walking in the way, and the foolish shall not err therein. He will guide you by his counsel, and afterwards receive you into glory. One of you after another shall follow your dear Pastor, perhaps before the end of this year, and four or five next year, and so on, till you all meet again in that heavenly city, where the *Lord God* Almighty and the *Lamb*, are the temple of it; the glory of *God* doth enlighten it, and the *Lamb* is the light thereof; and the inhabitants drink of the pure river of the water of life, proceeding out of the throne of *God* and the *Lamb;* and there shall be no more curse, but the throne of *God* and of the *Lamb* shall be in it: and his servants shall serve him, and they shall see his face, and his name shall be in their foreheads; for they shall be completely like him, when they shall see him as he is. But let me once more beseech you to notice

3. The *consequent obligations,* under which you are laid. Your Lord has said, "I will come unto you." *Believe him.* Take him at his word. Plead it before his throne of grace. Prove that you value his presence above every thing. Live under an abiding conviction, that without it, you must be comfortless, notwithstanding the presence of every temporal enjoyment; but with it, you must be happy, even under the pressure of every earthly calamity.

Let then the *expectation* that this promise will be accomplished, *moderate your sorrows,* on the present occasion, and on all others, and direct them into a proper channel. It is the presence of Christ which constitutes the perfected felicity of our dear departed friend: But Christ is really present with his church upon earth also: pray for more faith to realize that truth, and your heaven shall be begun below. He has said, "If any one love me, he will keep my words: and my Father will love him, and we will come unto him, and make our abode with him." And what is the loss, which the enjoyment of the presence of Christ, and of his Father, cannot compensate? or, what is the affliction, under which fellowship with the Father, and with his Son Jesus Christ, will not console you?

Let this promise enhance your *gratitude* for past mercies, and your *solicitude* to improve those which remain. It was from him, who ascended on high, after descending into the lowest parts of the earth, and who received gifts for men, that our dear brother received all his ministerial qualifications, as well as every Christian grace: and it was his blessing alone, which rendered him so successful, in winning souls to Christ. With him is the residue of. the Spirit. He has yet blessings in store to communicate. O live on his fullness! Though your beloved Pastor is gone, I trust that the benefit, which many of you received from his ministry, will never be lost. Ministers die, but Jesus lives; and his word endureth forever. You have also a prospect of still enjoying his ordinances. Look up for his gracious influence to attend them, knowing that neither is he who planteth any thing, nor he who watereth; but it is God who giveth the increase.

May the promise of Christ's presence excite your concern to *prepare for his coming.* Let it excite your watchfulness against every thing, which would be offensive to your blessed Lord. Christians, is there any thing in the daily course of your behaviour, or in the management of your families, of which you would be ashamed, if Christ were now upon earth in human nature, and took up his abode with you? And can you truly believe his Divinity, and not be afraid that he, whose, eyes are as a flame of fire, should see such transactions? Do you not believe that he even searches the reins and the hearts? and has he not said, that all the churches shall know it? Behold, he cometh frequently, as unexpected as a thief: Blessed is he who watcheth, and keepeth his garments, lest he walk naked, and they see his shame.

But now, without confining myself farther to the immediate language of the text, give me leave to address a few words, by way of a more *general improvement* of the late afflictive providence, both to the members of the Church statedly assembling in this place of worship, and the Congregation and Strangers present.

I address myself first to the CHURCH. You, my brethren, have, within these ten days, sustained the loss of a very affectionate and faithful Pastor; a young and active, and at the same time an able and judicious minister; who had approved himself among you for nine or ten years, and whose labours you hoped to enjoy for many years to come. But he is taken away in the midst of his usefulness, having but just completed the thirty-third year of his age. In such a trial, you have room to mourn. JESUS wept. And devout men made great lamentation at the death of *Stephen.*

Yet forget not to be thankful, that ever the Lord raised up such a minister, and gave you the chief benefit of his labours. It was the kindness of Providence that fixed him in this place, and continued him with you for several years. You have reason to bless God also, that he did not run in vain, nor labour in vain. Bless the Lord for giving so many seals to his ministry, and for enabling him to live so honourably, and to die so triumphantly.

And now, let each individual examine himself, how far he profited by the ministrations of this dear servant of Jesus Christ. If any of you put him out of his place, and idolized him; let such learn wisdom in future, and so account of us, as only the stewards of the mysteries of God. If any undervalued him, let them sincerely repent of that evil. And let all be concerned, that the benefit of his ministry may not die with him. Remember the interesting and important truths you professed to receive from him. Remember the affectionate and earnest exhortations, addressed to you by him, from this pulpit. Remember the consistent and lovely example which he set before you; and the evidence of the truth of religion, and the display of the faithfulness of God, which was made by his supports, under his painful and protracted affliction.

Consider, beloved, your *duty to his Family,* and shew the sincerity of your regard for your late dear Pastor, by your tender sympathy with his distressed Widow, and the substantial tokens of your affection to his five fatherless Children, whose tender years prevent them from forming any adequate conception of their unspeakable loss. May all the friends of the deceased, bear them and their afflicted mother on their hearts before the Lord; remembering how essential a part of pure and undefiled religion it is to pay kind attention to the orphan and the widow in their affliction; and accounting it an honour to imitate and subserve that glorious Being, in whom the fatherless findeth mercy, and who encourages the desolate widow to put her trust in him.

My dear brethren, forget not your *duty to one another* also, in this season of trial. While thus deprived of a pastor, to take the oversight of you in the Lord, watch over each other the more carefully in love. Forsake not the assembling of yourselves together, but stand fast in the Lord. Strengthen the hands of your *deacons,* at a time when the concerns of the church lie the heavier upon them, instead of indulging, as sometimes the case has been in other churches, a spirit of groundless jealousy respecting those whom you yourselves have called to that office, and who have shewn a conscientious and upright regard for your welfare.

In looking out for a minister, I trust, you will he careful to seek one of the same stamp with my late dear brother; one, who will guide you in the true narrow way, and guard you from error on the right hand and on the left; who will warn you against every sentiment which would dishonor God's moral *government,* as well as faithfully oppose whatever notion would disparage the riches of his glorious *grace.* May you choose a man equally zealous against self-righteousness, and against self-indulgence; who will preach salvation by Christ alone, and insist on deliverance from the power and love of sin; as a most essential part of that salvation. May God direct you to a minister, who shall answer to the description given by Paul of himself and his fellow labourers, "We preach Christ in you the hope of glory, warning every man and teaching every man in all wisdom; that we may present every man perfect in Christ Jesus." May he able to appeal to you, on his death bed, in the words of the same Apostle, "As we were allowed of God to be put in trust with the gospel, so we spake, not as pleasing men, but God, who trieth our hearts: not using flattering words, as ye know, nor a cloak of covetousness, God is witness; nor seeking glory of men; but we were gentle among you, even as a nurse cherisheth her children; so, being affectionately desirous of you, we were willing to have imparted unto you, not the gospel of God only, but also our own souls, because ye were dear unto us. Ye are witnesses, and God also, how holily, and justly, and how unblameably we behaved ourselves among you who believe: as ye know, how we exhorted, and comforted, and charged every one of you, as a father his children, that ye should walk worthy of God, who hath called you unto his kingdom and glory." Such a protestation, I am confident, your late beloved Pastor might have safely made, and I pray God, his successor may be assisted to imitate the same primitive example, and find a corresponding testimony in the conscience of every unprejudiced hearer.

At the same time, let me exhort you, my brethren, to manifest *genuine Christian candour* in your choice of another minister, and in all your subsequent conduct towards him. If he should not equal his predecessor in the popularity of his talents, the readiness of his utterance, or in every amiable qualification of still higher importance, yet if his heart be evidently devoted to God, do not despise him, nor undervalue him; but pray for him, encourage him, strengthen his hands in God. Make him not an offender for a word, nor for the want of a word. And do not magnify such infirmities as are common to the best of men in this state of imperfection.

Endeavour, brethren, *to be unanimous* in your choice. Let none oppose the general vote, merely to shew their consequence, or assert their liberty. Nor let others resolve upon having their own way, because they have a small majority of their mind: but endeavour to accommodate one another, as far as it is possible, without sacrificing truth or prudence. Only be sure that you seek a pastor that is a holy man of God, a faithful servant of Jesus Christ, who will naturally care for your souls.

Finally, beloved, let all be careful to walk worthy of the Lord, in the practice of all that is well-pleasing in his sight. And let it appear that God, by taking your late dear minister to heaven, has drawn you nearer to heaven. Remember that Christ is now in the midst of you, and that you hope soon to be with him in his kingdom, and to live and reign with him for ever. What manner of persons ought you then to be, in all holy conversation and godliness!

What I have said to the members of the *church*, will, for the most part, apply to such of the *stated* CONGREGATION, as are partakers of the grace of God.

But there are some, who constantly attended my dear brother's ministry, who are left unconverted. O what! shall I say to them! I earnestly pray, that they who heard him in vain while alive, may hear him now he is dead, so as to be made alive themselves. For, being dead, he yet speaketh. The history which all his friends can give you, of his life, and of his death, (his blessed death!) proclaims to you, the truth and excellence of the gospel. Do not you also remember that short, but most affecting address, which he made to you, the last time he ascended this pulpit, after brother Franklin of Coventry had been preaching? Then he told some, that his highest comfort, amidst the symptoms of approaching dissolution, which he then exhibited, was the expectation of meeting them in heaven; while he forewarned others of you, that his greatest anxiety arose from his fear of being obliged to witness against you, as despisers and rejecters of the glorious Redeemer. O that the recollection of that dying warning, enforced by all his own happy experience in succeeding months of suffering and superabounding consolation, might convince you of the vast importance of true religion, of the unspeakable worth of the gospel of Christ, and of the blessedness of being interested in his great salvation, and obtaining an inheritance among them who are sanctified, through faith in him.

Many may expect, especially those who are *strangers*, to hear a *character of the deceased;* but he chose this text to avoid much being said of himself, and though I should not scruple introducing whatever might tend to honour divine grace, and to promote your edification, yet I am unable to enter into a particular biographical detail at this time. And as to his character, those, who knew him well, need not my delineation of it, to make them remember it with high esteem, to their dying day; while others might suspect me of flattery, if I said but the half of what I cordially believe. One thing I will say, which I could say of very few others, though I have known many of the excellent of the earth, That I never saw, or heard of any thing respecting him, which grieved me unless it was his inattention to his health, and that I believe was owing to a mistaken idea of his constitution. If any of you know of other faults belonging to him, be careful to shun them; but O he sure to follow him, wherein he was a follower of Christ.

While his outward conduct was remarkably blameless and exemplary, he evidently had a deep, abiding, humbling sense of the evil of sin, of his own native depravity, and remaining sinfulness; of his absolute need of Christ as an atoning sacrifice, and the Lord his righteousness; and of the love of the Spirit, and the importance of his work as a sanctifier.—He lived a life of faith on the incarnate Son of God, as the blessed Mediator, who had loved him and given himself for him; and as Christ was all in all to him, his joy and his gain, in life and in death, so he took great delight in preaching Christ to others, as the only and all-sufficient Saviour; he earnestly longed, had it been permitted him by Providence, to have preached Christ to the heathen, and would have been glad to have carried the tidings of salvation by his blood, to the ends of the earth.

But, instead of giving a fuller account in my own words, I will give all strangers the means of forming a just idea of the man, and of the nature of his religion, by reading some of his letters, written three of them to myself, and two to the officers of this church, at different periods of his long illness; to which I shall add a few detached sentences, uttered nearer the close of his life, and taken down by his nearest relative.[25]

These will tend more to your edification who know the Redeemer, and more to the conviction of those who know him not, than any studied panegyric.

May they excite all present to pray from the heart, Let me live the *life*, as well as die the *death*, of the righteous; may the *commencement* of my profession, and may my *latter end* be like his. Amen and Amen.

---

[25] This material referred to here is found on pages 110 and following of this volume.

OTHER RELATED SOLID GROUND TITLES

THE MISSIONARY ENTERPRISE
A Collection of Discourses on Christian Missions

Fifteen outstanding addresses by leading gospel ministers on the critical subject of missions.

"The Moral Dignity of the Missionary Enterprise" by Francis Wayland
"Arguments for Missions" by Edward Dorr Griffin
"The Theory of Missions to the Heathen" by Rufus Anderson
"The Earth Filled with the Glory of the Lord" by Samuel Miller
"The Cross" by Richard Fuller
"Jesus the Great Missionary" by Edward N. Kirk
"Christ, A Home Missionary" by William B. Williams
"Messiah's Throne" by John M. Mason

PAUL THE MISSIONARY
Louis Berkhof

These four addresses were delivered in 1914 before the Southwest Indian Conference in Flagstaff, Arizona. In Berkhof's own words:

"Complying with this request, I lectured on three subjects pertaining to the life of Paul, the missionary par excellence, and in addition addressed the Conference on a subject that might be called the motto of Paul in his missionary labors, 'VICTORY THROUGH GRACE!' May they in some small measure help us to understand the life and work of that great apostle whose undying zeal laid the foundations of the Church in Gentile lands; and may his example be our guiding star in our missionary efforts."

Chapter One: PAUL'S PREPARATION FOR HIS GREAT TASK
Chapter Two: THE STRATEGIC ELEMENT IN PAUL'S WORK
Chapter Three: PAUL THE MISSIONARY PREACHER
Chapter Four: VICTORY THROUGH GRACE

King of the Cannibals: The Story of John G. Paton
Jim Cromarty

John MacArthur says, "This engrossing account of Paton's life and ministry will make him live again for a whole new generation. Cromarty's lively writing style makes this a book that is hard to put down." Stuart Olyott simply predicts, "No one can read this book and remain the same." A To Think About section concluding each chapter makes this perfect for Family Worship. First published in 1997.

OTHER SOLID GROUND TITLES

In addition to *A Heart for Missions* we are happy to offer the following titles to help equip you to serve the Lord of the Harvest.

Assurance of Faith by Louis Berkhof
The Backslider: *Nature, Symptoms & Recovery* by Andrew Fuller
My Brother's Keeper: *Letters to a Younger Brother* by J.W. Alexander
The Chief End of Man by John Hall
Church Member's Guide by John Angell James
Come Ye Apart: *Gospel Devotions* by J.R. Miller
Communicant's Companion by Matthew Henry
Divine Love: *Sermons on the Love of the Triune God* by John Eadie
The Doctrine of Justification by James Buchanan
Friendship: *The Master Passion* by H. Clay Trumbull
From the Pulpit to the Palm-Branch: *Memorial to C.H. Spurgeon*
Imago Christi: *The Example of Jesus Christ* by James Stalker
Jesus of Nazareth: *Character, Teaching & Miracles* by J.A. Broadus
The Man of Business by J.W. Alexander, W.B. Sprague and more
Manual for the Young by Charles Bridges
Notes on Galatians by J. Gresham Machen
Opening Scripture: *Hermeneutical Manual* by Patrick Fairbairn
Opening Up Ephesians by Peter Jeffery
Pastor's Sketches: *Case Studies with Troubled Souls* by I.S. Spencer
Pathway into the Psalter by William Binnie
Paul the Preacher: *Studies on Discourses in Acts* by John Eadie
Power of God unto Salvation by Benjamin B. Warfield
Secret of Communion with God by Matthew Henry
The Still Hour: *Communion with God in Prayer* by Austin Phelps
The Transfigured Life: *Selected Shorter Writings of J.R. Miller*
The Travels of True Godliness: *An Allegory* by Benjamin Keach
Whatsoever Things are True: *Discourses on Truth* by J.H. Thornwell
The Word & Prayer: *Devotions from Minor Prophets* by John Calvin

Call us Toll Free at 1-877-666-9469
Send us an e-mail at sgcb@charter.net
Visit us on line at solid-ground-books.com

Printed in the United States
51898LVS00005B/145-255